Assessment and Treatment of Older Adults

Assessment and Treatment of Older Adults

A Guide for Mental Health Professionals

Gregory A. Hinrichsen

AMERICAN PSYCHOLOGICAL ASSOCIATION
Washington, DC

The opinions and statements published are the responsibility of the authors, and such opinions and statements do not necessarily represent the policies of the American Psychological Association.

Published by
American Psychological Association
750 First Street, NE
Washington, DC 20002
https://www.apa.org

Order Department
https://www.apa.org/pubs/books
order@apa.org

In the U.K., Europe, Africa, and the Middle East, copies may be ordered from Eurospan
https://www.eurospanbookstore.com/apa
info@eurospangroup.com

Typeset in Charter by Circle Graphics, Inc., Reisterstown, MD

Printer: Sheridan Books, Chelsea, MI
Cover Designer: Mercury Publishing Services, Inc., Rockville, MD

Library of Congress Cataloging-in-Publication Data

Names: Hinrichsen, Gregory A., 1951- author.
Title: Assessment and treatment of older adults : a guide for mental health
    professionals / by Gregory A. Hinrichsen.
Description: Washington, DC : American Psychological Association, [2020] |
    Includes bibliographical references and index.
Identifiers: LCCN 2019007186 (print) | LCCN 2019009231 (ebook) |
    ISBN 9781433831393 (eBook) | ISBN 1433831392 (eBook) |
    ISBN 9781433831102 (pbk.) | ISBN 1433831104 (pbk.)
Subjects: LCSH: Older people—Mental health—Evaluation. | Older
    people—Psychology. | Geriatric psychiatry. | Older people—Mental health
    services—United States.
Classification: LCC RC451.4.A5 (ebook) | LCC RC451.4.A5 H555 2020 (print) |
    DDC 618.97/689—dc23
LC record available at https://lccn.loc.gov/2019007186

http://dx.doi.org/10.1037/0000146-000

Printed in the United States of America

10 9 8 7 6 5 4 3 2

For my sister, Sue—Lifelong friend

Contents

Acknowledgments

Over a long career, numerous people have made a difference in my professional life. Jane Eckert, ACSW, then at the Massachusetts Mental Health Center, was my first teacher about mental health and aging when I was a social services outreach worker in Boston. Barbara J. Felton, PhD, at New York University, was my academic mentor in graduate school and taught me the value of critical thinking and research and introduced me to the field of aging. Allen E. Willner, PhD, at Hillside Hospital, Long Island Jewish Medical Center, in New York, guided me on how to do psychotherapy with older adults. Kathleen F. Clougherty, ACSW, taught me how to conduct interpersonal psychotherapy, which made me a better therapist in my work with older adults. Deborah A. DiGilio, MPH, and Diane Elmore Borbon, PhD, MPH, schooled me in public policy and aging; it was from them that I learned the value of always having a seat at the table. U.S. Senator Ron Wyden of Oregon and his staff further built my knowledge of public policy and aging when I was an American Psychological Association Congressional Fellow in his office. Antonette M. Zeiss, PhD, from whom I have learned so much, offered me opportunities to work within the Department of Veterans Affairs on aging and other issues. Rosanne M. Leipzig, MD, PhD, at the Icahn School of Medicine at Mount Sinai in New York City, taught me much about geriatric medicine; she and I have ongoing collaborations.

I have had so many wonderful colleagues. An informal gathering of New York geropsychologists that we called "The New York Geropsychology

Group" was a professional home for many years and included Kathleen J. Byrne, PhD; Nanette A. Kramer, PhD; Vicki F. Passman, PhD; Amy J. Raphael, PhD; Rita P. Ryan, PhD; Eileen H. Rosendahl, PhD; Leah P. Siskin, PhD; Michael C. Smith, PhD; Richard A. Zweig, PhD; and others who were part of this convening of people who love their work with older adults. I have had many terrific professional colleagues—too many to mention—through my involvement in a variety of professional organizations, including the American Psychological Association (APA) Committee on Aging, APA's Society of Clinical Geropsychology, and the Council of Professional Geropsychology Training Programs. Thanks to my international colleagues Nancy A. Pachana, PhD, at the University of Queensland in Australia and Ken Laidlaw, PhD, now at the University of Exeter in England for opening the door to many professional opportunities abroad. Helen "Lena" Verdeli, PhD, at Teachers College, Columbia University, in New York City opened the door further to global mental health initiatives. The many students with whom I have worked have enriched my professional life; they include my now geropsychology colleagues Michele J. Karel, PhD; Erin E. Emery-Tiburcio, PhD; Eve H. Davison, PhD; and Marie-Genevieve Iselin, PhD.

My grandparents and parents taught me much about how to live the later years with dignity. I greatly appreciate the relationship I have with my five siblings—all of whom are now older than 60—with whom I share so much. My partner of 40 years, Rob Jerome, has been curious and enthusiastic about my career in aging and has read and faithfully edited many of the things that I have written. He now chronicles and honors the contributions of older athletes in his writing and photography.

Assessment and Treatment of Older Adults

INTRODUCTION

My first real job out of college was as a social services outreach worker to older residents of the Fenway neighborhood of Boston. The Fenway—perhaps best known as home of the Boston Red Sox baseball team—was not in good shape: Urban renewal efforts had dislocated residents, a rash of arsons had occurred, and street crime was common. Members of the community gathered to figure out what could be done. One big concern was with Fenway's longtime older residents who seemed to bear the brunt of the neighborhood's problems. A community task force was formed, and from it emerged a proposal for door-to-door social services outreach to all residents 62 years of age and older. The proposal was funded, and I was one of the three outreach workers. We met with older residents in their homes to assess for a range of social services, housing, benefits, and health and mental health problems, and then as needed, made referrals.

I presumed I would meet many beleaguered older people struggling to survive. In reality, it was quite the opposite. I met extraordinary older people, including a sizable group of never married career women who lived in the neighborhood because it was close to downtown Boston, where they worked. I learned my first lesson in gerontology: Most older adults are resilient, adaptive, reasonably happy, and have meaningful social connections. There were, of course, older residents with problems, and I directly observed what poverty, mental illness, chronic health problems, housing insecurity, and financial stresses looked like.

I was guided in this effort by experienced geriatric social workers from whom I learned much. I admired their commitment to and care for older people. Sensing my growing enthusiasm about aging, they asked if I might have interest in a career in aging. I replied that I intended to become a psychologist. "Are there psychologists who specialize in aging?" I asked. They knew psychologists who did research on aging but not any who were engaged in professional practice with older people. They said, however, that the population of the United States was aging and, undoubtedly in the future, all professional fields, including psychology, would develop aging-knowledgeable workforces. The year was 1976, and people 65 years of age and older constituted 10% of the U.S. population.

THE FUTURE AGING OF AMERICA ARRIVES

What my social worker colleagues had not advised me was that the lion's share of the growth of the aging population would arrive when I was an older adult. In 2007, the first members of the 75 million baby boomer population began to turn 65. In 2030, the percentage of the U.S. population 65 years and older will be 20%. Ten thousand baby boomers turn 65 *every single day*. My social work colleagues were overly optimistic about how the health and mental health professions would build an aging-knowledgeable workforce.

Just as the first group of aging baby boomers began to turn 65, the Institute of Medicine (2008) published a report that essentially said that the United States had not done a good job of planning for an aging society and had a woefully inadequate workforce to serve that population. There were not enough aging specialists and never would be, according to the report. A later report from the same institute further documented that the mental health and substance use workforce for older adults was thin (Institute of Medicine, 2012). In the end, the report concluded, older adults would receive health and mental health services from individuals who had little or no training related to aging. The challenge then would be to build foundational knowledge and competencies in the existing workforce so it could do a better job of serving older Americans.

OFF TO GRADUATE SCHOOL AND ON TO A CAREER IN AGING

I finished my job as an outreach worker, went to graduate school in New York, and was fortunate to have an academic mentor who was a psychologist who specialized in aging. I worked with her on a study of how older adults cope with chronic illness and other projects. I returned to the Fenway to gather dissertation data on how different residential environments impacted older residents' emotional and social well-being. There, I reconnected with my geriatric social work colleagues and some older residents whom I had first met when doing the outreach. A clinical psychology internship at Hillside Hospital, Long Island Jewish Medical Center, in New York included a year-long placement in a geriatric outpatient mental health clinic. Hillside Hospital became my professional home for 25 years, during which I saw older clients, did research on late-life depression and dementia, and created internship and postdoctoral training opportunities in geropsychology. I could not have imagined as a young social services outreach worker that the field of aging would bring me such varied and interesting professional opportunities.

Later in my career, through an American Psychological Association (APA) congressional fellowship, I was responsible for the aging legislative portfolio in the office of U.S. Senator Ron Wyden of Oregon. I then worked for the national mental health office of the U.S. Department of Veterans Affairs. Currently, I am on faculty in the Department of Geriatrics and Palliative Medicine at the Icahn School of Medicine at Mount Sinai and the Department of Counseling and Clinical Psychology at Teachers College, Columbia University, in New York City.

PSYCHOLOGY AND AGING

Unfortunately, my enthusiasm about aging has not been widely shared in psychology nor, for that matter, in most professional disciplines. Aging has been a hard sell, in part, I believe, because most individuals hold stereotypical and overly negative views of aging and older adults. Only 3% to 4% of psychologists have specialized training in aging (Hoge, Karel, Zeiss, Alegria, & Moye, 2015), which is not that different from other health and mental health professions (Bragg & Hansen, 2010). However, reflecting the growing U.S. population of older adults, almost 40% of psychologists now see some older adults in clinical practice (APA, 2016; Qualls, Segal, Norman, Niederehe, & Gallagher-Thompson, 2002), despite that few of them have formal training related to aging.

Only in the past 20 years has a field of geropsychology been substantively built. Therefore, until recently, few formal pathways have been available for those interested in becoming a geropsychologist. Similar challenges have existed for other mental health disciplines. When I entered psychology, a few clinical psychologists wrote of their work with older adults and expressed hope that the area would mature. The field of geropsychology—which has been variously known as "clinical aging," "clinical geropsychology," "applied aging," and "professional geropsychology"—first built on the larger field of academic gerontology to inform its applied work.

Although the foundation of professional geropsychology sits on almost 100 years of the study of aging and the psychology of aging, it also rests on more recent efforts. Those efforts include three training conferences on how to prepare individuals to become geropsychologists (Knight, Karel, Hinrichsen, Qualls, & Duffy, 2009); APA (2014) guidelines on professional practice with older adults; APA's designation of geropsychology as a specialty; a geropsychology specialty board within the American Board of Professional Psychology; the establishment of a number of geropsychology organizations within and outside of APA; and federal policy that includes psychiatry, psychology, social work, nursing, and others as eligible providers under Medicare, which pays the lion's share of mental health services for older adults (Hinrichsen, 2010).

THE CHALLENGE OF BUILDING FOUNDATIONAL GEROPSYCHOLOGY AND AGING COMPETENCY FOR POSTLICENSURE PROFESSIONALS

Some professionals without training in aging who are seeing older adults in clinical practice would like to gain foundational knowledge in this area. The practical challenge is where to gain that knowledge. Psychologists have two key guiding documents: The Pikes Peak model for training in professional geropsychology (Knight et al., 2009) and the APA "Guidelines for Psychological Practice With Older Adults" (APA Guidelines; APA, 2014). I hasten to add that other disciplines have created those own professional statements about recommended areas for knowledge and skills for those who serve older adults alone or in collaboration with others (e.g., American Association of Colleges of Nursing, 2016; Association of Gerontology in Higher Education, 2014; Galambos, Greene, Kropf, & Cohen, 2018; Interprofessional Education Collaborative, 2016; Williams et al., 2010). The Pikes Peak model outlines three domains of competence that should inform training in geropsychology: attitudes, knowledge, and skills. The APA Guidelines outline similar content with which psychologists who practice with older adults are encouraged to be familiar. The practical question is: What is foundational among the many areas recommended in the Pikes Peak model and the APA Guidelines? In other words, where do you start? This issue became increasingly important as my colleagues and I created professional training workshops for psychologists, social workers, and other mental health professionals interested in building basic knowledge about aging.

To address this issue, my colleagues and I, who are members of the Council of Professional Geropsychology Training Programs (CoPGTP), created a survey. CoPGTP is an organization of programs that provide training in geropsychology consistent with the Pikes Peak model. CoPGTP includes programs on the educational continuum from graduate school to postlicensure education. We surveyed 149 geropsychologists and asked which competencies among the many in the Pikes Peak model were most important for a postlicensure psychologist new to the aging field to learn first in the equivalent of a 2-day continuing education workshop. Survey results included recommendations that these five competencies be included: (a) attitudes about older adults and aging; (b) general knowledge of adult development and aging; (c) knowledge of the foundations of clinical practice with older adults; (d) knowledge of the foundations of assessment; and (e) knowledge of intervention, consultation, and other service provision (Hinrichsen, Emery-Tiburcio, Gooblar, & Molinari, 2018). Our hope is that these recommendations will yield greater uniformity in how introductory workshops and other venues on mental health and aging are created as well as bring about practical guidance for individuals who seek to build knowledge in this area.

ABOUT THIS BOOK

Purpose

The content of this book reflects CoPGTP recommendations on foundational attitudes and knowledge competencies in geropsychology (Hinrichsen et al., 2018). I also believe that the content reflects aging-relevant content often recommended by other mental health disciplines. This book is a broad overview of what I and others consider to be critical information for those mental health practitioners without prior aging background who are serving some older adults in clinical practice. The book is a primer for those who want to learn the professional lay of the land in geropsychology. It is not intended to be exhaustive in its coverage. What I hope the book does, however, is pique the reader's interest in learning more about geropsychology and more generally about aging. The book is also informed by many years of experience in conducting introductory mental health and aging continuing education workshops for psychologists, social workers, and related disciplines. Postlicensure professionals often attend the workshops to gain continuing education credits and to learn more about this area of practice. Practitioners are busy people who want to learn information in a way that is clearly conveyed and that has practical utility. Workshop participants also want to know about my own and other presenters' experience in working with older adults: "What kind of problems do you usually see?" "What do you find that works best in addressing this problem?" "Can you give me a clinical example of that?" "What assessment measures do you find work best?" "What would you do differently now than you did in the past?" "How do I get paid for my services?" "What's a good book on this topic?"

To that end, I have integrated my own clinical observations and experience into this book. Another person writing this book would use different examples, likely provide different emphases, and recommend different preferred approaches. I hope, however, that with content guided by the CoPGTP recommendations on foundational attitude and knowledge competencies, we each would cover the same issues informed by contemporary research and professional practice, albeit in different ways. Another caveat is that although my more than 40 years in the field of aging has encompassed a wide range of experience with varied problems and subpopulations of older adults, it has not included the full range of settings and populations that exist. I have chiefly worked in outpatient mental health and primary care medical settings in urban areas. I have not worked in long-term care settings where some psychologists work. I have general familiarity with late-life cognitive issues but am not a neuropsychologist. Some mental health conditions I rarely treat and try to refer.

Structure

This book has seven chapters. The first two chapters examine attitudes toward aging and basic facts about and perspectives on the aging process. These chapters are not clinically focused, but I hope after you read them you will find them clinically relevant. Chapters 3 and 4 are general overviews of issues in assessment and treatment of older clients. Chapter 5 reviews assessment and treatment of depression and anxiety and Chapter 6 discusses assessment and treatment of cognitive impairment and problem alcohol use and prescription drug misuse. Why have I chosen to focus on these four problem areas and not others? These areas are most commonly encountered in clinical practice. As a primer, this book intends to address foundational issues, and I believe these four problem areas are critical to working with older people. Chapter 7 summarizes key themes of the book and offers practical recommendations for those interested in further building knowledge and skills relevant to geropsychology. I end with some personal reflections on aging.

At the beginning of each chapter, I note how the chapter covers foundational attitude and knowledge competencies recommended by CoPGTP (Hinrichsen et al., 2018) and reflects recommended content from the Pikes Peak model for training in professional geropsychology (Knight et al., 2009) and the APA Guidelines (APA, 2014). For some readers, this material may not be of interest because it "gets into the weeds" of specific content. Yet for those who are interested in developing continuing education workshops in the area or want more guidance on further professional development, this material should be helpful. For the record, material in this introduction reflects content from the Attitudes domain of the Pikes Peak model for training in professional geropsychology (Knight et al., 2009), including items 1 (Work with older adults within their scope of competence and to seek consultation to make appropriate referrals when indicated) and 4 (Increase knowledge, understanding, and skills with respect to working with older adults through continuing education, training, supervision, and consultation). It also reflects content of the APA Guidelines (APA, 2014), including Guideline 1 (Psychologists are encouraged to work with older adults within their scope of competence). A case example[1] illustrates each of the four mental health problems chosen as a focus in the book. I have tried to provide continuity in the book with one case, Mabel Brown, which is discussed in several chapters. I have also reiterated the theme "I wasn't always this way," which is derived from Mrs. Brown's case throughout the book. It is a reminder that older adults seen in clinical practice have long and rich histories about which practitioners should be cognizant.

The volume includes two appendices. Appendix A summarizes resources listed by chapter. These resources include recommended books ("On My Bookshelf"), links to organizations or materials ("On My Favorite Links

---

[1]In all case examples, names and clinical material have been altered to protect client confidentiality.

Tab"), and a few scholarly articles ("An Article Worth Reading"). Appendix B includes a list of assessment instruments recommended in Chapters 3, 5, and 6 and provides information on how to obtain those instruments.

I loved writing this book. Throughout the writing, I was continually reminded of the contributions of my academic and practitioner colleagues who have built the field of aging, my many teachers, my open-hearted students, and the many extraordinary older adults I have met during my career. I hope that you will glean as much joy in professional work with older adults as I have.

1

THINKING ABOUT AGING AND WORK IN THE FIELD OF AGING

This chapter broadly discusses the topic of attitudes toward aging and older adults. Attitudes can affect behavior toward older people, including how health and mental health care professionals interact with them. Too often, people hold attitudes and beliefs about older adults that are negative and patronizing. Further complicating things, working with older adults can elicit unease about one's own aging—about which it is useful to be aware. This chapter begins with the case of Mabel Brown. Mrs. Brown is discussed in several chapters in this book to provide some continuity in the discussion of the various issues that bear on understanding and providing mental health services to older adults.

This chapter covers the Council of Professional Geropsychology Training Programs' recommended foundational knowledge competencies with respect to attitudes about aging and older adults (Hinrichsen, Emery-Tiburcio, Gooblar, & Molinari, 2018). Material in this chapter reflects content from the I. Attitudes domain of the Pikes Peak model for training in professional geropsychology (Knight, Karel, Hinrichsen, Qualls, & Duffy, 2009). It also reflects content from "Guidelines for Psychological Practice With Older Adults" (American Psychological Association [APA], 2014), including Guideline 1

http://dx.doi.org/10.1037/0000146-002
Assessment and Treatment of Older Adults: A Guide for Mental Health Professionals,
by Gregory A. Hinrichsen

(Psychologists are encouraged to work with older adults within their scope of competence) and Guideline 2 (Psychologists are encouraged to recognize how their attitudes and beliefs about aging and about older individuals may be relevant to their assessment and treatment of older adults, and to seek consultation or further education about these issues when indicated).

I'd like to introduce you to Mabel Brown, an older adult seen in clinical practice. She is discussed again in Chapters 2, 5, and 7.

CASE EXAMPLE OF MABEL BROWN: PART 1

Mrs. Mabel Brown was an 85-year-old, White, widowed, Catholic woman with a son and daughter. The geriatrician who was her medical provider referred her to me. She had been depressed for a year. Mrs. Brown refused many offers of an antidepressant medication from her doctor as well as referral to a mental health care provider. She finally and reluctantly agreed to see a psychologist. Her daughter, Carol, called me to set up an appointment. Carol explained that her mother had multiple medical problems, including diabetes, hypertension, impaired vision, a past back surgery, and problems with walking. She also felt her mother was depressed and wondered whether she had the beginning of "Alzheimer's" disease because she couldn't seem to concentrate and she forgot things. Carol brought her mother to the first appointment. Her mother slowly made her way into my office using a walker. She looked sad and scared. "I wasn't always this way," she said.

As I mentioned in the Introduction to this book, as a young person, my first job in the field of aging was as a social services outreach worker to older adults. "How old is older?" you might ask. My colleagues and I attempted to visit people 62 years of age and older. In advance of the visit, we left a flier under the doors of individuals we hoped to meet; the flier explained the purpose of our visit and provided the name of the agency, which had "senior citizens" in its title. Sometimes people in their sixties whom we visited refused to meet with us, saying, "I am no senior citizen!" I am now older and so are many of my friends. I occasionally hear some friends indignantly complain, "I was on the subway the other day and someone offered me a seat. What do they think I am, a senior citizen?" By my assessment, I (now at age 68) and many of my contemporaries could reasonably be perceived as "senior citizens." Why all the fuss?

UNEASE WITH AGING

For practitioners who work with older adults, reflection on one's own attitudes toward older people and one's own aging is a critical place to start. Researchers have well documented that most people have complicated and often negative feelings about aging. Although for most of our lives, the "aged" may seem like "them," for everyone who lives a full life, the aged will be eventually be "us." In most psychotherapy traditions, reflection on one's own thoughts, reactions, and feelings about clients is seen as useful. In the psychodynamic tradition, it is called *countertransference.* If a client is dealing with an issue that the therapist is struggling with, the therapist will try to be mindful of that and not let it get in the way of working in the best interest of the client. In the last 20 years of my career, building multicultural competency in health care providers has been emphasized (APA, 2002; APA Task Force on Re-Envisioning the Multicultural Guidelines for the 21st Century, 2017). If people are different from you, it's especially helpful to understand the background and experiences of those clients. For the practitioner, the aging issue has a complicated twist: Although you may not be old, you will be someday. You likely know older people and, on the basis of that, may believe you know something about aging. Or, you may be an older practitioner. Like most of us, practitioners have acquired preexisting notions about what old people are like that often are stereotypical. Attitudes about older people and one's own aging can therefore get in the way of doing the most effective treatment possible.

Part of the tangle of stereotypical attitudes toward older adults is the factually inaccurate information held about this age group. Gerontologist Erdman Palmore and his associates did many years of research on what the general public and health care professionals believed to be true about older people (Palmore, 1988). Both the public and health care professionals don't know some basic facts on aging. Most characterizations about older people overemphasize the negative and overestimate the prevalence of certain problems. Common "myths of aging" include the notions that most older people are depressed, sick, cognitively impaired, socially isolated, and inflexible (APA, 2014). Indeed, some older people have one or more of these problems but less commonly than generally thought. The next chapter discusses what is known about the physical, cognitive, mental, social, and psychological well-being of older adults. A contributor to misinformation and stereotyping has been that a group of people—who range in age from the conventionally defined beginning of old age (65 years) through the upper limit of the human life span (120 years)—is often referred to by one name: "the elderly." Older adults are quite diverse.

What do we mean by *elderly,* anyway? Reflecting ambivalence about aging, the names that have been used with the intent of respectfully characterizing individuals 65 years of age and older have changed over the years: "old," "aged," "elderly," "senior citizen," "golden ager," "older person," "older adult." National Public Radio reporter Ima Jaffe, who covers the older adult beat for this radio network, surveyed 2,700 listeners about their preferred term for the later stage of life (Jaffe, 2014). There wasn't enthusiasm for any of the names, although "older adult" was the most palatable. "Older adult" or "older person" are the preferred terms used by aging professionals and in most professional publications. From my point of view, "older" hedges the issue: Older than what? Of course, a host of negative and pejorative terms refer to older people: "old fogey," "geezer," "curmudgeon," "old goat," "old bird," "old codger," "old crone," "old witch," "old biddy." But do people actually use such terms these days?

I remember a professional gerontology article I read in graduate school in the early 1980s that was a content analysis of the messages in birthday cards that were thought to reflect attitudes toward older adults (Demos & Jache, 1981). They were uniformly negative and included the aforementioned pejorative terms for older people. In recent years—as my friends got older—I looked for age-positive birthday cards to send to them. "Geezer," "fogey," "curmudgeon," and other terms were common among them. I did find one card that seemed affirmative. It was a picture of a handsome older man in athletic attire blowing a whistle as would a sports referee. However, the message inside read, "Game Over—You're Old." The content of cards I perused portrayed older adults as incontinent, unattractive, forgetful, and pathetic. The apparent message was old age is a terrible time about which you just have to laugh. And keep in mind that these are greetings we send to people whom we apparently like. The reader is urged to check out a rack of birthday cards and form your own impression.

AGEISM

You likely have heard the term *ageism*. The term was coined by Robert Butler (1969), who was the first director of the National Institute on Aging, a major force in the field of aging who also founded the first academic department of geriatrics in a U.S. medical school (Mount Sinai School of Medicine, now the Icahn School of Medicine at Mount Sinai), which is, coincidentally, where I work. In the 1960s, when American society grappled with our terrible legacy of racism, he proposed the term *ageism* to characterize stereotypical and negative attitudes toward older people. Since the time that Butler initially introduced the term, *ageism* has been defined in different ways. The definition I like best is: "Ageism is defined as negative or positive stereotypes, prejudice and/or discrimination against (or to the advantage of) elderly people on the basis of their chronological age or on the basis of perception of them as being 'old' or 'elderly'" (Iversen, Larsen, & Solem, 2009 p. 15).

Most people, including professionals who work with older adults, would bristle at the idea that they might be "ageist." They believe that they treat older adults with respect and show no outward antipathy toward them. After all, most of us have or have had older relatives and may be older ourselves. Given that health and mental health professionals have been encouraged to reflect on their own beliefs and attitudes toward members of minority groups to enhance multicultural competence, I think it's reasonable for all of us to reflect on our attitudes, beliefs, and knowledge of the older adult population. The reason is because social scientists have well documented that social stereotyping is common and often invisible. Cognitive scientists speak of underlying cognitive schemas we all possess that shape our views of the world, other people, and ourselves. People are wired to simplify a highly complex social world to more efficiently maneuver through it. If we paused each time we met someone new to make complex judgments about who they are, what they are like, and what to expect from them, we'd never make it through the day. When working with older adults, it can pay rich dividends to pause and reflect on our views of aging others and our aging selves.

Doddering but Dear: Stereotyping of Older Adults

Researchers have documented stereotypes held about older adults. Two researchers summarized their findings about how older people are viewed as "doddering but dear" (Cuddy & Fiske, 2002). They used the *stereotype content model* that characterizes people along two dimensions: competence and warmth. For example, well-educated individuals are viewed as high in competence and high in warmth, whereas people on welfare are viewed as low in competence and low in warmth. Their studies found that older adults are viewed as low in competence and high in warmth—hence, "doddering but dear." Other researchers (Hummert, Garstka, Shaner, & Strahm, 1994) have found that young, middle-age, and older adults themselves hold both positive and negative stereotypes about older people. Their categories for positive stereotypes about older people include "golden ager," "perfect grandmother," and "John Wayne conservative." Negative stereotypes include "severely impaired," "despondent," "shrew" or "curmudgeon," and "recluse." Many of the negative stereotypes are found in the content of birthday cards for older adults, as noted earlier in this chapter. Another research approach (Kite, Stockdale, Whitley, & Johnson, 2005) has stressed that loss of social roles and the positive attributes associated with those roles may be as or more important than age alone in shaping attitudes toward older adults.

For example, if you are no longer working, you may be perceived as not possessing those characteristics often associated with working (e.g., motivated, productive). These perceptions have consequences for older people, which is discussed later in this chapter. I have spoken to older adults who have observed that when they tell a health care provider they are retired, the provider seems less interested in them than when they were employed. One of my retired older friends always wears a suit when he sees a health care provider because he believes it conveys the impression that he is in the business world. He feels he gets more time and attention.

Are older men versus older women stereotyped differently? Women are seen as entering later adulthood earlier and are judged less attractive than older men (Kite & Wagner, 2002). Does stereotyping vary by different cultures? One often hears that "the elderly are much more valued in Asian cultures," but research has documented that this view is highly exaggerated. The stereotyping of older people exists in all cultures, but the content is different among cultures (Ng, 2002). We know little about how age stereotyping varies by race or ethnicity within the United States.

Interestingly, however, once a person has more individualized information about an older adult, the stereotype weakens (Kite et al., 2005). A person may say about an aged relative, "Oh, my mother isn't like other elderly. She's happy, active, interested in many things, and sharp as a tack." That person may have an accurate view of his or her mother because the person knows her well yet possesses overly negative and stereotypical information about the larger group of which the mother is a part. Those in the aging field who train students sometimes ask them to meet older adults outside of clinical settings to get a more balanced view of older adults (e.g., in recreational groups, advocacy groups, religious faith congregations, their homes). My experience of meeting older adults in their homes as a young outreach worker gave me a much richer, diverse, and balanced view of older people that dispelled some of the usual negative stereotypes about older people I held at that time.

Behavior Toward Older People

Are people treated differently when they are perceived as being old or older? About 10 years ago, one of my colleagues, Becca Levy, and I did a presentation on ageism to the APA Council of Representatives (the organization's governing body) as part of a series of diversity trainings. We polled the audience and asked if they were older or had a relative who was older, and did they experience negative behavior by virtue of age. Seventy-nine percent said yes. Indeed, researchers have found that people perceived as old may be treated in both negatively and potentially favorable ways sometimes referred to as *age-differentiated behavior*. Some have argued that age-differentiated behavior becomes problematic when it "is either caused by inaccurate negative attitudes and beliefs about aging or older adults or has clear harmful impact on older adults" (Pasupathi & Löckenhoff, 2002, pp. 201–202). On the negative side of the ledger, older people may be spoken to in what has been called *overaccommodating speech*, which includes some or all of these elements: being overly polite, speaking loudly and slowly, talking in simple sentences, and taking less seriously what is said by them compared with younger individuals (Nelson, 2005). Older people are also more likely to experience *baby talk* or *elderspeak*, which is speaking words in an exaggerated way as if talking to a baby and in a high tone of voice. Most older adults find such behavior offensive. Moreover, despite federal laws against it, older adults contend with employment discrimination based on attitudes that, on the whole, they are less capable workers, even though this is not true (McCann & Giles, 2002).

On the positive side of the ledger, some older adults are advantaged by virtue of age. For example, some are offered seats on public transportation, which paradoxically, some older people find offensive. Certain public programs, such as Medicare and Social Security, were developed to advantage individuals by virtue of age. In some localities, older adults pay lower property taxes than younger homeowners. For example, I began to pay half fare in my local transit system when I turned age 65 (my transit card reads: "Gregory Hinrichsen, Senior Citizen"). Whether that is the best public policy was part of the "age versus need" debate in gerontology (Neugarten, 1982).

Attitude Toward One's Own Aging

"The strange case of prejudice against the older you. . . ."

(Nelson, 2011, p. 37)

"Prejudice against our feared future self. . . ."

(Nelson, 2005, p. 207)

"The enemy within. . . ."

(Levy, 2001, p. 578)

One of my psychology colleagues turned age 65 and shared his feelings of intense distress about this event. "I can't believe I'm this old. I don't look old, do I?," he pleaded. We talked a bit about what older adulthood meant, which, for him, included being physically unattractive, cognitively impaired, socially isolated, and unhappy. No wonder he didn't like turning 65. Where do these ideas come from? Psychologist Becca Levy (2009) has conducted research on how we acquire attitudes toward aging, the content of those attitudes, and their impact on us in later adulthood. From an early age, all of us acquire attitudes toward those who are seen as different from us based on gender, race, ethnicity, age, and other factors. If one is a member of a minority group about which there are negative characterizations, parents often tell their children they might encounter negative stereotypes about their group (e.g., lazy, dangerous, greedy, dishonest) and offer messages to the child that counter those stereotypes. Studies have found that even young children acquire stereotypical and generally negative attitudes toward older adults (Bergman, 2017). However, most children aren't taught information to counter those aging stereotypes, and they continue to be acquired throughout one's lifetime.

At some point, individuals perceive that they are now regarded as "old": You turn age 65, are offered a subway seat, asked if you are retired *yet*, or are mistaken for someone older than you believe you look. Levy (2009) argued that unconscious, underlying, long-standing, socially acquired beliefs and attitudes about aging become activated when you see yourself as an older adult. These attitudes may be positive or negative. In a series of especially interesting experiments, Levy (2009) demonstrated that if older adults are exposed to common negative, subliminal cues about aging, they will evidence behavior consistent with the stereotype. For example, if you ask older adults to complete a memory test and subliminally expose them to a cue about older people's being cognitively impaired, the older adult will perform more poorly than older people not exposed to the cue. Interestingly, the same is not true for younger people exposed to the same subliminal cues because they do not (yet) identify with being older and, therefore, the cue is not processed as relevant to them. Longitudinal research has demonstrated that both negative and positive attitudes toward aging from early life have long-term health outcomes as measured when they are old (Levy, Zonderman, Slade, & Ferrucci, 2009).

Health and mental health care professionals are not immune to the influence of attitudes toward their own aging. I used to work at a highly regarded mental health care facility and was one of the few staff with an interest in aging. I would talk to my colleagues who worked with younger populations about the challenges faced by some older clients I saw. I once talked with a colleague about an 85-year-old woman who was depressed, cognitively impaired, and had an array of medical problems. The colleague responded, "It if it gets to that point in my life, just shoot me."

For practitioners, the practical import of being more knowledgeable of the facts on aging is that knowledge may lead to better care for older adults. If you inaccurately believe that depression is common in older adults, you might be less likely to treat the condition with the same vigor as with younger adults. If you inaccurately believe that many older adults are alone and lonely, you might do less to help them find avenues for social engagement. If you believe the adage "You can't teach an old dog new tricks," you might be less likely to encourage an older adult to make meaningful life changes. If you think it is normative for older people to be cognitively impaired, you might be less motivated to assess for existing cognitive problems and refer for medical and neurological evaluations. If you are not aware of the substantive body of research that has demonstrated that most psychotherapeutic approaches are helpful for older adults with mental health problems, you may conclude that little can be done other than a bit of hand-holding.

Another practical import of being mindful of one's own reaction to working with older adults is that it may reveal thoughts and feelings that may bear on better or worse care in a professional enterprise that is built on the subtleties of patient–therapist interactions. If your first reaction to a depressed, frail older person is "I feel sorry for her," "What could I possibly do to help?" or "I hope that doesn't happen to me," then you may be less likely to help. How one feels about one's own aging and the aging of people close to you may become part of the therapeutic mix for better and for worse. If your underlying cognitive template for your own current or future aging self is one that says you will be frail, dotty, and unattractive, these "unconscious" views will likely enter the therapeutic room in ways that may not be evident to you. Older adults as a group are not unique in this regard, and the same cautions exists for individuals with backgrounds different than your own in terms of religion, race, ethnicity, socioeconomic status, gender, region of the country, sexual orientation, and gender identity—including the intersectionality of one or more of these with age (APA, 2002; APA Committee on Aging, 2009; APA Task Force on Re-Envisioning the Multicultural Guidelines for the 21st Century, 2017).

TREATMENT OF OLDER ADULTS BY HEALTH AND MENTAL HEALTH CARE PROFESSIONALS

Researchers consistently have found that older adults get poorer health care than younger adults across the continuum of care (APA Presidential Task Force on Integrated Health Care, 2007), especially older people who are minorities (APA Committee on Aging, 2009). The reasons for poorer care for older adults reflect a complex array of factors but likely begin with the fact that health care providers often hold negative stereotypes and factually inaccurate information about older patients, as does the general public (Pasupathi & Löckenhoff, 2002). Old age becomes a sort of black box for explaining (or not explaining) medical concerns of older adults. Medical diagnoses are missed or overlooked, and care is less proactive than with younger adults. Medical providers spend less time with older than younger patients despite that many older adults have more complex medical conditions. Medical information and treatment recommendations often are not clearly communicated. There is little discussion about end-of-life preferences with older people. Long-standing concerns exist about the treatment of older adults in long-term care facilities, including misuse of antipsychotic medications to manage behavioral problems, despite federal legislation that generally prohibits the use of such medications for that purpose. Further antipsychotic medications increase the risk for death in older adults with dementia. Despite slow improvements on the whole, the medical care "system" is not well suited for many older adults who have numerous medical conditions and take multiple medications.

Similar problems exist in the mental health care field. One of the first parents of the field of geropsychology, Robert Kastenbaum (1964), wrote in the article "The Reluctant Therapist" that many psychotherapists had little interest in providing services to older people. Even today, older adults underuse mental health services and are more likely be given psychotropic medication than psychotherapy services, despite their preference for psychotherapy services (Alliance for Aging Research, 2003; Areán, Alvidrez, Barrera, Robinson, & Hicks, 2002). Suicidal thoughts in older adults often are not recognized or treated as well as with younger adults, despite that a subgroup of older adults has the highest rates of suicide in the U.S. population (a topic discussed in Chapter 5, this volume). These issues are often more pronounced for minority older people (APA Committee on Aging, 2009).

Concerns about psychologists' (and other mental health care professionals') lack of knowledge and interest in older adults are long-standing. Lack of knowledge of older adults can adversely affect treatment outcomes (Gatz & Pearson, 1988); furthermore, undergraduate psychology texts lack information about aging (Whitbourne & Hulicka, 1990) and some research psychologists have failed to use appropriate study designs that misattribute age differences to age and not to other factors (Schaie, 1989, 1994). Psychologists rate the prognosis for improvement in mental health problems for older people as worse in older compared with younger adults (James & Haley, 1995). Nonetheless, in psychology and other fields, much progress has been made in the past 20 years. That progress has included, as noted in the Introduction, the establishment of a well-articulated framework for training people in the psychology of how to assess and treat late-life mental health problems (Knight et al., 2009), guidelines for the provision of psychological services to the older adult population (APA, 2014), and other professional developments that will likely improve care.

HISTORY, PUBLIC POLICY, AND AGING

"Being old in American today is remarkably similar to and incredibly different from conditions in past times. Old age clearly has assets and liabilities, and it arouses a mixture of feelings that transcend time and space" (Achenbaum, 1978, p. 1). So begins Andrew Achenbaum's classic book on the history of aging in the United States: *Old Age in the New Land: The American Experience Since 1790*. During my career, I have often heard people remark, "It's too bad we don't take care of the elderly like we used to when everyone lived together." The comment reflects nostalgia for the "good old days," when things were better and people "really cared about old people." But the story is far more complicated. In prior years, older adults often lived with adult children because most were impoverished and had no other options. Rates of suicide for older people living in the beginning of the 20th century were many times higher than they are today. Like almost any topic in gerontology, multiple strands of influence intertwine to weave the fabric of aging. And those strands continually are woven and rewoven over time. As Achenbaum (1978) noted, similarities and differences exist about how older people are viewed when comparing the 18th century with the 21st century. Ambivalence about aging is present in both eras and across cultures (Bodner, 2017).

Attitudes toward aging are shaped by historical era, religion, culture, gender, sexual orientation, socioeconomic status, and the interactions among them. In some historical eras, older adults are viewed as possessing unique knowledge and experience that contribute to the larger community. In some religious traditions, old age as seen as evidence of God's blessing of longevity to the righteous or opportunities to fulfill religious commands to care for one's parents (Bodner, 2017; Cole, 1992). Given that attitudes about women vary among cultures, so will attitudes about older women compared with older men. Traditionally, some cultures have collectivistic values (Eastern cultures are often cited) in which older adults are seen an integral part of the collective for which all members have responsibility. However, cultural values are reshaped over time. Although many Eastern cultures may be more collectivistic than Western cultures, those cultures are in evolution. Recent work has questioned the assumption that modern Eastern societies have more favorable attitudes toward older adults than Western societies (North & Fiske, 2015).

Attitudes toward older adults are reflected in the public policy arena and change over time. When I came into the aging filed, there was increasing concern about the "plight of the elderly" through media portrayals of poor, frightened, isolated old people living in crime-ridden urban neighborhoods. One story frequently told was of old people who were so poor that they had to eat dog food. (This story was not true.) Gerontologist Robert Butler (1975) wrote the Pulitzer prizewinning book *Why Survive? Being Old in America*, which was a polemic about the terrible state of affairs for older adults. Building on those and other concerns, Medicare and Medicaid, a nationwide system for assistance for the aged through the Older Americans Act of 1965, were established, and improvements in Social Security were made, Just a decade later, the political winds had shifted: Older adults were beginning to be viewed as a drain on society, and some said they should make way for the younger generation. These days, older adults tend to be characterized in political realms as the "silver tsunami" that will overwhelm the society with their need for support (some disparagingly referred to as "greedy geezers") and a Social Security system that will go bankrupt. All of these portrayals are highly simplified and dichotomized, map onto existing stereotypes, and are inaccurate or so highly simplified they distort the facts (Schulz & Binstock, 2006).

How the larger society views older adults influences how political figures and policymakers will or will not address existing problems or engage the older population. Political and historical views of older adults may influence practitioners' views of older adults but also make it more or less likely that mental health services will be reimbursed or that larger efforts to improve the well-being of older adults are supported. For some practitioners, broader concerns about older people have led to advocacy for them in the local, state, and national policy arenas (Hinrichsen et al., 2010). I know some of those individuals and appreciate that their efforts, in concert with others, have led to better support for aging services, including better reimbursement for mental health practitioners who serve older people.

MULTICULTURAL VIEW OF AGING

"All individuals exist in social, political, historical, and economic contexts, and psychologists are increasingly called upon to understand the influence of these contexts on individuals' behavior" (APA, 2002, p. 1). This is the introductory statement from the APA *Guidelines on Multicultural Education, Training, Research, Practice, and Organizational Change for Psychologists.* The most recent revision of these guidelines (APA Task Force on Re-Envisioning the Multicultural Guidelines for the 21st Century, 2017) emphasizes the diversity within each of these and other factors and the complex "intersectionality" among race, ethnicity, language, sexual orientation, gender identity, age, disability, social class, religious or spiritual concerns, country of origin, and other issues. Other professional organizations have similar statements.

Imagine you have a first appointment with a widowed 90-year-old African American woman who uses a wheelchair. She has three sons and is accompanied to the appointment by her daughter-in-law. You learn that she grew up in the rural South, spent much of her life in New York, worked as a nurse on the staff of the same institution where you work, and is religiously committed. What facts do you think might shape your initial impressions of her? She is in a wheelchair? She is 90? She is religiously committed? She worked for the same institution as you? She was a health care professional like your? She is a New Yorker? She was a Southerner? Her daughter in law accompanied her? She is middle class? She is a woman? She is African American?

Some of my mental health colleagues have enthusiastically welcomed the emphasis on cultivating multicultural awareness and sensitivity. Privately, others have expressed reservations and feel as if they are being lectured to. "We're mental health providers. For goodness's sake, we're schooled to be sensitive to people. We don't need to be told to do that." I appreciate their concerns and believe there are better and worse ways to approach building greater knowledge and sensitivity to individuals different than us. And yet, as a geropsychologist, I continue to be troubled by offhanded remarks about aging (e.g., "Just shoot me when I'm old") from colleagues who, by all accounts, are thoughtful, kind, and highly capable clinicians. I love the term *cultural humility*: The world is so complex—and so are people—and we need to reflect on what we know and don't know. One of my first supervisors said that best quality that a therapist can have is "intense curiosity" about his or her clients. I think that the vast majority of mental health practitioners are, by nature, curious, open-hearted people.

That curiosity and open-heartedness will be your best friend as you, the practitioner, see older clients. In the preceding example, as you begin to work with a 90-year-old African American woman, you will move beyond age, race, and gender to better understand the blending of those statuses with other factors in her life, including her experience of her own history and how she makes sense of it. Your curiosity and open-heartedness may spark greater curiosity for the client herself in understanding and addressing the obstacles that brought her to your office. You may also learn something from her that you can use to reflect on in your own older adulthood.

SUMMARY

Some geropsychologists view attitudes toward aging as the key foundational lesson for those who provide health and mental health services to older adults (Knight, 2018). A rich literature documents that stereotyping of older adults is common, often unexamined, and affects behavior toward them (us). For mental health care professionals, greater mindfulness about attitudes toward preconceptions of aging, including one's own aging, will often generate a more complex understanding of their older clients and how to better care for them.

2 FACTS ABOUT AGING AND THE LIFESPAN DEVELOPMENTAL PERSPECTIVE

Unfortunately, too many practitioners labored through graduate school with what seemed to be many courses on theory, statistics, and related topics to get to what they wanted to do: Practice with clients. I don't think we do a very good job in graduate education of engaging students to appreciate and even love the research foundations of practice. The field of geropsychology is relatively new; it sprung out of the larger field of academic gerontology and more specifically within what is now commonly referred to as *adult development and aging* or sometimes as *lifespan developmental psychology*. (*Note: Gerontology* is the larger field of the study of aging. All the major disciplines [e.g., sociology, economics, biology, anthropology, psychology, medicine, public policy] have individuals who research aging-related aspects of their respective disciplines.) For those practitioners who work with older adults, it can be so helpful to understand fundamental issues of what is known about older people. It is helpful because it builds an appreciation of the many forces that shape people from childhood into older adulthood, and this information hopefully will

http://dx.doi.org/10.1037/0000146-003
Assessment and Treatment of Older Adults: A Guide for Mental Health Professionals, by Gregory A. Hinrichsen

deepen your appreciation of the older individual who comes to your office. Knowledge of what is "usual" about older adults will help you to appreciate what is "unusual" about your older clients with respect to the problems they have and the strengths they possess. To that end, in this chapter, I review fundamental issues related to aging and demography, biology, health, how people successful adapt, methods to study change over time, successful aging, mental abilities, emotions, well-being, personality, social dynamics, and work or retirement.

This chapter covers the Council of Professional Geropsychology Training Programs' recommended foundational knowledge competencies with respect to general knowledge about adult development and aging (Hinrichsen, Emery-Tiburcio, Gooblar, & Molinari, 2018). Material in this chapter reflects content from the Pikes Peak model for training in professional geropsychology (Knight, Karel, Hinrichsen, Qualls, & Duffy, 2009), including II. Knowledge Base, A. General Knowledge About Adult Development, Aging, and the Older Population. It also addresses content from "Guidelines for Psychological Practice With Older Adults" (American Psychological Association [APA], 2014), including Guideline 3 (Psychologists strive to gain knowledge about theory and research in aging), Guideline 4 (Psychologists strive to be aware of the social/psychological dynamics of the aging process), Guideline 5 (Psychologists strive to understand diversity in the aging process), and Guideline 6 (Psychologists strive to be familiar with current information about biological and health-related aspects of aging).

WHO IS OLD?

How do we define who is *old* (e.g., elderly, older, senior citizen)? Conventionally, the entry into older adulthood has been set at 65 years of age. Why 65? This was the age that pension eligibility was established in the first old-age pension system in Germany in the 19th century. It was also used as the criterion for Social Security eligibility in the United States when that program was established in the 1930s.

Gerontologists soon learned the intellectual folly of aggregating people from age 65 onward into one monolithic group and began to slice the gerontological pie into smaller pieces: the *young-old* (ages 65–74), *old-old* (ages 75–84), and *oldest old* (age 85 and older). In recent years. the pie has been sliced into even finer pieces to include *centenarians* (those older than 100 years of age) and *supercentenarians* (those 110 years and older).

DEMOGRAPHICS

It is sometimes said that demography is destiny. What that means is that the size and composition of a population of a nation have powerful and real-life consequences for the people who live there. In some nations, almost half of the population is under 25 years of age with few older adults; frequently, too many younger people are competing for the available jobs, so social unrest may result. The percentage of the population of Uganda that is 65 years of age and older, for example, is 2% and is projected to grow to only 3.4% by 2050. Currently, the percentage of the population of Japan age 65 years and older is almost 27% and will grow to 40% by the year 2050 (Federal Interagency Forum on Aging-Related Statistics, 2016). Furthermore, Japan has little in-migration compared with countries like the United States and Canada.

It is sometimes said that America's population is aging because "people are living longer." That's partially true. For those who reach age 65, additional years have been added. For example, in 1950, the average life expectancy for individuals 65 years of age was 13.9 years. In 2007, it was 18.6 years (National Center for Health Statistics, 2011). Therefore, in my lifetime, 65-year-olds can expect to live about 5 years longer than my great grandparents. (*Note: Life expectancy* is the average number of years that people will live from a particular age. For example, you could estimate life expectancy from birth, age 50, age 65, and so on. *Life expectancy* is often confused with *lifespan*, which is the upper limit in age that a human can live: about 120 years.) A bigger contributor to the "aging of America" is that many more people live to later years than they did 100 years ago. In 1900, the life expectancy from birth was 47.3 years. In 2007, it was 77.9 years (National Center for Health Statistics, 2011). This huge increase in life expectancy is related to improvements in health and public health that have significantly reduced childhood deaths and death from infectious disease during adulthood during the past century.

The other important contributor to the aging of America is the aging of the *baby boomers*, those individuals born between 1946 and 1964. In the 1930s and early 1940s, people had fewer children than usual because of the economically and socially disruptive effects of the Great Depression and World War II. At the end of the war, all of this pent-up reproductive power was unleashed; the result was that an unusually large number of children were born in about a 20-year period. (Sometimes the vivid image of the "pig in the python" is used to represent the movement of baby boomers as they go through the life cycle.) The impact of this demographic was a sharp demand for schools as baby boomers entered childhood and a demand for housing when they started jobs and formed families. In a few years, the impact will be a demand for health and long-term care services as they enter late older adulthood. Figure 2.1 illustrates different aspects of the baby boomer demographic phenomena. You can see how dramatic the percentage increase of the U.S. population is once the first of the baby boomers turn age 65. And the absolute number of individuals 65 years and older grows dramatically as a function of not only the aging of the baby boomers but also the increase in the total U.S. population. As of this writing, the leading edge of baby boomers is 71 years of age. The health of most of them is generally good. But in 10 years—as they move from being the young-old to the old-old—most will have increasing health problems, which will be associated with increased use of health- and related services. The practical import for the mental health practitioner of today is that you will see increasing numbers of older adults seeking services. And for mental health practitioners 10 years from now, the number of older adults seeking services will be even larger.

Population aging can be further understood by the individuals within it who vary by: race, ethnicity, country of origin, region of the country, gender, socioeconomic status, sexual orientation, and other factors (APA Committee on Aging, 2009). The diversity within older adulthood is equally or more important than the generalities about a particular generation. Among the old-old is a higher percentage of women versus men because, at age 65, the life expectancy of women is about 2.5 years longer than men (Federal Interagency Forum on Aging Related Statistics, 2016). Most (78.3%) of the current cohort of older adults is non-Hispanic White (see Figure 2.2). Ten percent of older people live in poverty, but rates vary significantly by race or ethnicity (White, 7.8% vs. Black, 19%). The percentage of the population that was 65 years of age in 2014 was 14.5%, but that percentage varies by state. In Florida, the percentage is 19.1% versus 9.4% in Alaska. And all of these numbers will change in coming years. For example, it is estimated that by 2060, only 54.6% of the United States will be non-Hispanic White (compared with 78.5% today; Federal Interagency Forum on Aging-Related Statistics, 2016).

BIOLOGY OF AGING

As a graduate student, I read about structural alterations in the eye starting in one's 40s that result in vision changes. One of these changes—a condition called *presbyopia*—makes it harder to see things at close range. Like

FIGURE 2.1. The Impact of the Baby Boom Generation on Aging in the United States

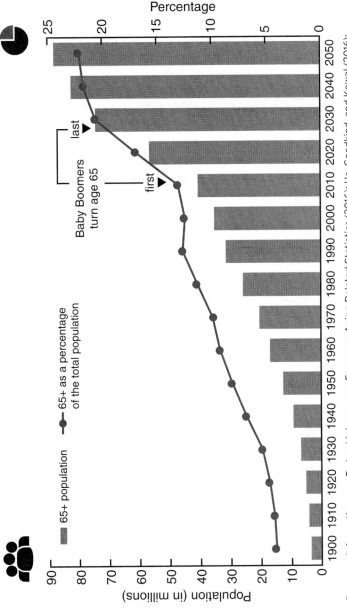

For more information, see Federal Interagency Forum on Aging-Related Statistics (2016); He, Goodkind, and Kowal (2016); West, Cole, Goodkind, and He (2014); and U.S. Census Bureau (2011). From "Population Aging in the United States: A Global Perspective," by Federal Interagency Forum on Aging-Related Statistics, n.d. (https://agingstats.gov/images/olderamericans_agingpopulation.pdf). In the public domain.

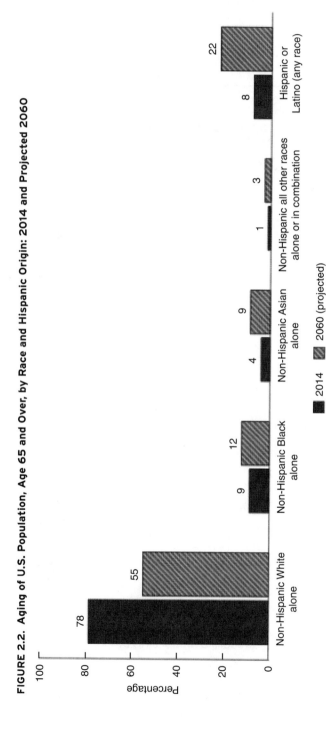

FIGURE 2.2. Aging of U.S. Population, Age 65 and Over, by Race and Hispanic Origin: 2014 and Projected 2060

From "Older Americans 2016: Key Indicators of Well-Being," by Federal Interagency Forum on Aging-Related Statistics, 2016 (https://agingstats.gov/docs/LatestReport/Older-Americans-2016-Key-Indicators-of-WellBeing.pdf). In the public domain.

clockwork, at age 40, I began to squint to see things and realized I needed reading glasses, the strength of which grows stronger each decade. In later years, I have found it harder to drive at night because I don't see as sharply as in younger years. The reality is that our bodies begin to wear out over time. Why is that? Several theories offer explanations for the biological fact of aging. One stream of thought—*programmed longevity*—is that organisms are programmed to age and eventually die: The number of times that cells can divide over time is limited, and a change or weakening of the hormonal and immune systems occurs that increases susceptibility to disease. Another stream of thought is the *wear-and-tear theory of aging*: Parts of the body wear out; the cross-linking of cells with each other stiffens the constituent parts of the body, including organs; biological by-products called free radicals damage organs; and DNA damage occurs over time (Jin, 2010). In the end, whatever the biological forces at work associated with aging, they interact with the environment and lifestyle in ways that may hasten or slow the aging process.

Evidence of the biological changes associated with aging is clear in the mirror and as we peruse photographs of ourselves and others over the years. With aging, the skin becomes thinner and less elastic with associated wrinkling. Hair grays and thins. The voice changes, which often includes a lowering of pitch and volume and decreasing resonance. Bodily changes associated with aging include middle-age weight gain followed by later life weight loss and a reduction in the ratio of muscle mass to fat. Bones thin especially for women as they age. In addition to the need for reading glasses, other vision changes associated with aging include a decrease in the amount of light that enters the eye, which is one reason why older adults have more difficulty driving at night than younger people. The lens of the eye often darkens, so cataract surgery may be required later in life. Changes in hearing commonly occur with aging and can be exacerbated by lifestyle issues from earlier life (e.g., exposure to loud noise). One common hearing condition is *presbycusis*, which is evident in problems hearing high-pitched tones. There are some declines in ability to taste and smell (National Institute on Aging, n.d.).

What is the import of this information for the practitioner? For some clients, these biological changes make it harder to engage in life activities. You can work with your clients to explore options to increase daily activities, despite sight and hearing problems. Other clients are emotionally distressed about these changes. Distress may reflect negative attitudes toward aging that are acquired throughout life about which the client may be unaware (see Chapter 1, this volume). Knowledge of common hearing and vision changes helps the clinician to enhance communication with the client and, for example, avoid misattributing hearing problems to cognitive problems. Knowledge of these common biological changes builds the clinician's credibility in discussions with medical providers with whom coordination about a client may be needed.

PHYSICAL AND FUNCTIONAL HEALTH

You've probably heard the expression "If you've got your health, you've got everything." I beg to differ. I know perfectly healthy people who are deeply unhappy and people with many health problems who lead active, happy lives. The truth is that when we get older, most of us have an increasing number of health problems. I provide psychological services in a geriatric primary care medical clinic. When I am referred a new client, I review the client's electronic medical record, which lists all current diagnosable medical problems and associated medications. Sometimes the list is very, very long, but when I conduct a first interview with that client, often I wouldn't know the individual had health problems from appearance or demeanor. Furthermore, the issue for which the client was referred to me might have nothing to do with health concerns. That being said, health-related issues are often directly or indirectly part of the reason that older adults are referred for mental health services. An important distinction is between acute health problems, which often develop over a short period and immediately affect one's health, versus chronic health problems, which develop over longer periods, often do not disappear, and require long-term treatment or management. Older adults have fewer acute health problems and more chronic health problems than younger adults.

In Figure 2.3, you can see the most common chronic health conditions in older adults. Hypertension and arthritis top the list, and the percentages vary somewhat based on gender. When I look at a medical chart, I often see one or more of the medical conditions listed. People 65 years and older take an average of almost four and a half medications per day (AARP, 2005), and 45% report having two or three chronic health conditions (National Institute on Aging, 2016). Despite having chronic health conditions, how do older people subjectively rate their health? As can be seen in Figure 2.4, the majority of people 65 years and older view their health as good or excellent. Self-rated health is judged less favorably in older age groups, but even among those 85 years of age and older, the majority judge their health as good to excellent. For the reader interested in learning more about health

FIGURE 2.3. Percentage of People Age 65 and Over Who Reported Having Selected Chronic Health Conditions, by Sex, 2013–2014

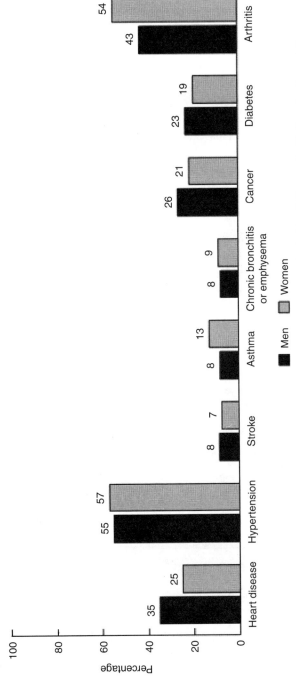

Data based on a 2-year average from 2013–2014. Reference population: These data refer to the civilian noninstitutionalized population. Chronic health conditions in older Americans, by gender. From "'Older Americans 2016: Key Indicators of Well-Being," by Federal Interagency Forum on Aging-Related Statistics, 2016 (https://agingstats.gov/docs/LatestReport/Older-Americans-2016-Key-Indicators-of-WellBeing.pdf). In the public domain.

FIGURE 2.4. Percentage of People Age 65 and Over With Respondent-Assessed Good to Excellent Health Status, by Age Group and Race and Hispanic Origin, 2012–2014

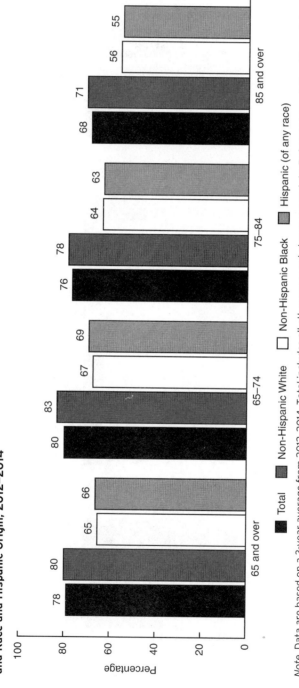

Note. Data are based on a 3-year average from 2012–2014. Total includes all other races not shown separately. Reference population: These data refer to the civilian noninstitutionalized population. Self-assessed health in older Americans, by age group and race and Hispanic origin. From "Older Americans 2016: Key Indicators of Well-Being," by Federal Interagency Forum on Aging-Related Statistics, 2016 (https://agingstats.gov/docs/LatestReport/Older-Americans-2016-Key-Indicators-of-WellBeing.pdf). In the public domain.

and health care for varied cultural groups of older adults, Stanford University School of Medicine's ethnogeriatric website is a good resource. See Appendix A for the link.

For most older people, health issues become more practically meaningful as they limit ability to go about daily life. Two concepts are important: activities of daily living (ADLs) and instrumental activities of daily living (IADLs). *ADLs* are functions fundamental to self-care and include bathing, toileting, walking, transferring in and out of bed or a chair, dressing, and eating. *IADLs* are important for an individual to live independently in the community and include ability to use a telephone, perform housework, prepare a meal, shop, and manage money. One fairly recent study found that, of Medicare beneficiaries 65 years and older, 11.7% had IADL limitations but no ADL problems, 20% had one to two ADL limitations, 5.8% had three to four ADL limitations, 2.8% had five to six ADL limitations, and 3.7% were in long-term care (Federal Interagency Forum on Aging-Related Statistics, 2016).

Most practitioners working with older adults will see clients who have one or more medical conditions for which they are taking medications and that may or may not limit their functioning. Older adults may be seeking psychotherapeutic services to better manage issues tied to a medical problem. Practitioners become more credible providers to their clients when they have basic knowledge of the medical problems often seen in older adults and therefore are in a better position to explore options to adapt more successfully to them. Basic familiarity with medications taken for health conditions and their possible side effects will assist the practitioner to know when it may be helpful to contact the medication prescriber to alert him or her to some possible untoward effects of those medications, including symptoms like anxiety, depression, insomnia, agitation, memory loss, and confusion.

LIFESPAN DEVELOPMENTAL PERSPECTIVE: MANY STRANDS THAT ARE WOVEN AND REWOVEN THROUGHOUT LIFE

Kurt Lewin (1951), one of the founders of social psychology, said, "There's nothing so practical as a good theory" (p. 169). The roots of the field of geropsychology are in studies of aging. Psychology has a long tradition of studying developmental processes from birth through adolescence. For those who provide services to children and adolescents, an understanding of the usual processes of earlier life development undergirds efforts to help young people who are having problems. Those who have taken developmental psychology courses learned about early life development, but they rarely learn theories and about research on adulthood and later adulthood.

What is called a "lifespan developmental perspective" offers a way for viewing (and also researching) life beyond adolescence that I believe enriches and informs mental health practice with older adults.

Lifespan developmental psychologists study behavioral change and constancy from birth to death, although those in the aging field focus on adulthood and later adulthood. There is a long tradition of psychologists, psychiatrists, psychoanalysts, and others who have thought about old age and its relationship to the human lifespan. In 1922, noted American psychologist G. Stanley Hall wrote the book *Senescence: The Last Half of Life* (Hall, 1922), which reflected his broader thoughts about aging and the life course as well as struggles with his own aging (Cole, 1984). The work of psychoanalyst Erik Erikson (1959) is perhaps best known to mental health care providers because he extended and enriched traditional, psychoanalytic concepts about development through the entire life course. He proposed that psychosocial development involved trying to manage the tensions or conflicts ("crises") through eight stages of life. The last three stages are intimacy versus isolation, which is the challenge for younger adults of finding an intimate partner (ages 21–39); generativity versus stagnation, which is finding meaning and purpose in the middle years often by giving to others (40–65); and ego integrity versus despair, which is making sense of one's life (65 and older). His stages of psychosocial development are appealing and well-known and have formed the basis of some research. A subsequent book by Erikson and his wife elaborated on and extended his theory to include very old age (Erikson & Erikson, 1998).

As Swiss psychologist Jean Piaget was an important influence in theorizing about and researching child development, German psychologist Paul Baltes was equally influential in the fields of aging and of lifespan development. There are many components to his theories and his work, some of which I briefly summarize. His work and that of others form the *lifespan developmental perspective*: In contrast to simplistic overly positive or overly negative stereotypical characterizations of older adults, the lifespan perspective views the process of aging as complex and dynamic. For those of us who work with older adults, the notion that the lives of our older clients are complex and dynamic makes a great deal of sense. Our academic colleagues help us to better conceptualize the lifespan and generate evidence to support existing theories.

The following are key concepts in the lifespan developmental perspective (Baltes, Lindenberger, & Staudinger, 2006).

- Human development is a lifelong process (vs. the belief that development ends after adolescence).

- Development involves both gains and losses ("multidirectionality" vs. seeing aging only as a series of losses).

- People's abilities can change over the life course ("plasticity" vs. seeing aging as a process of increasing rigidity).

- Development exists within particular historical contexts ("historical embeddedness" vs. seeing individuals as developing independent of history and culture).

- Human development is influenced by many forces, including biological, psychological, sociocultural, and life cycle (studying human development is multidisciplinary vs. seeing aging as a "medical problem").

These forces are at work in different ways throughout the lifespan. Biological forces include those evident in, for example, the physical and sexual maturity of young people and the physical changes seen in older adulthood, including wrinkling and reduction in efficiency and capacity of organ systems. Psychological forces include personality, emotion, and cognition. Sociocultural forces include societal, interpersonal, cultural, and ethnic factors. Life-cycle forces are evident in how biological, psychological, and social forces affect people in different ways at different segments of the life cycle.

Although Baltes viewed adult development as full of potential, he was also clear-eyed that aging also involves losses and that not all is possible in the later years. Childhood is characterized as a period of rapid growth; middle adulthood, by maintenance of those gains; and old age, as regulation and management of loss (Baltes, 1997). Biological forces at work often diminish physical and mental capacities of older adults. Optimal aging involves maximizing gains and minimizing losses. Younger individuals also try to maximize gains and minimize losses but typically have relatively fewer losses. How did Baltes propose that people accomplish this? Like other theorists, he viewed individuals as active responders to life problems (vs. the view of older adults as passive victims of forces over which they have little control). His model for understanding how people minimize losses and maximize gains is selection, optimization, and compensation. As older people contend with age-related losses, they may limit the scope of what they do and choose activities that best suit their current abilities (selection). They then may make an extra effort to maximize their ability to perform what is needed as part of the activity (optimization). If there are limitations in their ability to perform the chosen action, they will engage in compensatory efforts (compensation). He used proverbs to illustrate each: for selection, "Those who follow every path, never reach any destination"; for optimization, "Practice makes perfect"; for compensation, "There are many hands; what one cannot do, the other will" (Freund & Baltes, 2002).

The best illustration of the model of selection, optimization, and compensation was provided by Baltes himself (1997):

> When the concert pianist Arthur Rubinstein, as an 80-year-old, was asked in a television interview how he managed to maintain such a high level of expert piano playing, he hinted at the coordination of three strategies. First, Rubinstein said that he played fewer pieces (selection); second, he indicated that he now practiced these pieces more often (optimization); and third he suggested that to counteract his loss of mechanical speed, he now used a kind of impression management, such as introducing slower play before fast segments, so to make the latter appear faster (compensation). (p. 371)

I find Baltes's theory of selection, optimization, and compensation practical in work with older adults. Sometimes older clients say that they don't feel that they have the physical, functional, emotional, or cognitive capacity to engage in activities that they previously have enjoyed. The problem can be further complicated by preexisting negative attitudes toward aging (e.g., "You're old. What can you expect?") as well as the presence of depressive and anxiety symptoms or disorders. Engaging a client to take stock of current abilities and limitations can lead to a review and selection of options for activities (selection). The therapist can then work with the client to review and practice efforts that would be needed to engage in the chosen activity (optimization). If the client feels he or she cannot perform some dimensions of the chosen activity, explore other ways to do them or get help from others (compensation).

A woman I recently saw is another good example of selection, optimization, and compensation. She had founded a civic organization in earlier years that was successful and for which she always had been the spokesperson. In her 90s, she had sight and hearing losses, as well as increasing difficulty remembering names. She found organizational meetings that she continued to lead increasingly stressful because of those hearing, sight, and memory difficulties. Many members of the group looked up to her not only for her contributions to the group but as a model of "successful aging." However, she considered resigning from the organization, yet she knew that would be a big loss for herself. After much thought, she decided to attend only the most important meetings (selection); practice the names of meeting presenters in advance of the event (optimization); and have her daughter accompany her to meetings, stand by her side, and quietly remind her of the names of individuals she interacted with (compensation).

AGE, PERIOD, COHORT: KEY CONCEPTS IN THE STUDY OF LIFESPAN DEVELOPMENTAL PSYCHOLOGY

Please bear with me for a brief discussion of methodological issues in the study of aging. They have relevance to clinical practice (really). When psychologists first began to give standardized intelligence tests, they found that older adults did more poorly on them than younger adults. Some concluded that something about aging diminished intelligence. Eventually, researchers began to understand it was not so much aging that was related to lower IQ scores but that older adults had less access to higher education in their younger years (than their later age cohorts) that influenced test performance.

Researchers have distinguished among three important influences in studying aging. One of the intellectual giants in this area is K. Warner Schaie, whose Seattle longitudinal studies have contributed enormously to our understanding of stability and change in mental abilities as well as the best methods to study that process (Schaie, 1994). Age effects are tied to aging only—most notably, biological aging. *Period effects* (also known as *time-of-measurement*) are recent events to which individuals of all age groups are exposed collectively, such as war and economic crisis. (As a New Yorker, I think about the immediate emotional impact of the September 11, 2001, attack on the World Trade Center complex.) *Cohort effects* are those experiences uniquely shared by members of group. I am sure that you are familiar with names coined for different generational groups (e.g., baby boomers, Generation X, millennials). The challenge for lifespan developmental researchers is to try to disentangle age, period, and cohort influences. Cross-sectional, longitudinal, and a combination of cross-sectional and longitudinal studies ("sequential designs") are used in this effort (Cavanaugh & Whitbourne, 2003). *Cross-sectional studies* examine differences at one point in time among different age groups. *Longitudinal studies* follow individuals over time. Combinations of cross-sectional and longitudinal studies follow different groups of people over time and yield findings that better identify differences based on age, period, and cohort (Schaie, Willis, & Pennak, 2005). Of course, things can get more complicated. The distinct abilities that are measured by "intelligence" may have different trajectories of gain or loss over time that vary by each generation (Schaie et al., 2005). Using the preceding example, if a study of perceived safety were being conducted at the time of the attack on the World Trade Center complex, it might vary by age groups.

Keeping these concepts in mind will help practitioners to think more complexly about their clients. Consideration of cohort influences is especially important for practitioners because each cohort or group of older adults will be different from the cohort or group that came before or after. Over my career, I have seen several cohorts of older adults—those of my grandparents' generation, my parents' generation, and my own generation. What they all shared was that they were older but differed in their collective life experiences. I remember one of my clients, who was on the leading edge of the baby boomer generation, talking about her experience of taking hallucinogens in her youth. I had never heard an older adult talk about that topic and realized that she was part of a generation in which some individuals experimented with perception-altering drugs in a way that was rare for my grandparents' or parents' generation. Generational experiences vary by other factors, including race, ethnicity, gender, sexual orientation, social class, and other statuses. That is, within each generation are subgroups of individuals who have life experiences that are conditioned by being a member of that subgroup (APA Committee on Aging, 2009). Subgroup experiences may be more important in shaping experience than those of the larger generational cohort. From my perspective, it is all so beautifully complex in a way that can come alive working with individual clients.

AGING "SUCCESSFULLY"

Are there better ways to live your younger years so that your later years are happier and healthier? Are there better ways to live your later years so that you are happier and healthier? In 1998, geriatrician John Rowe and psychologist Robert Kahn wrote the book *Successful Aging*. Their work was supported by the MacArthur Foundation (best known for its "genius awards"). Their work, which reflected more than 10 years of research by people from many disciplines, led to this definition: "We therefore define successful aging as the ability to maintain three key behaviors or characteristics: low risk of disease and disease-related disability; high mental and physical function; and active engagement with life" (Rowe & Kahn, 1998, p. 38). After reading their book, my first thought was that I saw many older adults with health problems and cognitive difficulties who also were struggling with engagement in life. Would Rowe and Kahn consider them aging failures? Their work generated much discussion and controversy about the notion of "successful aging" and factors that lead to a better quality of life for older adults. There still does not appear to be a professional consensus on what is *successful aging* (Depp & Jeste, 2006). That topic, however, is not a new one for the field of gerontology, which sought early on to better understand the factors tied to a better old age (Havinghurst, 1961). Favorable genetics and good health practices in earlier life are tied to longevity and better late life. Social connectedness and certain psychological attributes (e.g., positive attitudes) are tied to better emotional well-being in older people. Good physical health, physical activity, and engagement with others promote the retention of cognitive abilities. Wisdom and spirituality are tied to better late-life well-being. (See Depp, Vahia, & Jeste, 2012, for a brief review.) Socioeconomic and cultural factors are integral to how "success" in late life is understood. Economically disadvantaged older adults are much more likely to have health problems in later life, and different cultural views exist regarding what late-life characteristics might be seen more or less favorably (e.g., embeddedness in family structures, personal independence).

In one qualitative study, older adults said that successful aging involved not so much freedom from health problems but their ability to adapt and compensate for them (Montross et al., 2006). Based on my many years of clinical work with older adults, I would agree with this observation. Most older people are not surprised that they have health problems; often they are surprised if they don't have them. The usual therapeutic goal is how to more successfully contend with health, cognitive, and other concerns to maximize functioning and enhance emotional and social well-being. This perspective is also consistent with Baltes's (1997) model of selection, optimization, and compensation.

When people ask me how they can better plan for their own aging, I say the first step is to think about your "future self" as an older adult. In caring for your future self, you can do things when you are younger that will maximize your late-life options. These efforts include engaging in financial planning (i.e., money put away for late life), preparing legal documents (e.g., will, power of attorney, advance directives), building a stable and hopefully rewarding work life (e.g., managing work–life balance), taking steps to promote better health (e.g., nutrition, exercise, sleep, health checkups), and building and sustaining social connections (APA Committee on Aging, 2018). For people who are now older, they can continue to take steps to make their later years better—and practitioners can play an important role in helping older adults to identify available options.

MENTAL ABILITIES IN LATER LIFE

The study of mental abilities is a broad and complex area of research. Some researchers examine "intelligence" and its components; others study specific cognitive abilities, the assessment of which is the province of neuropsychologists and neuroscientists. For practitioners, the practical questions often are: Is my client showing signs of cognitive decline about which I should be concerned? What are normal changes in mental abilities for older adults? Can anything be done about preserving mental abilities? If a client is contending with cognitive loss, how might this be handled therapeutically? In this section, I highlight central issues in the conceptualization of late-life mental abilities as well as important findings.

I return to Paul Baltes, the German psychologist who influenced many generations of researchers. In a seminal article, he wrote, "My colleagues and I have tried to understand both what is possible as we grow older, and what is not. . . . We have attempted to keep reality in sight so as not to succumb to naïve romanticism" (Baltes, 1993, p. 580). For those who have studied intelligence, a long-standing distinction has been between fluid intelligence and crystallized intelligence. For Baltes (and others) *fluid intelligence* (which he called *mechanics*) is the biological basis of mental activity that he likened to computer hardware. Fluid intelligence is the product of evolution and is evident in such mental abilities as memory and speed of processing. *Crystallized intelligence* (which he called *pragmatics*) is the product of all the experiences an individual has as part of a given culture. Baltes likened crystallized intelligence to computer software; it is evident in writing and reading skills, the understanding of language, and the retention of information about the world. Fluid intelligence begins to lessen in the twenties, whereas crystallized intelligence generally increases over the lifespan. These two processes vary considerably among individuals, but it is clear that fluid intelligence declines with aging, and in very late life, decrements in crystallized intelligence generally are evident. However, as we've discussed, individuals use selection, optimization, and compensation to balance cognitive losses and resources to achieve their goals.

K. Warner Schaie's work on cognitive aging began in 1956, when he started the Seattle longitudinal study, which has collected data at 7-year intervals through 2005. Over time, 6,000 have participated in the studies. He and his colleagues have published more than 300 articles from their data (Schaie, 1994). I summarize a few major findings from that work:

- Over the lifespan, changes in intellectual abilities occur but are not uniform and vary, depending on the component of intelligence that is measured—that is, an overall IQ score is not the most accurate measure of intellectual ability. Fluid intelligence declines earlier than crystallized intelligence. There is considerable variability in these patterns of loss among individuals. Most individuals show evidence of sustained ability in one or more intellectual abilities, even in late adulthood.

- Cohort or generational differences in patterns of change in components of mental abilities occur over the lifespan, thus attesting to the influence of varied life experiences on intelligence.

- Better cognitive aging is associated with the absence of disease, including cardiovascular disease; better socioeconomic status; engagement in a complex and intellectually stimulating environment; a flexible personality; life with a spouse who functions at a high cognitive level; and other factors (Schaie, 1989, 1994).

When seeing older clients, practitioners can appreciate that a slowing of mental quickness is to be expected and is not necessarily evidence of a cognitive disorder. Most older adults retain most mental abilities—typically those evident in crystallized intelligence—and draw on them to cope with and adapt to life circumstances. Considerable variability exists among older adults with respect to mental abilities and their respective change over the lifespan (vs. a stereotypical characterization of older people as dotty or demented). When clients ask what can be done to preserve cognitive health, the practitioner can point to maintenance of good health and engagement with others. Baltes's (1997) notion of selection, optimization, and compensation informs the practitioner's effort to help the client cope with cognitive losses and meaningfully engage in the world and with others.

EMOTIONS AND EMOTIONAL WELL-BEING IN LATER LIFE

In 2010, *The Economist* magazine had this title on the cover: "The joy of growing old (or why life begins at 46)." In that issue, an article ("The U-Bend of Life: Age and Happiness," 2010) discussed research attesting that, on the whole, as people grow older, they grow happier. Old = Happy? That equation does not correspond to the commonly computed math that Old = Depressed, Despondent, Dispirited. Indeed, researchers consistently have found that emotional well-being (e.g., positive affect, happiness, well-being) improves over the lifespan well into the 60s and beyond. Many very old people are happier than most younger people. These findings are evident in both cross-sectional and longitudinal studies (Carstensen et al., 2011). As discussed in Chapter 3 of this volume, older adults have lower rates of depression and anxiety than younger adults (Blazer, 2003). Anger decreases as people grow older (Magai, 2001). Most older adults experience better well-being in their later years compared with their younger years, despite increasing health-related problems; this effect has been called the *paradox of aging*. But the paradox can be better understood when we view aging through the lifespan developmental psychological lens. On the whole, people are adaptive and resilient in contrast with the commonly held view that older adults are passive responders to the accumulation of life's problems over which they have little control and that emotionally wear them down. Baltes's (1997) process of selection, optimization, and compensation may be one means by which individuals successfully contend with late-life losses in a way that preserves or enhances well-being. Psychologist Laura Carstensen (Carstensen, Isaacowitz, & Charles, 1999) has found that as people age, they focus on those relationships that give them the most emotional meaning—what she called *socioemotional selectivity*. Also, life generally builds a reservoir of experiences that helps people better manage its challenges.

Other components of emotional processing characteristic of older adults include generally appraising circumstances as more positive, experiencing fewer feelings of regret, and experiencing a more complex range of emotions and regulating them better than younger people. However, those older adults who score high on measures of neuroticism (e.g., are emotionally reactive, dwell on negative events—often since younger adulthood) do not evidence improvements of well-being over their lifetimes. Furthermore, older adults with cognitive problems, those experiencing personal loss, or those contending with prolonged life stress are less capable of maintaining well-being (Charles & Carstensen, 2010). Practitioners who work with older adults do see individuals who score high on neuroticism, have personal and cognitive loss, and are contending with prolonged life stress (e.g., health problems, caring for a family member with health problems). The practical import of this research for practitioners is that many older adults experience and maintain relatively high levels of emotional well-being; however, those older people seen in clinical practice often are not doing so at the time they are seeking help. Some clients have had lifelong problems with maintaining emotional balance, and late life brings another set of challenges that they are less capable of handling than others. Other clients are contending with the onset or exacerbation of late-life problems (e.g., loss of loved ones, chronic stress in care for a loved one, cognitive loss) that temporarily erode well-being (as evident in depressive, anxiety, and other symptoms) and for which the practitioner can help improve well-being.

PERSONALITY

If you look at many birthday cards, you will conclude that old age brings rigidity of personality. Many generations of researchers have studied stability or change in personality across the lifespan and have come to a different conclusion. What is *personality*? That topic has been debated since scholars began to conceptualize and study it. One definition that most would agree on is: "relatively stable patterns of thoughts, feelings, and behaviors over time and context" (Griffin, Mroczek, & Wesbecher, 2015, p. 218). The origins and nature of personality reflect three broad schools of thought: stage theories, studies of traits, and social–cognitive approaches (Boron, Schaie, & Willis, 2010). As part of the first school of theories, Freud (1923) proposed that personality was a function of the id, ego, and superego and associated processes that evolved in a series of developmental stages. Building on Freud and others, Erikson (1959) posited that personality develops through the dynamic tensions of eight stages of the lifespan. His later two stages include midlife's generativity versus stagnation and then late-life's ego integrity versus despair. Stage theories have been a challenge to study. How do you measure successful resolution of, for example, Erikson's stage crises? How do you study how "unsuccessful" resolution of one stage impacts subsequent stages? The second approach to personality has been the study of stability or changes in personality traits over time. This is a highly researched area, but some have questioned whether findings may be missing important components of the personality process that have not been measured in most studies. The third area, social–cognitive, has examined how perceptions of self change over time in a dynamic process of interactions between the individual and the larger environment or life experiences. I briefly summarize salient findings from the traits and social–cognitive approaches to personality.

Paul Costa and Robert McCrae have spent their professional lifetimes studying stability or change in personality primarily using the five-factor model (McCrae & Costa, 2008). The model has consistently found that five factors best represent the components of personality: extraversion, agreeableness, conscientiousness, neuroticism, and openness. They and others have found relative stability of these components by looking at mean change of them over time and at their *rank order consistency*, which is the degree to which the five components are higher or lower in relation to each other (Griffin et al., 2015). From childhood to older adulthood, the consistency of traits increases. Nonetheless, some changes are evident with a decrease in neuroticism and an increase in agreeableness and consciousness as people age (Mroczek, Spiro, & Griffin, 2006). Personality has practical consequences. High levels of neuroticism and low levels of extroversion are tied to mortality; and high neuroticism and low agreeableness are associated with poorer health (Mroczek et al., 2006). Critiques of this research are that it does not measure changes in these factors over time within individuals ("intraindividual differences") and that these differences may be masked by looking at changes in groups of people that may, in effect, cancel them out. That is, some people may show changes in personality over time in one direction or the other, and others may not. Life experiences (e.g., parenthood, divorce, health problems) impact personality traits in ways that reflect an interaction between individuals and their environment (versus the impermeability of traits over time; Mroczek et al., 2006).

Some have argued that personality traits only tell part of the story and that other processes are at work, such as those proposed by Baltes (1997) and his colleagues that view individuals as adaptive and active responders to changing life circumstances in their lives. The third approach to the study and conceptualization of personality, social–cognitive, emphasizes how the individual's perception of self over time interacts with changing life circumstances. Carstensen's socioemotional selectivity theory (Carstensen et al., 2011) is part of this group of approaches to personality in which individuals are seen to shape and reshape their interaction with the world—mindful of the remaining time in their lives—to maintain emotional and social well-being. Others have suggested that people's sense of themselves is organized and reorganized to successfully (or unsuccessfully) integrate new information about self and the world (Whitbourne & Connolly, 1999). Other work has posited that people are guided by a sense of "possible selves" over their lives, which includes their sense of who they were, who they are, and who they will be in the future (including who they fear they might become; Markus & Nurius, 1986; Ryff, 1991).

For practitioners, this body of work attests to both stability and change in older adults (vs. the assumption that old age is associated with the onset of a set of undesirable personality characteristics, e.g., rigidity, disagreeableness). Personality change is not the goal of psychotherapy; rather, in working with the person, practitioners will be mindful of the basic components of the individual's personality. Some older adults possess neurotic characteristics that complicate their current and past lives. Others possess potentially favorable personality characteristics (e.g., openness, extraversion) that have served and may now serve them well in contending with life challenges. The practitioner adapts psychotherapy to whom the individual is and then works with adaptive processes (e.g., selection, optimization, and compensation; shaping of sense of self) and psychotherapeutic tools to help the older person better contend with current life stressors, thus enhancing functioning and emotional well-being.

SOCIAL DYNAMICS OF LATER LIFE

Gerontologists had early concerns about the social well-being of older adults. Sociologists observed that as people entered later adulthood, they lost social roles (e.g., worker, parent). Social roles are not just a vehicle for making connections with others; they also have norms and values associated with them. Mindful of that, some have referred to the "rolelessness and normlessness" of later life (Rosow, 1976). Without those roles, older adults are at risk of winnowing social networks; indeed, early work documented smaller networks in older compared with younger individuals (Cumming & Henry, 1961). The notion that older adults are prone to social isolation is consistent with a widely held view of older people. Findings of 50 years of research is that for the vast majority of older Americans, social isolation and loneliness are highly unusual; instead, good social connections are the norm.

Here are a few facts about the social dynamics of later life:

- The size of older adults' social networks is smaller than when they were younger, but they are more satisfied with those relationships than younger individuals.

- Older adults say they have better ties with their children, better marriages, and more positive friendships than younger adults.

- Older adults report fewer conflicts with others than do younger adults.

- When older adults do have conflicts with others, they report fewer negative emotions, such as anger, than do younger adults (Luong, Charles, & Fingerman, 2011).

Why might these facts be? Carstensen's socioemotional selectivity theory (Carstensen et al., 1999) offers one compelling explanation: With awareness of the decreasing number of remaining years of life, individuals prioritize relationships that are most emotionally sustaining and meaningful to them and reduce those social connections that are not or that are fraught with problems. Although the sheer size of older adults' social networks is smaller than that of younger adults, the relationships are, on the whole, more satisfying compared with younger individuals. It also appears that many older people have developed greater expertise in managing interpersonal relationships than when they were younger (Hess & Auman, 2001). Carstensen's work is consistent with the lifespan developmental perspective that views people as adaptive and active responders to life's gains and losses. More meaningful and satisfying relationships undoubtedly contribute to the high rates of subjective well-being evident in older people (Carstensen et al., 2011).

Psychologist and gerontologist Toni Antonucci offered another perspective on social relationships through her convoy model of social relationships (Antonucci, Ajrouch, & Birditt, 2014). Throughout their lives, most people are part of a network of relationships through which they give and receive support, that varies in closeness, and that changes over time. (For me, the notion of convoy elicits the image of a group people surrounding and protecting the individual as he or she marches through life.) The model integrates many aspects of social relationships (e.g., quality, function, size, structure), has demonstrated consistency and change in social relationships, and has been influential in the study of this area.

The quality of social relationships has a big impact on older (as well as younger) adults. Among older adults, better social relationships consistently have been tied to better physical health, cognitive functioning, and emotional well-being. Conversely, problematic social ties that include conflict are associated with poor physical health, poor emotional well-being, and poor cognitive functioning (Rook & Charles, 2017). Factors that increase the likelihood of interpersonal conflict include stressful life circumstances; the giving or receiving of care to others; personality characteristics, such as neuroticism; and cognitive impairment. Furthermore, loss of spouse, other family members, and friends becomes increasingly common in later life, and these losses can have a detrimental effect on emotional, physical, and social well-being (Rook & Charles, 2017). The astute reader will note that among those older adults seen in clinical practice, conflict with others and death of loved ones are common foci of psychotherapy; and clinical research has indicated that most older people will benefit from most psychotherapies (Scogin & Shah, 2012).

Family Relationships

Some readers have seen the Norman Rockwell painting *Freedom from Want* that depicts what appears to be grandparents serving a holiday turkey at a dinner table filled with smiling faces of several generations of family members. The painting represents an idealized vision of the American family from another era. Indeed, American families look different today from those of an earlier era, including the one in which I grew up. Family is part of the "convoy" (Antonucci et al., 2014) of relationships that may protect us throughout the life course and to which we contribute. "Conventional families" have two married people of the opposite sex who have biologically related children, and the couple remains together throughout their lives. Sociologists have documented that within those families, normative expectations exist about family obligations to each other. Usually, the expectation is that in late life, if an older person needs care, family members will provide it. But family relationships are much different today than in earlier eras. Among the aging baby boomer generation, higher rates of divorce, remarriage, and blended families exist than in earlier generations. More people have or have had partnerships with or without children that were not formalized by marriage than in the past. Same-sex (i.e., gay, lesbian) relationships exist, some of which include children and some of which, in recent years, have been formalized by marriage. Some individuals include nonrelated persons as part of their families, which sometimes is called *fictive kin*. The baby boomer generation married later and had fewer children than their parents' generation. All of these factors raise interesting questions about what late-life family relationships will look like for the baby boomer generation. In view of these varied family structures, what are the social norms that will guide which family member(s) will provide care to the aging individual who needs help? For a person with a blended family, will the biologically related child have primary responsibility for the aged parent, the geographically closest stepchild, or both? There is some research on this question, but the coming years will reveal which ties are more or less durable in later life for this generation of older adults (Roberto & Blieszner, 2015). Caregiving issues are a common focus of psychotherapy with older adults and their families; this topic is discussed in more detail in Chapters 4, 5, and 6. Older adults have a range of family relationships, including those with siblings, grandchildren, and more distant kin. Most engage in leisure activities, and many contribute to their communities by volunteering. Involvement in religious and faith communities is common. For the sake of brevity, however, I offer a summary of basic facts and issues related to older couples, their adult children, and friends.

Older Couples

At age 65, 58.6% of people are married (24.4%, widowed; 12.2%, divorced; and 4.8%, never married). At age 85 and older, only 32.1% of people are married. Older men are much more likely to be married than women (age 65 and older: 72.4% of men vs. 47.6 % of women; age 85 and older: 58.6% of men vs. 17.4% of women; Federal Interagency Forum on Aging-Related Statistics, 2016). There are practical consequences for women associated with these different rates of marriage. Women are more likely to be widowed and single in later life and less likely than men to remarry. Being widowed or divorced is tied to an increased risk of financial insecurity. Marital status only tells part of the story of late-life intimate partnerships. Some older couples live together but do not marry; some do not live together but still consider themselves committed to each other ("living apart together").

The quality of relationships among married older adults is better than that of younger adults and has emotional and physical health benefits (Roberto & Weaver, 2019). However, older couples have more disagreements about intergenerational relationships, personal habits, and allocation of household tasks than younger couples (Roberto & Weaver, 2019) Marriage is experienced differently by men than women ("his" and "her" marriage; Blieszner & Roberto, 2012). Late-life widowhood and divorce have negative emotional and physical consequences, especially for men. Older couples have their fair share of problems. Those in persistently ambivalent or hostile relationships face negative physical health and emotional consequences, and late-life divorce takes its own emotional and financial toll. Historical differences, financial strain, health problems in one or both partners, differences over children, and many other issues kindle or add to interpersonal stresses (Rook & Charles, 2017). More older adults are divorcing or separating today than in the past (in 1980, 5.3% vs. in 2016, 14%; Administration on Aging, 2016). Contrary to the stereotype of older adults' lacking interest in sex, studies have shown consistently that some older adults remain sexually active well into their eighties and nineties. However, frequency of engagement in sexual behavior declines over time. One large study found that among those among those 57 to 64 years of age, 84% of men and 61% of women engaged in some form of sexual behavior in contrast to those 75 to 85 years of which 38% of men and 24% of women did. The vast majority of older adults identify as heterosexual; 10% indicate a sexual orientation other than that. Not having an available partner and having health problems both reduce the likelihood that older people will engage in sexual activity (Hillman, 2012).

Adult Children

Most older adults (89%) have at least one living child, and 80% of older people have grandchildren. The number of childless older women is higher for the baby boomer cohort compared with earlier age cohorts (16% vs. 7.5%; Roberto & Weaver, 2019). In a widely cited article from many years ago, Ethel Shanas (1979) addressed the "social myth" that adult children abandon their older parents, which is

> the widely held belief that in contemporary American society old people are alienated from their families, particularly from their children. . . . Many older people when describing their active involvement with their children and grandchildren will say, "But of course my family is different." (p. 3)

In contrast to the stereotype that older adults are "abandoned" by their adult children, most research has demonstrated that older parent–adult child relationships are generally good—there is regular contact, mutual affection, broadly shared values, exchange of resources, and feelings of obligation to each other (Bengtson, Giarrusso, Mabry, & Silverstein, 2002). But commonly, tensions exist in these close relationships over how much time the adult children or grandchildren spend with the older person or their children's partners, and how the grandchildren are raised. In my clinical practice, these are common issues raised by older people seeking psychotherapy related to relationship problems with their children.

Friends

Friendships are important in the lives of most older adults. Friendships are voluntary and usually between individuals who view themselves as equals. Durations of friendships vary from short-term relationships to lifetime friendships. Friendships vary in intensity and closeness. The size and nature of friendships change over the life course. Older people generally choose friends from their own age group. Women's friendships are generally different from those of men. This difference has been characterized as women's "face-to-face" (confiding) friendships in contrast to men's "side-by-side" (sharing activities) friendships. Older women's friend relationships are more sizable and more actively maintained, and women have more interest in developing new relationships than men. Furthermore, older women's relationships are characterized more by self-disclosure and mutual emotional support than those of men (Blieszner & Roberto, 2012; Cavanaugh & Blanchard-Fields, 2015).

From young adulthood, the number of friendships declines as many individuals marry or partner and have children (Atchley & Barusch, 2004). The closeness and size of friendships vary over the life course. According to socioemotional selectivity theory, as people get older, they often reduce the number of friendships and other relationships to focus on those that are most emotionally rewarding and meaningful (Carstensen et al., 1999). Friendships provide many benefits: emotional support, validation, instrumental support, and practical advice. Friendships are associated with elevated self-esteem, happiness, reduced loneliness, and better health (Blieszner & Roberto, 2012; Cavanaugh & Blanchard-Fields, 2015). Problems exist in friendships too. Friendships may diminish in closeness when one or both friends geographically relocates, shared interests diminish, or one or both friends has health problems. Friendships may strain or end because of perceived slights, betrayals, or other fractures. However, most older adults are relatively tolerant of behaviors in their friends that irritate them, and it is uncommon for older adults to terminate friendship relationships (Blieszner & Roberto, 2012). It is worth mentioning that sometimes older adults consider relatives to be "friends," which likely attests to the strength and meaningfulness of the relationship.

WORK, RETIREMENT, AND LATE-LIFE ECONOMIC SECURITY

When I was a young man, I remember listening to a song from an album by the then popular singers Paul Simon and Art Garfunkel. The song was about older people and had a voice-over from an older woman who referred to older people without money as "pathetic." For some reason, the pathos of older people without money has concerned me throughout my life—perhaps reflecting my own fears of not having adequate income in later life. Having enough money in later life rests on the foundation of one's work history, access to a pension or individual retirement plan, ability and willingness to save money, the amount of Social Security, and other factors.

Early gerontological concerns about retirement from work were focused on men's adjustment to retirement. A common assumption was retirement was difficult for many men because of the loss of a meaningful social role (Rosow, 1976). Research demonstrated that most men made a reasonably good emotional and social adjustment to retirement, but it depended on various issues, including whether retirement was voluntary or not (Sheppard, 1976). Involuntary loss of work could result from a layoff or termination (i.e., being fired), mandatory retirement, health problems, or other factors that led to a loss of desired employment. Mandatory retirement in later life once was seen as a means of "making way" for a younger labor force. Mandatory retirement was, of course, a problem for those who didn't want to retire. The problem of mandatory retirement for older adults was partially remedied with federal legislation in the 1980s that generally prohibited that practice. However, older workers continue to face discrimination in the workforce. As many more women entered the labor force beginning in the 1960s, the discussion of work and retirement began to include them.

Concerns about later life work and retirement shifted further. "If the 20th century was about getting older workers out of the labor force, the 21st century may well be about keeping them in" (Rix, 2006). Indeed, "workforce participation rates'" for men and women between the ages of 65 and 69 have steadily increased since the 1980s (Federal Interagency Forum on Aging-Related Statistics, 2016). With the anticipation of a large number of baby boomers' retiring from the workforce, concern was raised about workforce shortages and ways in which older adults could be retained in employment beyond the usual retirement age of 65. Studies showed that employers viewed many older adults as good workers, despite decrements in some cognitive, sensory, and physical abilities. A lifespan developmental perspective that views people as resilient and adaptive has framed some discussions of how most older workers succeed in their jobs. Policy recommendations have been made for how to retain older workers by offering part-time or shared work options. Furthermore, "retirement" is no longer viewed as binary (working vs. retired) as in an earlier era but as a process that includes anticipation and planning for retirement, phased retirement, part-time work, retirement, and even return to employment after retirement (Sterns & Dawson, 2012). Successful adjustment to life in post-retirement includes a plan for it, the existence and quality of a marital or partner relationship, financial resources, physical and psychological health, how one came to retire, and other factors (Sterns & McQuown, 2015).

The good news is that rates of federally defined poverty for older adults has markedly declined from 28.5% in 1966 to 10% in 2014 (Federal Interagency Forum on Aging-Related Statistics, 2016). The bad news is that many current older adults and baby boomers who will soon enter later adulthood will not have enough money to live in a way that they have been used to. They may not be officially "poor," but they may feel that way. In what has been dubbed "the looming retirement income crisis," studies have shown that only a small fraction of middle-aged adults feel confident that they will have enough money in the later years. There is a $6.6 trillion-dollar deficit between what Americans have saved for retirement and what they should have saved to live the way they are used to. In 2015, the average Social Security benefit was $1,328 per month with two thirds of people 65 years and older depending on Social Security for half their income (Kingson & Checksfield, 2015). In clinical practice, I am beginning to see older adults very distressed about their economic circumstances and at a loss about what to do to improve them. One older client told me that when he runs out of money, he will kill himself. "Rather dead than homeless," he said matter-of-factly.

How did things get this way? Many fewer individuals get pensions than in an earlier era. (I hasten to add: Minority older adults were much less likely to get them than majority older adults.) The 401(k) plans, individual retirement plans, and their financial cousins have reduced the actual amount of money that has been invested in retirement compared with a pension (a "defined benefit") system (Kingson & Checksfield, 2015). Furthermore, individuals have been left the responsibility for making and managing contributions to these plans and have not done a very good job of it. Jacob Hacker (2008) called this the "great risk shift"; that is, we have shifted collective responsibility for late-life economic security from the larger society to the individual—with regrettable consequences. For clients without adequate late-life economic resources, I discuss options that are often recommended: Work longer, save more, spend less, leave retirement and work part time, apply for federal or state or local benefits, and ask family members for support.

But the larger story of work, retirement, and late-life economic security varies considerably among people. Women have less money than men in later life. The rate of poverty for men 65 years and older is 7.4%, but for women, it is 12.1% (Federal Interagency Forum on Aging-Related Statistics, 2016) Racial and ethnic minorities have had fewer occupational opportunities in younger years than majority adults, and therefore often are less able to save money for retirement or have access to pensions. Rates of poverty for people 65 and older vary dramatically by race or ethnicity: non-Hispanic White, 7.8%; Hispanic, 18.1%; Black, 19.2% (Federal Interagency Forum on Aging-Related Statistics, 2016).

CASE EXAMPLE OF MABEL BROWN: PART 2

> Mrs. Mabel Brown (introduced in Chapter 1) was the 85-year-old White, widowed Catholic woman with a daughter and a son who was referred by her primary care provider because of concern that she was depressed. She had diabetes, high blood pressure, vision problems, and an earlier back surgery, and needed a walker to ambulate. Her daughter, Carol, who brought her to the first appointment, felt that her mother was depressed and possibly had "Alzheimer's" disease. Mrs. Brown was reluctant to see a mental health provider.
>
> Mrs. Brown was born in 1933 during the great economic depression. In 1954, at age 21—the beginning of adulthood—the United States was entering into a period of rapidly growing economic prosperity.

How do you think these factors might have affected the way she viewed the world? She was reticent about seeing a mental health care provider. What generational perspectives about mental health problems might bear on that reluctance? She is widowed and has an adult daughter involved in her care. How common would it be that a woman of her age would be widowed? Have an adult daughter who helped her? What role would you expect her son to play in her care? As you begin to think about doing an initial intake with her, what would you be interested in learning about her background that would help to more effectively engage and work with her?

SUMMARY–WITH CAUTIONS ABOUT GENERALIZATIONS

For those of you who have read this chapter, I appreciate your patience and interest. I have broadly reviewed what I considered important facts, issues, and themes that come from these many areas of research on older adults. As you see older clients, I hope you will reflect on these topics, asking yourself whether and how these general issues apply to a particular client. I think that this information will enrich your understanding and appreciation of your older clients. If you are interested in learning more, take a look at the resources in Appendix A.

I believe a lifespan developmental perspective makes a lot of empirical and clinical sense. It sees older adults as adaptive responders to the joys and challenges of life. Older adulthood brings the realities that the body is wearing down and time is increasingly limited. Most older adults adapt to those realities and maintain reasonably good social and emotional well-being. Older adults experience both stability and change as well as loss and gain during the course of life. But some older people get stuck and look to mental health care practitioners like you to draw on their own resources and to acquire new tools and perspectives from you.

When I make a categorical statement about older adults based on research findings, I always find a *but* lingering in the back of my mind (e.g., "but that might not always be true for all older adults and may depend on . . ."). In graduate school, I learned about the difference between the "nomothetic" and the "idiographic." (I have had to look up the meaning of those terms intermittently throughout my career. *Nomo* and *idios* come from Greek. Nomo means law; idios, private.) The social and psychological sciences seek to identify generalities about people—the *nomothetic*. Mental health practitioners are often interested in the experience of the individual client—the *idiographic*. A tension exists between the two. Social scientists have critiqued practitioners for overgeneralizing from their own select sample of individual clients based on "clinical experience"; and practitioners have critiqued academics for making broad generalities that don't apply to all or even most of their clients. Psychology's answer to this tension was the scientist–practitioner model, which has guided graduate education in clinical psychology. That is, practitioners can generate important hypotheses based on clinical experience, which can then be tested.

One other issue about which we should be mindful in making generalizations about older adults (and other groups) is understanding how general conclusions may differ by sex, race, ethnicity, immigration status, rural or urban residence and upbringing, socioeconomic status, sexual orientation, and other relevant factors. When we make generalizations about the current cohort of older adults (which is predominantly White), those generalizations—with respect to some of the topics discussed in this chapter, such as health, emotions, cognition, personality, and social dynamics—may be similar or different in subgroups of older Americans. And those generalizations may not fully hold true for a prior or future cohort of older adults. Researchers increasingly have been cautious about broad generalizations without attention to similarities and differences that may vary by subgroups. Practitioners increasingly appreciate the need to consider similarities and differences among clients from different backgrounds—which has been characterized as *multicultural competency*. Although practitioners may believe that we look at our clients as individuals, we also carry assumptions about them about which we may not be aware, including inaccurate and stereotypical characterizations based on age and other factors. In the end, practitioners should take satisfaction in the skills we have acquired, embrace humility in knowing that sometimes we do not know, and cultivate curiosity in continuing to learn more about the people we serve and what researchers have found.

3 OVERVIEW OF ASSESSMENT

At this point, I hope that you have begun to embrace the notion that most older people are resilient, reasonably happy, and socially engaged—and are so despite aging bodies and changes in cognitive functioning. Like younger adults, older adults contend with intermittent (and sometimes persistent) life obstacles that affect the way they feel, think, and function. A minority of older people contend with diagnosable mental disorders or with what is sometimes called clinically significant distress. Both can benefit from the services of a mental health professional. An even smaller number of older people face a lifetime of mental health difficulties (including what has been called sometimes serious and persistent mental illness) and now have their own late-life version of those difficulties. In this chapter, I discuss the prevalence of late-life mental disorders, the diagnostic and assessment intake process, and recommendations for optimizing an intake with older adults. I also discuss common life problems some older adults face that emerge in a diagnostic and assessment intake and are a frequent focus of psychotherapy. I assume that the reader is adept in the general conduct of a mental health assessment and the diagnostic categories of the *Diagnostic and Statistical*

http://dx.doi.org/10.1037/0000146-004
Assessment and Treatment of Older Adults: A Guide for Mental Health Professionals,
by Gregory A. Hinrichsen

Manual of Mental Disorders (fifth ed. [*DSM–5*]; American Psychiatric Association, 2013) and therefore can focus on those issues that are specific to older clients.

This chapter covers the Council of Professional Geropsychology Training Programs' recommended foundational knowledge competencies with respect to foundations of clinical practice and assessment of older adults (Hinrichsen, Emery-Tiburcio, Gooblar, & Molinari, 2018). Material in this chapter reflects content from the Pikes Peak model for training in professional geropsychology (Knight, Karel, Hinrichsen, Qualls, & Duffy, 2009), including II. Knowledge Base, C. Knowledge of Assessment of Older Adults. It also addresses content from "Guidelines for Psychological Practice with Older Adults" (American Psychological Association [APA], 2014), including Guideline 7 (Psychologists strive to be familiar with current knowledge about cognitive changes in older adults), Guideline 8 (Psychologists strive to understand the functional capacity of older adults in the social and physical environment), Guideline 9 (Psychologists strive to be knowledgeable about psychopathology within the aging population and cognizant of the prevalence and nature of that psychopathology when providing services to older adults), Guideline 10 (Psychologists strive to be familiar with the theory, research, and practice of various methods of assessment with older adults, and knowledgeable of assessment instruments that are culturally and psychometrically suitable for use with them), Guideline 11 (Psychologists strive to develop skill in accommodating older adults' specific characteristics and the assessment contexts), and Guideline 12 (Psychologists strive to develop skills at conducting and interpreting cognitive and functional ability evaluations).

HOW COMMON ARE MENTAL DISORDERS IN OLDER ADULTS?

A few years ago, some of my geropsychology colleagues synthesized existing evidence to estimate the *prevalence* (i.e., the percentage frequency) of mental disorders in different groups of people 65 years of age and older (Karel, Gatz, & Smyer, 2012). They distinguished between older adults living in the community versus older adults in residential care. The prevalence of *dementia* (a progressive loss of mental ability, now called *major neurocognitive disorder*) climbed steadily as people grew older: 1.4% (65–69 years), 2.9% (70–74), 7.6% (75–59), 18.6% (80–84), 32.7% (85–89), and 37.4% (90 and older); the overall prevalence was 10% in people 65 years of age and older. The prevalence of mental disorders, excluding dementia in the community, held fairly steady across late life: 9.6% (65–74), 6.8% (75–84), and 8.1% (85 and older); the overall prevalence was 8.5%. In residential care, the prevalence of mental disorders (not including dementia) was 31.5%—underscoring how common mental disorders are in that setting. Overall, the prevalence of all mental disorders, including dementia in the community and residential care, was 20.4%.

How do these rates compare with those in younger adults? The issue is important because knowledge about and attitudes toward older adults skew in the negative direction. With the exception of dementia, older adults have much less than half the rates of mental disorders than younger adults (Gum, King-Kallimanis, & Kohn, 2009). In my experience, mental health practitioners routinely guess that 30% to 50% of community-residing older adults are seriously depressed. As you can see from Table 3.1, only 2.6% of people 65 years and older have a diagnosable mood disorder and, with the exception of dementia, their rates of other mental disorders are much lower than younger adults. When teaching, I find that some audience members do not believe those figures based on their own clinical experience: "I see lots of depressed older people in clinical practice," they say. Thinking about it, older adults with mental health problems who actually see a practitioner are not a representative sample of all older adults. (Imagine if a cancer doctor assumed most people had cancer because that doctor saw cancer patients every day.) My former statistics professor, Jacob Cohen, coined the term *clinician's illusion* (Cohen & Cohen, 1984), by which he meant that clinicians may inaccurately generalize from the select group of clients they see to the larger population from which they come. I believe that another factor

TABLE 3.1. Prevalence of Anxiety, Mood, and Substance Abuse Disorder, by Age Group, Over 1 Year

Mental disorder	Age group			
	18-44	45-64	65 and older	All ages combined
Anxiety	20.7%	18.7%	7.0%	17.8%
Mood	10.2%	8.0%	2.6%	8.3%
Substance abuse	3.6%	1.0%	0%	2.2%
Any	27.6%	22.4%	8.5%	22.8%

Note. Anxiety disorders include panic disorder, agoraphobia without panic, specific phobia, social phobia, generalized anxiety, and posttraumatic stress. Mood disorders include major depressive, dysthymia, and bipolar I and II. Substance abuse disorders include alcohol abuse and drug abuse. From "Prevalence of Mood, Anxiety, and Substance-Abuse Disorders for Older Americans in the National Comorbidity Survey-Replication," by A. M. Gum, B. King-Kallimanis, and R. Kohn, 2009, *American Journal of Geriatric Psychiatry, 17,* p. 774. Copyright 2009 by Elsevier. Adapted with permission.

contributes to these overestimates of depression: the common negative assumptions about most older adults that were discussed in Chapter 1.

The take-home message for practitioners: Older adults are at increasing risk of dementia; those living in the community have much lower rates of mental disorders than younger adults; and those living in residential facilities often have mental disorders, including dementia.

Keeping in mind some lessons from Chapter 2 on age cohort, these rates may differ between generations of older adults, each of which may possess unique vulnerability or resilience to one or more mental disorders. Some have speculated that the now exiting group of older adults—that former television news anchor Tom Brokaw (1999) dubbed the "greatest generation"—had a high degree of emotional heartiness and coping abilities that decreased their vulnerability to mental disorders in late life. Some have speculated that perhaps lacking some of the characteristics of their parents' generation, the baby boomers will have higher rates of mental disorder in later life. Time will tell.

REFERRAL

In advance of the diagnostic and assessment intake is the referral for that service. Who will make the referral of an older adult for evaluation depends on the setting where you serve. I get referrals from the medical doctors and other staff in my primary care clinic. Some mental health practitioners working in medical inpatient or rehabilitation settings also get referrals from colleagues within the institution. In mental health settings, referral for services may come from the staff member who assigns them or the provider who does an initial assessment. For those with independent practices, referrals often come from a variety of sources but commonly from medical and social services providers, family members, and older persons who self-refer. Those who work in long-term care settings usually get referrals from staff members concerned about residents who appear to be having difficulties. It can be useful to get initial information from the referrer to determine why a mental health evaluation might be needed and whether the identified problem is one that you believe you are suited to evaluate and potentially treat (La Rue & Watson, 1998). For example, you might be referred an actively suicidal, psychotic, or apparently delirious older individual who—in your judgment—may need acute hospitalization before an outpatient evaluation. It is prudent to clarify the individual's insurance coverage because older adults increasingly are in Medicare managed care plans (Medicare Advantage Plans, sometimes called "Part C") in which you may not be a provider. Furthermore, because some older adults have vision and sight problems, encourage them to bring needed glasses and hearing aids to the initial assessment visit.

DIAGNOSTIC AND ASSESSMENT INTAKE

For some older people, the assessment process will look quite similar to that conducted with younger individuals. These older people are typically the young-old (see Chapter 2 for a definition) who are cognitively intact and have relatively few medical problems. However, the diagnostic picture can get more complex with older people who have multiple medical conditions, medications, or health care providers or who may evidence cognitive deficits (Mohlman et al., 2012). Sorting out what is medical from what is psychological (or both) can be challenging even for the geriatrically seasoned professional and may require input from or coordination with health care providers. Older people often come with one or more sensory deficits (e.g., hearing, sight) or physical limitations that may require attention or adaptation of the assessment enterprise. Furthermore, they frequently come for assessment at the behest of someone else—a health care provider, social services worker, community program, or relative—and with varying degrees of understanding of, or interest in, a mental health evaluation.

Many mental health assessment instruments generally have been developed for or normed on younger individuals. In use with older adults, they may lack data for their psychometric usefulness and may or may not be a good choice, or they need to be conducted with caution (Edelstein et al., 2007). Some assessment tools evidence differences based on race; practitioners should be cognizant of those differences (American Psychological Association Committee on Aging, 2009).

Assessment Environment

Older individuals may have functional limitations that might need to be accommodated. For a while, I had a small independent practice and considered renting space from a colleague. My first consideration was whether entry into the office required climbing stairs because I knew some clients would use walkers or wheelchairs. Fortunately, the office was on the first floor and didn't have any stairs. However, the bathroom didn't have grab bars or much room to maneuver a walker, which I advised potential clients. Most institutional settings are disability friendly these days.

For those who work in inpatient or rehabilitation settings or long-term care settings, finding a quiet and relatively private place for an evaluation may be a challenge. In these and other environments, background noise may make it more difficult for the older client to hear. Inadequate illumination or glare from lights or from an outside window may affect the client's ability to see. It is important to ask the client whether he or she is having problems hearing, seeing, or understanding you; otherwise you might misinterpret communication problems as cognitive deficits. For those with hearing deficits I ask, "Which is your better ear?" and then physically locate myself accordingly. Some providers print forms in large type that they ask the client to complete. I find that as long as older adults bring needed reading glasses, regular-sized type usually is adequate.

Interpersonal and Communication Environment

Some older adults referred by others do not really want to come for an evaluation. Some have never seen a mental health provider before or hold unfavorable views of the profession. I have even found that some older adults who believed I was a medical doctor came to see me for a medical assessment either because they misunderstood or a family member misrepresented the nature of the visit because, otherwise, their relative would not see a mental health professional. In outpatient settings, a family member often accompanies the older adult. Some family members assume that they will be part of the whole evaluation process. Even if the older individual seems significantly cognitively impaired, it is important to have time alone with the potential client and to get permission for involvement of the accompanying person. Most family members can be helpful—but it's important to keep in mind that may not always the case.

If providers hold overly positive or overly negative views of older adults, those views are likely to come into play verbally or nonverbally in the first meeting. Providers with overly positive views may overlook problems, and those with overly negative views tend to overemphasize problems without taking into account preexisting strengths and history of resilience (Knight, 2018). (See Chapter 1, this volume, for a discussion about attitudes toward older adults.) The Gerontological Society of America (2012) published the booklet *Communicating With Older Adults: An Evidence-Based Review of What Really Works* for practitioners who work with older adults (see Appendix A for a link to the booklet). Although the recommendations were created for a broad array of health and social services providers, most of them are useful for mental health care providers. Recommendations include the following:

- Recognize the tendency to stereotype older adults, then conduct your own assessment.

- Avoid *elderspeak*, speech that might be seen as patronizing to an older person.
- Monitor and control your nonverbal behavior.
- Minimize background noise.
- Express understanding and compassion to help older patients manage fear and uncertainty related to the aging process and chronic disease.
- Verify listener comprehension during a conversation.

The following are additional suggestions on how practitioners might optimally engage older adults on an initial visit.

Be Friendly but Not Overly Familiar

I usually engage in small talk with the older person as we walk from the waiting room to the office. "Did you find the place okay?" "How was the traffic?" "Such a cold day, yes?" I don't presume to call an older adult by a first name unless he or she asks me to. If I don't know a woman's marital status, I use "Ms." If I know that the potential client has an advanced degree by which he or she has been referred to as "doctor," I use that honorific. If I will be seeing a client on an ongoing basis, I ask about his or her preferred form of address. In most intakes, I try to use a little humor to put the client at ease, and I try to use everyday language versus anything that might sound like jargon.

Orient to the Tasks for the Intake

To ease the client into the intake process, I say something like, "I'm going to ask you a lot of questions today. Forgive me if I'm a bit businesslike, but we are going to cover a lot of ground in the next hour."

Set Limits, as Needed

Some older adults may believe their role in the interview is to give extended and detailed narratives of recent or past events. In such a case, I redirect, saying something like,

> We won't be going into details in this visit. As I said at the beginning, we've got a lot of ground to cover. But if it makes sense for us to see each other for future visits, we'll have plenty of time to talk at length about this.

Most older adults respond to direction, and many have learned in visits with their medical doctors that professional appointments are time limited.

Occasionally, some clients are—in mental health parlance—highly tangential and circumstantial or—in everyday language—overly talkative and not on task. This behavior is sometimes diagnostic of cognitive problems, anxiety, or other issues, especially if the person does not respond to repeated redirection (Gerolimatos, Gregg, & Edelstein, 2014). In such a case, I continue to redirect and explain why. If a client becomes distressed during the course of the interview when talking about a topic, I might say, "I know that I am asking you some very personal and difficult questions. I can see that this is bringing up a lot of feelings for you." Some older adults are puzzled or annoyed that they are asked screening questions related to history of sexual, physical or domestic abuse, or use of drugs and alcohol. So, I say, "I ask everyone these questions. Sometimes people have these kinds of problems. If I understand correctly, you don't."

Give Feedback and Ask for Questions

I give feedback about my initial impressions at the end of every intake and ask the client if he or she has any questions. I tell clients that they are free to ask questions about my professional background. I find that some older adults do an Internet search on my name in advance of the visit and know quite a bit about me! (I was recently unnerved when an older woman told me that she knew I came from a family of six children. I asked how she knew that. She had found my mother's obituary online.) I do not presume that the client will return for another visit, even when needed; I always ask. If I recommend a course of psychotherapy, I ask the client if that is something he or she desires. Most individuals say yes and appreciate being asked.

Interview Structure and Content

A practical issue for most professionals is limitation of time for doing an initial assessment. In my clinic setting, I have 55 minutes. By setting up expectations about the format of the interview at the beginning and directing the client, as needed, I can complete the interview in that time.

Most providers have their own structure for doing a diagnostic and assessment intake. In addition, paperwork requirements vary among institutions and practices.

General Inquiry and Confidentiality

After introducing myself and describing the structure of the interview, I ask the older adult, "So why have you come to see me today?" Much information can be gained by this general inquiry, including the client's perspective on what problems may be of concern to that client or to others as well as information that may be relevant to the mental status exam. I limit time for this discussion to 5 to 10 minutes. I explain that the interview is confidential and will not be shared with others—including family members—without the client's permission. I make exceptions to this confidentiality rule, for example, when there is a concern that the client may be at risk for harm to self and others. (In many states, practitioners must report suspected elder abuse.) Alas, some professionals assume that because someone has accompanied an older person to an appointment, the practitioner can share information with that accompanying person without the client's permission.

Basic Background Information

Work Status. Do not presume that by virtue of age someone is retired. I ask the client, "Are you still working?" (One of my psychology colleagues is 97 years old and sees clients 2 days a week and supervises psychology interns.) If clients are not working, I ask when they stopped and why. Others substantively contribute to organizations on a volunteer basis, which might be viewed as an uncompensated job. As noted in Chapter 2, retirement is often phased, and voluntary (vs. involuntary) retirement is tied to better adjustment (Sterns & McQuown, 2015).

Marital Status. Asking about marital status may not tell the whole story. Some older adults have important and enduring relationships with individuals to whom they are not married or with whom they do not live (Blieszner & Roberto, 2012).

Sexually Active? Ask whether the older adult is sexually active. Most older adults may be more comfortable talking about the topic than you are. (In graduate school, I remember one gerontologist's remarking that older adults are more comfortable talking about their sex lives than how much money they have.)

Sexual Orientation. Ask about sexual orientation. I realize this question might be uncomfortable for some practitioners and older adults, but asking it might build immediate rapport with an older person who happens to be a gay or lesbian individual (Hillman & Hinrichsen, 2014). For long-standing married individuals, I ask, "Can I presume you're heterosexual?" (When one widowed man in his 80s responded, "Generally," a fruitful discussion followed. His interest in having a relationship with a man was the focus of psychotherapy. I'm glad I asked.) For others, I'll ask directly, "What is your sexual orientation?" For some older adults, raising the topic might prompt remarks, such as, "I'm straight, but my granddaughter is a lesbian, which bothers me," which could be a topic for further exploration.

Gender Identity. Awareness has grown about gender identity, and a variety of professional guidelines exist on this issue (APA, 2015). Although, in my career, I have not worked with an older adult who has expressed concerns about gender identity (but, on reflection, did I do an adequate job of giving therapeutic space for discussion of the topic?) or is transgender, in some settings, this issue may be more common. Not far from where I live in New York City is the organization SAGE (Advocacy & Services for LGBT Elders) that sponsors New York City-funded senior centers for gay, lesbian, bisexual, and transgender (GLBT, also known by the acronym LGBT) older people throughout the city. In those settings, questions about sexual orientation and gender identity are front and center in any interview. Recently, one of my colleagues who works in an inpatient rehabilitation setting consulted with me about how to most respectively treat an older transgender woman with physical and cognitive disabilities on that unit.

Ethnic and Racial Identity and Faith and Spirituality. I find out a bit about the client's ethnic and racial identity and ask whether he or she was raised in a particular faith. Sometimes practitioners make assumptions about race and ethnicity on the basis of appearance that may not be those of the client. How the client characterizes race and ethnicity may reflect the primacy that is placed on one or more aspects of them. One older woman commented, "I don't like being called African American because I was born in Canada." Another said, "My parents were Jewish, but I do not consider myself Jewish." It can be useful to discern whether faith and spirituality are important in the individual's life now because they may inform how the client views current problems and how religious faith can be a resource for contending with those problems. One female client with multiple medical problems who identified as Christian said to me, "Jesus will give me no burden heavier than I can carry." Later, during the course of psychotherapy, I learned how this perspective was pivotal in her efforts to make sense of her medical problems and to better contend with them.

Emergency Contact. I ask if there is someone who can be designated as an emergency contact. Those clients who cannot identify a contact are often socially isolated. I also do a brief review of immediate family and where they live and obtain a subjective assessment of the quality of the relationship (from very poor to very good). This information gives me a general sense of strengths and problems in social connectedness.

Military Service. I also ask about military service history. Almost half of men 65 years and older have served in the military (Federal Interagency

Forum on Aging-Related Statistics, 2016). Some clients appreciate being asked the question and acknowledged for their contribution to our country. If an individual has served, I ask about any combat experience, which may have had psychological effects and may potentially be a focus of treatment (Clark, Rouse, Spangler, & Moye, 2018).

Physical Health

Assessment of physical health and medication use in a mental health intake usually requires much more attention with older compared with younger adults. In the geriatric primary care medical clinic where I work, past and current health history as well as prescribed medications and over-the-counter medications are available in the electronic medical chart. In other health and long-term care settings, this information should be readily available in the client's chart. When I had an independent practice, I asked clients, in advance of the first visit, to bring a list of medical problems and prescribed and over-the-counter medications to the first visit as well as the name, address, and phone of the primary care physician.

Most older people have one or more chronic illnesses and prescribed medications (AARP, 2005). If a client has multiple medical problems, I ask which one or two are of them are of most concern and to what extent health problems limit functioning. I ask about whether the individual experiences pain. The Numeric Rating Scale for pain (Jacox, Carr, & Payne, 1994) is recommended for those in pain; it simply asks the individual to rate pain on a scale from 0 (*no pain*) to 10 (*unbearable pain*). (See Appendix B for links to websites that have this measure and other instruments mentioned in this and other chapters.) As noted in Chapter 2, formal or informal assessment of limitations in activities of daily living (ADLs; e.g., bathing, toileting, walking, transferring in and out of bed or chair, dressing, eating) and instrumental activities of daily living (IADLs; e.g., use telephone, perform housework, prepare meals, shop, manage money) is helpful. If needed, recommended instruments include The Lawton Instrumental Activities of Daily Living (IADL) Scale (Lawton & Brody, 1969) and the Katz Index of Independence in Activities of Daily Living (ADL) scale (Katz, Downs, Cash, & Grotz, 1970). I also note assistive devices that the older person uses (e.g., walker, wheelchair, cane, glasses, hearing aid).

Mental Health

Gathering mental health history can be a challenge, especially from people who have received services throughout their lives. Usually people can only give a general sense of mental health issues with which they have contended: providers they saw, treatments they received, and medications they have taken. If need be, the clinician can obtain other information in future visits. I inquire about whether the individual has ever been hospitalized for a mental disorder or has made a suicide attempt. Most older adults can give a history of significant mental health problems in biologically related relatives. Of course, obtaining information about currently prescribed psychoactive medications is of particular interest, including over-the-counter medications. I'm interested when a client is using over-the-counter medications for sleep because their use is a good clue that the individual has insomnia. As previously mentioned, I assume that mental health providers reading this book are familiar with the *DSM–5* (American Psychiatric Association, 2013) diagnostic system, so I have not discussed criteria for specific disorders.

Alcohol and Other Substance Use

I ask about tobacco and caffeine use. I rarely see many older adults who use tobacco but do see many former smokers. Half of men 65 years and older and almost one-third of women in that age group are former cigarette smokers; 8.5% of older adults currently smoke cigarettes (Federal Interagency Forum on Aging-Related Statistics, 2016). Many older adults drink caffeine, but some do not realize that drinking caffeine in the afternoon or evening can interfere with sleep. Consistent with epidemiological data that illicit drug use is uncommon in older people, (Gum et al., 2009), I see few who use so called street drugs (e.g., opioids, cocaine, methamphetamine), but I do see some baby boomers who report using nonprescribed marijuana, whereas, earlier in my career, this was quite rare. Many older adults drink alcohol (40%; National Institute on Alcohol Abuse and Alcoholism [NIAAA], n.d.), so a careful inquiry is useful here as well as assessment of whether the person is taking psychoactive medications in a manner inconsistent with prescriber recommendations. See Chapter 6 for a more detailed discussion about alcohol problems and the misuse of prescription medications.

Physical and Sexual Abuse History

Earlier in my career, I did not routinely ask older adults about history of physical or sexual abuse. Once I did, though, I was surprised how many women reported sexual abuse in their younger years. I saw a woman in her nineties who had only recently told her family about a teenage rape, which resulted in posttraumatic stress disorder (PTSD) symptoms throughout her adult life. (I hasten to add that after a course of cognitive processing therapy [Resick, Monson, & Chard, 2016], her symptoms were markedly reduced.) In response to my question about sexual abuse, another woman told me that in college, a man broke into her dorm room and repeatedly raped her. She advised me that rape counseling at that time was helpful and that she did not have PTSD symptoms after that counseling. Most commonly, women who report sexual abuse describe episodes of inappropriate sexual touching by relatives when they were children or teenagers. Some older men and women report physical abuse as children by parents—some behaviors that, during an earlier era, were regarded as acceptable child-rearing methods by some. One older man said that he did not understand why he had experienced a lifetime of violent dreams until, when he was in his fifties, a relative told him that when the man was a toddler, the man's father repeatedly and violently beat him—events about which he did not have conscious recollection. Sometimes physical abuse takes place within intimate relationships. The take-home message is that it is important to ask. Most older adults appreciate that someone asked—whether the issue is a focus of treatment or not.

Elder mistreatment or *abuse* is "an intentional action or inaction that results in significant physical or emotional harm to a person who is vulnerable because of age-related factors" (Mosqueda & Olsen, 2015, p. 667). One must be alert for this possibility when evaluating older adults, and many states require the reporting of suspicion of abuse (as defined by the individual state) to the designated entity. Practitioners need to be aware of reporting requirements. One in 10 older adults has been subject to abuse, of which there are four broad types: sexual and physical abuse, financial exploitation or abuse, psychological or emotional abuse, and neglect. Older adults can both be objects of abuse and perpetrators of abuse. Financial exploitation or abuse is the most common type. Risk for abuse among older adults is greater for those with dementia, people living in a long-term care facility, and women (Mosqueda & Olsen, 2015). Mosqueda and Olsen (2015) summarized common abuse scenarios that include the following:

- a family member who is a caregiver to relative with dementia,
- a person with substance use or mental illness who is caring for an individual with dementia,
- a professional person who takes advantage of a socially isolated older person,
- intentional exploitation of a vulnerable individual by being ingratiating or feigning romantic interest,
- financial scams (e.g., telemarketing, computer, government impostors),
- abuse within a long-term care facility, and
- problematic family dynamics that result in abuse of an older person.

With respect to the scenario of problematic family dynamics that result in abuse, I interviewed a caregiving daughter who complained that her now frail older mother treated her harshly throughout her life. "Now it's payback time," she casually remarked. A recommended screening tool is the Elder Assessment Instrument (Fulmer, Paveza, Abraham, & Fairchild, 2000). Elder abuse or neglect may raise issues of capacity of the older individual; see Chapter 6 for a discussion of the capacity assessment of older adults.

Life History

I ask older adults to give a broad and brief chronology of their life histories. Personally, I find this part of the interview to be the most interesting because I learn about people's origins, successes, disappointments, and often their personal resilience. I also get a glimpse into American and world history from the perspective of an individual person who has lived through it. Over the years, I have learned about World War II through the eyes of a Jewish man who survived the Auschwitz concentration camp, a German woman who grew up in wartime Germany, a woman who lived through the bombing of London by the Germans, and an American man who took part in the military invasion of Normandy. I have learned about American history from the perspectives of African Americans who grew up in the rural South and whose parents were sharecroppers; White men who grew up in wealth, attended prestigious schools, and ran large corporations; White women who forged opportunities for themselves in earlier eras when they didn't have easy access to higher level positions in the workplace; immigrants who made lives for themselves in a new land; and gay and lesbian people who lived in an earlier era of criminalization of sexual orientation.

As discussed in Chapter 2, the elements of a lifespan developmental perspective are evident in the narratives that people give with respect to influences of age, period, and cohort (Schaie, Willis, & Pennak, 2005); the psychosocial dynamics of each life stage (Erikson, 1959; Levinson, 1986); and how selection, optimization, and compensation (Freund & Baltes, 2002) come into play in later life. The challenge is to do the assessment intake briefly and efficiently. I often want to hear more—and clients often want to tell me more than time permits. In this section of the intake, I am chiefly interested in family of origin, seminal childhood experiences, education, work history, marriage or partnerships, whether the individual has had children, and current life circumstances (e.g., widowed, divorced, working, volunteering). What may be unique among older adults is that there is an awful lot of history to cover. I keep the conversation moving along by saying something like, "And then what happened?" "What did you do after graduating from high school?" If the client chooses to see me in the future, I can always ask for more life information as it pertains to the focus of psychotherapy.

A number of other issues are relevant to conducting a diagnostic and assessment intake with older people. They include the use of screening instruments geared toward older adults, medical and cognitive concerns, the use of information from multiple sources, and an understanding of the client's life issues that may become a focus of future treatment.

Screening Instruments Relevant to Older Clients

Taking into consideration general cautions about the use of assessment instruments that have not been normed on older adults, screening assessments can be useful in an initial intake. Especially for those who are unfamiliar with mental health and aging, screening instruments are an efficient way of asking relevant questions that may lead to further inquiry and sometimes a formal diagnosis. Some mental health and aging practitioners have favored instruments, and each instrument has advantages and disadvantages. Many of the screening instruments recommended in this chapter may be found on the website of the Hartford Institute of Geriatric Nursing, New York University College of Nursing (see Appendix B for the link to that website). What is especially useful about the Hartford Nursing website is that experts make a recommendation of one or two instruments for a clinical problem (e.g., cognitive problems, depression, elder abuse) based on psychometric properties and on advantages or disadvantages of the instrument for older adults. The actual instrument can be found on the website, which makes things so much easier for clinicians who are trying to track down individual measures.

Practitioners might administer some instruments in their entirely but find others useful to generally inform the kind of questions that they ask the client. For example, if an older adult does not drink alcohol, usually there is no need to administer an alcohol screening instrument. I routinely administer a screen for depression, anxiety, and cognitive functioning and then, as needed, may administer other assessment instruments or use the content of the instrument to inform my inquiry. I often have other screening instruments for disorders I don't commonly see (e.g., PTSD, obsessive–compulsive disorder) in my back pocket because they are an efficient way of covering relevant questions that may inform making a diagnosis.

Medical and Cognitive Issues

It is really important that older adults with mental health problems regularly see a physical health care provider. Depression, anxiety, and cognitive impairment and other symptoms might be caused by underlying medical problems or prescribed medications. Problem alcohol use and prescription drug misuse may lead to medical problems. Over the years, I have had depressed older adults referred to me who had thyroid problems that, when remediated, were no longer depressed; older people with cognitive impairment who had a condition called *normal pressure hydrocephalus* (accumulation of cerebrospinal fluid in the brain), which, when remediated, halted the progression of cognitive problems; older clients with anxiety that was exacerbated by medications they were taking for medical problems; and older people with alcohol problems who had nutritional deficits, falls, and cognitive problems as a result of chronic alcohol use.

In the introduction to his widely used book *Handbook of Assessment in Clinical Gerontology*, Lichtenberg (2010) emphasized the importance of basic knowledge of medical problems and syndromes with which many older adults contend. In the assessment of older adults, he noted challenges that include the blurring of normal compared with clinical aging as well as identifying pathological from normal processes, stereotypical "ageist" assumptions that muddy the assessment process, the importance of a team approach to assessment, and the utility of brief assessments and multiple sources of information.

Multiple Sources of Information
Along with Lichtenberg, most geropsychologists advocate the use of multiple sources of information (Edelstein, Drozdick, & Ciliberti, 2010). These include client self-report, report of others, clinician observation, and the use of assessment instruments. I find the best source of information is the older adult him- or herself. However, generational issues (i.e., historical embeddedness, cohort effects) may influence how individuals experience or report mood and behavior (Baltes, Lindenberger, & Staudinger, 2006).

Reliance on self-report becomes problematic if the older adult has cognitive problems. In an assessment interview, some have suggested that older adults are more likely than younger people to say they "don't know," refuse to answer certain types of questions, evidence caution in their responses, or minimize symptoms (Edelstein et al., 2010). In my experience, some but not most older adults evidence these interview behaviors.

Report of others can be a critical source of information but is also subject to bias. Family members and—among older adults seen in care settings—staff can often provide useful information. But family members may have biased views of the older adult based on their shared life history, may be reluctant to acknowledge existing problems, or may exaggerate existing problems based on stereotypical views of aging.

Residential setting staff members may overemphasize problematic behavior of older residents because of the practical difficulties they create for care staff and underreport other behaviors that are evidence of resilience.

Within the assessment interview, the clinician's observation of the older adult's behavior is critical and foundational in the mental status examination. However, clinician observations usually are made within a time-limited diagnostic interview in a setting that is unfamiliar and perhaps intimidating to the older adult.

Well-designed screening instruments yield critical information about thoughts, behaviors, and physical and other symptoms that reflect an underlying diagnostic entity. Yet, many screening instruments have not been normed on older adults or have limitations in use with older adults. Furthermore, assessment instruments may have differential utility in subgroups of older adults who have varying cultural or ethnic/regional background as well as levels of education (Edelstein et al., 2010). Use of multiple sources of information greatly increases the likelihood that practitioners can make a reasonable diagnostic assessment—and, if other sources of information become available at a later time, a practitioner can modify the diagnostic assessment. With all these cautions noted, however, I generally find there is a convergence of client self-report, family report, health provider perspectives, my observation, and data from screening instruments.

In the assessment of older adults, Lichtenberg (2010) cautioned,

> In my clinical consultation I am often surprised, and indeed alarmed, at the misapplication of symptoms to a diagnosis: delirium confused with dementia; dementia unrecognized in the context of disability or life-long psychiatric conditions; end of life conditions of frailty going unrecognized; and aging equating with incapacity. (p. xv)

For practitioners new to working with older adults, basic familiarity with assessment issues will enhance their capacity to make better assessments but also lead to an appreciation of the need to refer some clients to medical doctors, neuropsychologists, and geropsychology specialists.

Life Problems That May Be the Focus of Treatment

Regardless of the client's age, mental health practitioners are interested in understanding what life issues may be contributing to the client's emotional distress or other symptoms. In the assessment of older adults, it is foundational to know what is normative for older people and what is not. If the clinician incorrectly assumes that it is common for older people to feel socially isolated, the clinician may be less likely to see this as a problem focus. As Edelstein et al. (2010) noted, mental health practitioners often conduct assessment and treatment through one of two perspectives: One approach is trait oriented (i.e., psychodynamic psychotherapy) and the other is more behavioral (i.e., behavioral therapy, cognitive therapy, cognitive behavior therapy [CBT]). I would add a third: interpersonal (i.e., interpersonal psychotherapy; Weissman, Markowitz, & Klerman, 2018). In an intake interview, those who are guided by their favored perspective will likely be attending to issues that relate to that perspective. For example, a psychodynamic therapist may be interested in early life themes that appear to be evident now in late life. A behavioral therapist often is interested in changes in availability of pleasurable activities for an older adult, whereas a cognitive therapist may be interested in the way that the older adult views current life circumstances, including unhelpful thought patterns. Interpersonal psychotherapists may be quite interested in life changes that may impact the availability and quality of relationships. And one's preferred perspective also informs how the practitioner may establish initial therapeutic goals and judge their outcome (Strupp & Hadley, 1977). In Chapters 5 and 6, I review treatment approaches that have been found effective for older adults; those approaches focus on depression, anxiety, cognitive impairment, and problem alcohol use or prescription drug misuse.

Four domains of problems are often evident among older adults seeking psychological services. In the diagnostic and assessment intake, the practitioner identifies one or more that might be a focus of future treatment. The four problem domains of interpersonal psychotherapy (Hinrichsen & Clougherty, 2006) nicely encompass most of these issues: life transitions, interpersonal disputes, grief, and social isolation or loneliness. (See Chapter 4 for a more detailed discussion of these four domains.) To distill this further, I have found that the lion's share of psychotherapy issues with older adults is tied to the client's physical and cognitive health and to the physical and cognitive health of others. Onset or exacerbation of the client's physical and cognitive health problems can lead to practical and emotional stresses associated with those problems. Onset of physical or cognitive health problems in a spouse or partner may lead to conflict with the spouse or partner or with family members around that care, to financial strains, and to increasing isolation from others as one becomes "engulfed" in the caregiving role. Older adults are more likely to see a spouse or partner, siblings, and friends die compared with younger individuals—with the associated experience of grief and loss. I have met older adults who have outlived every meaningful relationship they have had in their lives. The lifespan developmental perspective (discussed in Chapter 2) directly addresses the reality of late-life cognitive and physical changes and how most individuals adapt to those changes (Baltes et al., 2006). I often say to prospective clients, "You've handled so many things well in your life. Now you've hit a rough patch. So, let's work together so you can better handle what you're dealing with now."

DEPRESSION, ANXIETY, COGNITIVE IMPAIRMENT, AND PROBLEM ALCOHOL USE OR PRESCRIPTION DRUG MISUSE: FOCAL POINTS

Older adults experience the full range of mental disorders, including psychotic, bipolar, obsessive–compulsive, sleep, personality, and others. Chapter 5 reviews the assessment and treatment of depression and anxiety, and Chapter 6 focuses on cognitive impairment and problem alcohol use and prescription drug misuse. So why did I choose to focus specifically on these particular disorders in this book? In community prevalence studies of older people, depression, anxiety, and cognitive impairment are most common of the disorders (Gum et al., 2009). One recent study found that depression, anxiety, cognitive impairment, and alcohol or substance use are the most common mental health problems seen among older adults in primary care (McCombe et al., 2018). In my clinical practice and those of my colleagues, these disorders also are most commonly seen, and they are all reviewed in contemporary books on mental health and aging. Although the onset of new substance abuse disorders in community-residing older adult is rare, 40% of older adults drink alcohol (NIAAA, n.d.) and about one quarter receive medications that have potential for abuse (Simoni-Wastila & Yang, 2006). In clinical practice, one sees older adults who are engaging in problematic use of alcohol or are being prescribed or are using mood-altering prescription medications in a way that can be problematic. For those new to mental health and aging, it is helpful to possess tools for assessing and engaging older clients and have strategies to reduce problem alcohol use and prescription drug misuse.

Nonetheless, I would like to briefly mention two issues that practitioners often see with older adults: insomnia and personality disorders (PDs). About 20% of older adults experience sleep problems—and sleep problems frequently are interwoven with anxiety, depression, cognitive impairment, and alcohol or substance misuse (Bélanger, LeBlanc, & Morin, 2012). Many different sleep disorders exist, but insomnia (problems falling asleep, staying asleep, or waking up too early) is common among them. Sleep disorders can be effectively treated (McCurry, Logsdon, Teri, & Vitiello, 2007), but they first need to be assessed. Cognitive behavior therapy for insomnia (CBT-I) is a highly effective treatment for insomnia in younger and older adults (Bélanger et al., 2012; Perlis, Jungquist, Smith, & Posner, 2008). One potential problem, among others, for older adults with insomnia is that they may be treated with sleep medications for extended periods, and those medications include a risk for falls (Bloom et al., 2009). I often am referred older adults who have taken sleep medications for many years because of insomnia who want to discontinue them, or their primary care physicians want them to discontinue them. In my clinical experience, most older people who are willing to take part in CBT-I do discontinue medications, and the vast majority make substantive improvement in the insomnia.

In an excellent review of the topic of PDs in later life, Balsis and his colleagues wrote:

> People with personality disorders (PDs) have disturbed patterns of thinking and poorly formed self-concepts. They often display rigid and inflexible responses in social settings that compromise their abilities to develop relationships. To make matters worse, people with PDs are typically unaware of or have limited insight into these problems. (Balsis, Zweig, & Molinari, 2015, p. 79)

I believe all of us have evaluated or worked with clients who evidence one or more of these characteristics. Estimates of the percentage of older adults seen in clinical practice with a PD varies widely (from 5 to 64%!). There are debates about whether PDs change over a person's lifetime (Do they get better?), whether existing *DSM–5* (American Psychiatric Association, 2013) criteria are well-suited for older adults, what the best methods are for assessing PDs in older people, how a lifespan developmental perspective enhances our understanding of PDs, how late life may be a better or worse "fit" for older adults with different types of PDs, and other important questions (Balsis et al., 2015; Segal, Coolidge, & Rosowsky, 2006). The challenge for many older adults with PDs is that they often become increasingly dependent on others as health problems mount—and they may have fewer people on whom they can depend and are often less capable of managing relationships with care providers than most other older people. Segal et al. (2006) developed a useful framework—goodness-of-fit—for working with older adults with PD that includes changing both client and caregiver behaviors (e.g., long-term care staff) to reduce interpersonal demands on the older adult and improve functioning.

SUMMARY

That rates of mental disorders (with the exception of cognitive impairment) are lower in community-residing older than in younger adults should give the clinician pause to examine the common assumptions that many older adults are depressed and dispirited. That being said, practitioners will see that minority of older people who do have mental health problems. A diagnostic and assessment intake with an older client covers much of the same territory that is covered with a younger adult but with notable differences. In view of sensory and age-associated cognitive changes, the clinician and the client benefit by maximizing communication: minimizing environmental distractors, engaging the client in a friendly but not overly familiar and patronizing way, setting limits respectfully for those who have problems staying on task, giving feedback, and asking questions of the client to make sure he or she understands and feels understood.

Usually the older client's life is embedded in other health or social services systems and with family and friends. With cognizance of the client's right to confidentiality, engaging and coordinating with others can optimize care for the older person, especially the individual who is cognitively impaired or is having substantive problems with day-to-day functioning,

Unlike many younger adults, most older adults have one or more chronic health problems for which they are receiving treatment with one or more medications. Therefore, the clinician needs to inquire about medically relevant issues to a degree that is less common with younger adults. Sometimes mental health symptoms are caused by or intertwined with medical problems or medications. By definition, older adults come with long life histories that challenge the clinician to cover a lot of ground in an initial intake—and challenges the client to be as focused as possible. Some clinicians may find that asking older people about "sensitive topics" like substance use, sexual abuse, sexual functioning or orientation is uncomfortable. I find, however, that older people may be more comfortable talking about these topics than providers. Finally, it is important to recognize that older clients are not sum of their symptoms or the diagnostic categories that can be applied to them. Most older people come with a long history of having solved earlier life problems. Now, they may have a late-life version of those problems often reflected in distress associated with life transitions, disputes with others, grief, and social isolation or loneliness.

4 OVERVIEW OF TREATMENT

In this chapter, I highlight a broad range of issues relevant to providing treatment to older adults. These issues include an integrative model for doing psychotherapy, common problems seen in psychotherapy, treatments found to be effective, the role of the environment on well-being, settings in which mental health services are usually delivered, the importance of interdisciplinary collaboration, and ethical considerations. I conclude the chapter with a discussion of social services and reimbursement issues.

This chapter covers the Council of Professional Geropsychology Training Program's recommended foundational knowledge competencies with respect to intervention, consultation, and other service provision (Hinrichsen, Emery-Tiburcio, Gooblar, & Molinari, 2018). Material in this chapter reflects content from the Pikes Peak model for training in professional geropsychology (Knight, Karel, Hinrichsen, Qualls, & Duffy, 2009), including II. Knowledge Base, D. Knowledge of Intervention, Consultation, and Other Service Provision. III. Skills competencies: A. Skills: Professional Geropsychology Functioning, item 7 (documentation, billing, reimbursement). It also addresses content from "Guidelines for Psychological Practice With

http://dx.doi.org/10.1037/0000146-005
Assessment and Treatment of Older Adults: A Guide for Mental Health Professionals, by Gregory A. Hinrichsen

Older Adults" (American Psychological Association [APA], 2014), including Guideline 13 (Psychologists strive to be familiar with the theory, research, and practice of various methods of intervention with older adults, particularly with current research evidence about their efficacy with this age group), Guideline 14 (Psychologists strive to be familiar with and develop skill in applying culturally sensitive, specific psychotherapeutic interventions and environmental modifications with older adults and their families, including adapting interventions for use with this age group), Guideline 15 (Psychologists strive to understand and address issues pertaining to the provision of services in the specific settings in which older adults are typically located or encountered), Guideline 18 (In working with older adults, psychologists are encouraged to understand the importance of interfacing with other disciplines, and to make referrals to other disciplines and/or to work with them in collaborative teams and across a range of sites, as appropriate), Guideline 19 (Psychologists strive to understand the specific ethical and/or legal issues entailed in providing services to older adults), and Guideline 20 (Psychologists strive to be knowledgeable about public policy and state and federal laws and regulations related to the provision of and reimbursement for psychological services to older adults and the business of practice).

MODEL FOR ADAPTING PSYCHOTHERAPY TO OLDER ADULTS

Geropsychologist Bob Knight has blended many of the elements of issues discussed in earlier chapters to inform assessment and treatment of older adults. His model is called the *contextual adult lifespan theory for adapting psychotherapy* (CALTAP; Knight & Pachana, 2015). He has argued that psychotherapy with older adults often is similar to that conducted with younger adults, and when informed by a broad understanding of later adulthood, the therapeutic relationship and psychotherapy outcomes are enhanced.

By now, elements of Knight's model should be familiar to the reader:

- *Developmental forces:* The process of adult development brings both positives and negatives. Growing older is tied to physical and cognitive slowing as well as enhanced emotional regulation, interpersonal expertise, and breath of life experience. Exceptions to these gains may be evident in individuals with personality disorders.

- *Specific challenges:* Late life brings its own set of problems, most notably, health and cognitive issues for the older person him- or herself or in care of aging loved ones.

- *Social context:* The social context and environment in which an older person lives influence late-life adjustment. Older adults living in institutional or age-segregated facilities, for example, contend with different social dynamics than those living elsewhere. Older adults are often engaged with community or institutional programs, including health delivery institutions, that serve the aged. Experiences with these programs can favorably or unfavorably affect the well-being of older adults.

- *Cohort influences:* Age cohort experiences shape who we are and how we see the world.

- *Cultural context:* Age cohort experiences are nested in the larger culture or subcultures from which we come. Among many influences, cohort and culture likely shape our expectations about our own old age and the aging of others.

COMMON LIFE PROBLEMS AS A FOCUS OF PSYCHOTHERAPY WITH OLDER ADULTS

One of my colleagues remarked that if you don't have problems in your life, you are likely dead. Often, later adulthood is viewed as full of problems that depress and deplete most older adults. As I have discussed, this view is not true. Likely because of negative expectations about old age acquired throughout life, late life can become a sort of Rorschach blot onto which people project their fears. Like younger adults, however, older adults experience life problems but usually a different version of them than in earlier life. That version is often associated with increasing risk of health problems in themselves, their spouses or partners, and their contemporaries. With each year of life, the closer you are to your own death and that of your contemporaries; and if you live a very long life, you'll see a lot of people die before you.

Although research has found that many older adults better manage relationship issues than in earlier life, some have interpersonal difficulties. A minority of older people have had long-standing difficulties in establishing and maintaining relationships, and others have experienced social isolation only later in life for varied reasons. In this section, I discuss common life problems often seen in psychotherapy with older adults that also usually are interwoven with depressive or anxiety disorders as well as depressive or anxiety symptoms. I have organized the discussion of these problems based on the four-problem foci of a psychotherapy I often use in clinical practice, which is interpersonal psychotherapy for depression: life transitions, interpersonal disputes, grief, and social isolation or loneliness. Interpersonal psychotherapy is a time-limited psychotherapy that I have found especially useful in the treatment of depression; I discuss this topic more in Chapter 5 of this volume (Hinrichsen, 2008).

Life Transitions

Psychologist Daniel Levinson's (1986) view of the lifespan emphasizes the importance of the transitions that people face between different eras of their lives. Each life era has its own unique rewards and problems. Each era eventually comes to an end, and there is a transitional period to another era during which the person must take stock of the old life and the new life. Life transitions are often stressful. We know that the stress of life changes increases the risk for depression and anxiety in younger as well as older adults (Edelstein, Bamonti, Gregg, & Gerolimatos, 2015; Fiske, Wetherell, & Gatz, 2009; Miloyan, Byrne, & Pachana, 2014). Using the language of sociology, life transitions often involve the loss or acquisition of a new role (George, 1993; Munk, 2014). Social roles are associated with norms and values and are sort of social templates that guide us in how to behave and give us a sense of who we are (e.g., "I'm a student." "I'm a mother," "I'm a psychologist"). As Levinson (1986) argued, loss or changes in life roles can be disconcerting, confusing, and emotionally distressing. Life transitions offer new possibilities. They also may include challenges involving health problems, caregiving issues, job loss or retirement, money problems, child rearing of grandchildren, and relocation.

Medical Problems

Onset or exacerbation of health problems is a common life transition among older adults seen in clinical practice. Persons with medical problems acquire the "role" of a "medical patient" who is contending with the emotional and practical consequences of health issues. Challenges a person with medical problems faces may include interacting with medical personnel and institutions, comprehending medical information, dealing with insurance paperwork, paying for unreimbursed care, following medical recommendations (e.g., changing diet; monitoring medical parameters, such as blood pressure or glucose; taking medications), adapting to functional limitations of health problems, explaining to others the change in medical status or functional limitations, negotiating changes in daily responsibilities with spouses or partners, and managing emotional distress and uncertainty about the future.

Caregiving
Providing care to a family member (typically a spouse or partner) can be both rewarding and stressful. The issues that may prompt the need for care are varied but typically include medical problems, mental health problems, and cognitive problems. Care for family members with dementia can be especially stressful (Miloyan et al., 2014; Zarit & Heid, 2015).

Job Loss or Retirement
Although most older adults adapt well to the transition out of work, for others, that transition is difficult. Retirement may be especially difficult if one does not have control over it (e.g., termination of employment) and if it is not planned for (Sterns & McQuown, 2015). Clients in psychotherapy with job loss or retirement often have concerns about the loss of social supports and friendships from work, lack of meaning, difficulties in establishing a new life pattern, and changes in the relationship with their spouse or partner—all of which are more difficult if the older adults are concurrently depressed or anxious.

Financial Problems
As noted in Chapter 2, some older adults have limited financial resources because of a history of poor earnings, lack of access to retirement benefits, poor planning, unexpected life expenses that have depleted retirement savings, and other factors. In clinical practice, I have seen increasing numbers of my baby boomer generation express anxiety and worry about their current or future financial circumstances They may have transitioned from the economic role status of a middle-class person to that of a low-income person.

Grandparents Parenting Grandchildren
Some older adults have found that they are required to care for grandchildren because their own children are facing life challenges that make it difficult or impossible to provide the care themselves. Issues may include an adult child's death, mental illness, substance abuse, job loss, and incarceration. Although providing care to one's grandchildren may yield special rewards, it may also be associated with financial stress, loss of meaningful social and recreational pursuits, perceived inadequacy in parenting the

grandchildren, and problems in the relationship of older grandparent couples (Hayslip, Maiden, Page, & Dolbin-MacNab, 2015).

Residential Move

Some older adults may move residences either voluntarily or involuntarily. In my clinical work, common problems include move to another part of the country for a hoped for better life that did not work out, move to an assisted living facility that did not meet expectations, and move into a nursing home because of increasing health problems.

Interpersonal Disputes

As discussed in Chapter 2, most older adults evidence better capacity to manage interpersonal relationships than younger adults and selectively invest in relationships that are more meaningful to them than in younger years. However, a minority of older people have had interpersonal difficulties throughout their lives or interpersonal problems that arise in the later years. Late-life interpersonal problems can be prompted or exacerbated by financial, medical, or other stresses. Medical problems may change and strain relationships (e.g., dependence on family members, the need for increased contact with family members whom the older adult had previously kept at a distance). Sensory or cognitive loss may make interactions with other people more difficult and may lead to misunderstanding and interpersonal distancing. Acute and chronic interpersonal conflict have been associated consistently with emotional distress, poor health, functional impairment, slowed recovery from medical illness, and increased risk of death (Krause & Hayward, 2015; Rook & Charles, 2017). In clinical practice, problems with other people—tied to depression, anxiety, and general emotional distress—are a common focus of psychotherapy. The following are the most common interpersonal issues that I have found in outpatient practice with older adults.

Marital or Partner Disputes

Some older couples have never gotten along well but have stayed together. Now in later life, things are much worse. Early in my career, I remember seeing a couple who said that, in retrospect, they were ill matched. The husband remarked, "I realized that my wife and I probably needed counseling when, in the middle of heated argument, I grabbed her, threw her on the ground, and began to choke her." Providing care to a now-ill spouse with whom one has not had a good relationship may be especially difficult.

Some older couples have found that conflict may be kindled on retirement of one or both members of the couple (e.g., She: "Doesn't he have anywhere to go?" He: "Isn't this my home too?"; Lee & Shehan, 1989). Other couples have had what they have characterized as a reasonably "good marriage" but begin to experience conflict because of late-life medical or other stresses. Some older couples are in conflict about the degree of financial support that is provided to an adult child who—for a variety of reasons—is living with them or is financially dependent on them.

Adult Children

Studies have shown that most older adults have reasonably good relations with their adult children (Shanas, 1979), but those relationships vary in quality and some are troubled. Some older people seek psychotherapy because of conflict with an adult child. Common problems include long-standing differences that are now worse, differences in expectations about the frequency of visiting with the adult child or grandchildren, unhappiness with how the grandchildren are being raised, conflict with the adult child's spouse or partner, and financial or emotional over-reliance of the adult child on the older person. For example, I worked with a depressed and anxious woman whose son called her weekly to demand money and belittled her for being so selfish. She sought help to better understand why she continued to give money to her son even though she didn't want to.

Health Care Providers or Institutions

Older adults increasingly interact with health care institutions, social services providers, and individual caregivers. Interactions with these players may lead to frustration, anger, and discouragement. Occasionally, I have heard a client exclaim, "I hate this hospital!" and then list unsatisfying interactions with doctors, support staff, and administrators. (I hasten to add: Sometimes clients have perfectly justified reasons for their frustration but get stuck in how to negotiate these difficulties.) Another issue is conflict or disappointment with a home health aide who helps the older person or family member. Comments I have heard include: "That aide treats me like I'm a child!" "She always shows up late," "She doesn't seem to like me," and "She has three children and no husband." Among my colleagues who work in long-term care settings, conflicts with staff, including nurse aides, is a common focus of psychotherapy. I believe inherent to home-based support from an aide is role confusion: Is the aide a friend? An employee? Something in between?

Grief

I recently gave the presentation "Grief in Later Life" to a group of older adults in a senior center and was surprised at how well attended it was. I asked, "How many of you have lost an important person in your life?" Everyone raised their hand, including me. I was also surprised at how eager many people were to share their stories of lost loved ones and how the deaths of those loved ones were at the same time painful, poignant, and beautiful. Gerontologists have had long-standing concerns about what it is like for older adults who are at increasing risk of loss of a spouse, other family members, and friends.

By age 85, 80% of women and 40% of men have lost a spouse (Rosenzweig, Prigerson, Miller, & Reynolds, 1997). Spousal loss in later life is so common for women that it is sometimes characterized as a normal, expectable life event. The ubiquity of late-life spousal loss for women prompted Phyllis Silverman to create a mutual support model—"widow-to-widow"—in the 1960s (Silverman, 2004); it is still used today. Psychologist George Bonanno's work has challenged many assumptions about the process and potential complications of grief or bereavement. Contrary to what is commonly believed, he and his colleagues found that there are no set stages of grief and that failure to grieve in a certain ways does not result in further problems later (Bonanno et al., 2002; Bonanno, Wortman, & Nesse, 2004; Neimeyer & Holland, 2015). Bonanno et al. (2002, 2004) also found that two thirds of older adults evidence resilience in the grieving process—with few symptoms of depression—and that about 10% evidence a reduction in depressive symptoms after the death of a spouse! The best explanation for that 10% reduction is that these individuals had poor or stressful caregiving relationships with their spouses that were tied to depressive symptoms, which were reduced after the death of the spouse. They did find, however, that almost 10% of older widows and widowers had a chronic grief trajectory. Those individuals evidence what has been called complicated grief, and they likely are candidates for psychotherapeutic interventions.

Researcher Holly Prigerson and others have tried to characterize what differentiates usual, "normal" grief from complicated grief. The general view these days is that *complicated grief* might be seen as an attachment disorder with such symptoms as yearning and preoccupation for the dead person, strong feelings of loneliness, a sense that a part of one has died, avoidance of reminders of the dead person, bitterness, problems moving on, a purposeless life, and numbness (Prigerson et al., 2009). (These symptoms appear to have some correspondence with those of posttraumatic stress disorder.) I recently saw an older woman who was preoccupied with the idea that, one day, her husband would die—even though he was in good health. She said that if her husband died, "I would lose part of myself," "My life would be meaningless," and "I'd kill myself." I suspected that she was at increased risk for complicated grief and perhaps at risk for suicidal behavior if her husband did predecease her. I had another patient who made similar statements that if her mother died, her life would be over. When her mother did die, she was distressed but—much to her surprise—grieved her mother's death and then moved on to a life without her. Bonanno (2009) argued that the vast majority of older adults who have lost a spouse do not need psychotherapy and that offering it to them may pathologize what is a normal process. However, a minority of those with complicated grief can benefit by grief-focused psychotherapies.

Older adults, of course, experience loss of other important relationships, including those with siblings, friends, and sometimes adult children or grandchildren. The impact of the death of a sibling in later life may result in loss of a confidant and companion and prompt feelings of vulnerability and thoughts about one's own death (Cicirelli, 2009). Some have suggested that about 10% of people older than age 60 will experience the death of an adult child, yet research on this topic is quite small (Van Humbeeck et al., 2013). In clinical practice, I have seen older adults seek mental health services around the past or more recent death of an adult child who had experienced chronic or acute illness. Normatively, older adults do not think that an adult child will predecease them—a life experience that psychologist Bernice Neugarten (1968) called an *off-time event* (De Vries, Davis, Wortman, & Lehman, 1997; Van Humbeeck et al., 2013). The death of a grandchild is an even more off-time event that may shake one's beliefs about the fairness of life, engender feelings of survivor guilt, and result in emotional pain by witnessing the grief of one's own adult child (Fry, 1997). Death of friends may be quite difficult for some. Some friendships endure from childhood and are irreplaceable. For some older adults, friends become the equivalent of family members. For older lesbian and gay people, friends may become the "family of choice" and have greater meaning and salience for them than for other older people (Travis & Kimmel, 2014). Some older adults experience grief on the death of a beloved companion animal.

Social Isolation or Loneliness

As noted in Chapter 2, the field of gerontology historically has had concerns about potential social isolation and loneliness in later life. More recent work has demonstrated that many older adults choose to reduce the size of their social connections to selectively invest in those that are most meaningful and satisfying (Carstensen, Isaacowitz, & Charles, 1999). However, a minority of older adults subjectively feel lonely and are socially isolated. One recent study suggested that 8% of older adults feel lonely "often" (AARP Foundation, n.d.). There has been renewed interest in the topic of loneliness and social isolation in the aging field. Some have suggested that the current cohort of older adults may be at greater risk of social isolation and loneliness than in earlier years because of increasing numbers of unmarried persons, divorce, and less engagement in community organizations than in previous eras (Holt-Lunstad, 2017). Time will tell whether societal changes increase rates of social isolation and loneliness in older people. Some risk factors for subjectively feeling lonely in older people include not being married, having three or fewer friends, socializing less than once a week, and having family strains (Ryerson, 2017). Loneliness is tied to an increased risk of death and health problems; social isolation is associated with depression and dementia (Holt-Lunstad, 2017).

In outpatient practice, I have not worked frequently with individuals for whom the chief concern is loneliness and social isolation perhaps because most older adults seek mental health services at the behest of a family member or friend. Older people who are not socially connected and are feeling lonely are less likely to have people in their lives who facilitate access to mental health services. However, I have a geropsychology colleague who provides mental health services in people's homes. I asked her about how often she works with socially isolated and lonely older adults. Her reply: "Sometimes, but not as often as you might think. Even if they are lonely, their chief concern is medical problems." I asked another colleague who works in long-term care about how often her clients feel lonely. She replied, "Sometimes, but older residents' chief concerns have to do with managing issues with other residents and staff." Among older adults with whom I have worked, social isolation and feelings of loneliness often exist within the context of depression, and once the depression improves, clients often report feeling less lonely and having more interest in and ability to engage in social relationships.

PSYCHOTHERAPEUTIC TREATMENTS DEMONSTRATED TO HAVE WORKED WITH OLDER ADULTS

When I began to practice psychology in the early 1980s, little empirical evidence was available to answer the question, Does psychotherapy work with older people? There was skepticism—in my view, fueled by negative stereotypes about older people's being too rigid to change—that older people would benefit from psychotherapy. Today, we know that most major psychotherapeutic treatments found to be effective for younger adults—when informed by a foundational understanding of late life—are effective for older people. These also include psychopharmacological treatments for mental disorders.

In the past 20 years, the health and mental health professions have emphasized that, optimally, practitioners should use treatments that have been shown to work based on good research (Chambless et al., 2006). Geropsychologist Forrest Scogin and his colleagues have summarized psychological treatments that have been found to work for older adults for depression, anxiety, dementia-related problems, and insomnia (Scogin, 2007; Scogin & Shah, 2012). Most of the evidence is for individual treatments. Three treatment approaches that have been found effective are unique to older adults: (a) reminiscence therapy, (b) behavioral treatments to manage problematic behaviors in older adults with dementia, and (c) treatments to reduce distress in caregivers of older adults with health problems as well as dementia. The second and third approaches are discussed in Chapter 6. The bottom line is that most psychotherapies that work for younger adults also work for older adults. One caveat is that most of the psychotherapy studies of older adults have included chiefly White people in their 60s and 70s who do not have substantive cognitive deficits. For me, the question is not so much do recognized psychotherapies work most older adults, but these questions: How do they work for very old people with multiple medical problems, significant functional limitations, or cognitive deficits? How might psychotherapies need to be adapted for these individuals as well as older adults with varied cultural backgrounds (APA Committee on Aging, 2009)?

LIVING ENVIRONMENTS AND SOCIAL AND PSYCHOLOGICAL WELL-BEING

I want to briefly note the role of the environment in social connectedness, day-to-day functioning, and well-being. There has been long-standing interest in gerontology in how aspects of the immediate environment (e.g., community, neighborhood, building) play a role in enhancing not only social connectedness in older adults but also their functioning and well-being. Psychologist Powell Lawton did some of the most important work in this area and, along with others, demonstrated that living in housing environments (i.e., age-congregated "senior citizen" housing) that offered easy access to age peers increased social and emotional well-being among those who chose to live in such housing compared with those who did not (Lawton & Cohen, 1974).

My own doctoral dissertation was on this topic, and I also found that living in urban apartment buildings with more fellow older adults was associated with more friendships and better morale compared with other settings (Hinrichsen, 1985). In what he called the *environmental docility hypothesis*, Lawton (1990) argued that as individuals become less capable (e.g., have increasing health, functional, cognitive problems) they become increasingly dependent on the immediate environment for their functional, social, and emotional well-being. A social work colleague recently told me that one of her clients was discharged from a short-term stay in a nursing home following hip replacement surgery. With distress, my colleague remarked, "She lives in an apartment on the fifth floor that does not have an elevator." The practical consequence for her client was that it would be difficult to get out of her apartment, which might result in social isolation, difficulty in getting to medical appointments, and even difficulty getting food. An elevator would likely make her life much different. Furthermore, the physical layout of a home or apartment might make a big difference in whether the older person can remain there. An older person who requires a wheelchair and lives in an apartment with doors that are not wide enough to accommodate it or in a house with multiple levels might not be able to remain there. Older adults who live in rural areas without easy access to transportation or those in high-crime urban neighborhoods may be at increased of social isolation (Kaye, 2017; Portacolone, 2017). The practical import of this research for practitioners is to be mindful of where the older person lives and how it might facilitate or impede social engagement with others and day-to-day functioning.

SETTINGS FOR DELIVERY OF MENTAL HEALTH SERVICES TO OLDER ADULTS

Mental health services are delivered to older people in many of the settings in which services are delivered to younger adults: outpatient mental health clinics, outpatient independent practice, outpatient day or partial hospital mental health programs, and inpatient mental health. Increasingly mental health services are delivered to younger and older people in outpatient medical settings (Armento & Stanley, 2014). Practitioners are called on to see older adults in inpatient medical units and rehabilitation programs.

Some practitioners work with seriously ill older people in hospice or pallia-tive care programs. Older adults predominate as residents of long-term care settings, notably assisted living residences and nursing homes. Sometimes services are delivered to older adults in community-based programs, such as a senior citizen center. Within the U.S. Department of Veterans Affairs (VA) health care system, mental health services are delivered to older and younger adults across the continuum of services provided by the VA. It is worth emphasizing, that the VA health care system serves a sizable number of older adults who are veterans, and the VA has been a leader in the devel-opment of geriatric health and mental health services (Zeiss & Karlin, 2010).

Some psychologists exclusively work in long-term care settings as inde-pendent providers or as part of nursing home "groups"—typically private, for-profit organizations. A small number of mental health care providers deliver services within the older adult's home (Yang, Garis, Jackson, & McClure, 2009) typically to clients who have physical health problems that make it difficult for them to leave their homes. Over my career, I have delivered services to older adults in a wide range of settings: outpatient mental health clinic, outpatient medical clinic, mental health day hospital, inpatient mental health, and community-based services.

INTERDISCIPLINARY COLLABORATION

Most health care systems are ill suited to serve older adults who have multiple medical conditions, are prescribed multiple medications, have problems functioning, and may need concurrent social and home-based supports (APA Presidential Task Force on Integrated Health Care, 2007). Add mental health problems to the mix and things really get complicated. A recurrent theme in the mental health and aging literature is that health and mental health care providers need to work collaboratively. Who could argue with that? But the reality is that care is often fragmented and care coordination is, at best, an occasional phone call between providers.

Poorly coordinated or poorly integrated care usually result in worse care and poorer outcomes compared with coordinated care. In my view, the one notable exception is the VA health care system. Different terms are used to described the process of professionals working in concert with each other: interprofessional geriatric health care, interdisciplinary teams, col-laborative care, and others (Steffen, Zeiss, & Karel, 2014). The take-home message for practitioners who see older adults is that they need to make the effort to reach out to other providers at the onset of care and, as needed, on an ongoing basis. I hasten to add that family members are usually involved in the care of an older adult—and care is optimally coordinated with family members—but with permission from the client.

ETHICAL ISSUES

Laws relevant to mental health practice, reporting requirements for suspected abuse of older adults, and related matters vary by state. Each professional discipline has its own ethical guidelines that share common principles. Ethical issues apply to all aspects of the work of each profession, including what is considered adequate preparation to serve different groups of clients or address clinical problems. The topic of ethics and aging encompasses so many issues that books, like one in Appendix A, can be written about the topic.

For me, the recurring ethical issue in working with older adults is that of balancing safety with autonomy. For example, how do I best work with an older adult with cognitive impairment so that the client can be as independent as possible yet reduce the likelihood of that client's getting harmed? I find that some professionals are most interested in optimizing the client's safety without fully taking into consideration what the client wants or the psychological impact of overly restricting daily life. Geropsychologist Michele Karel (2011, pp. 115–116) nicely summarized key ethical and legal issues relevant to older adults:

- Older adults are more likely to have cognitive deficits that may impair their ability to make decisions. How can decisions be best made with or for them?

- Collaboration among professionals is important in serving older adults, yet how can confidentiality be protected at the same time?

- Families and other members of the older person's social world are important, yet how can they be engaged ethically in decisions about the older client and, at the same time, the practitioner maintains the client confidentiality?

- In institutional settings, how can older people be best served, yet their rights to privacy and self-determination be maintained?

- Impaired older adults are at increased risk for exploitation, abuse, and neglect. How can they be protected, and yet their ability to self-determine be balanced?

- Many older people contend with end-of-life decision making. How can decision-making be best facilitated?

- How can cultural and other diversity factors be integrated into the preceding issues in a way that best honors the older adult's wishes and preferences?

Practitioners make explicit or implicit decisions about the older adult's capacity to engage in a range of life activities: making medical decisions, managing money, living independently, operating an automobile, engaging in sex, or making a will (American Bar Association and APA, 2008). Awareness of state laws and professional ethics, self-reflection, and consultation with colleagues and other professionals relevant to ethical dilemmas are important.

ONGOING ASSESSMENT IN PSYCHOTHERAPY

In graduate school, I read an article on the tripartite model of assessing psychotherapy outcomes (Strupp & Hadley, 1977). The article proposed that mental health outcomes in psychotherapy should be seen through the lens of society that wants well-functioning individuals, the client who usually wants reduction in distress, and the therapist who is interested in a psychologically healthy individual. Sometimes these desired outcomes converge, but sometimes they do not. Furthermore, how one defines *well-functioning*, *client satisfaction*, and *psychologically healthy* reflects certain assumptions and biases. The tripartite model continues to make a lot of sense to me, especially in working with older adults. Colleagues who work in long-term care facilities say that they often get referrals from staff members ("society") who are concerned about a disruptive and noncooperative resident. A good outcome of psychotherapy for the staff member might be a more cooperative resident, yet for the resident, it might be a change in institutional policy and staff behavior that results in a reduction in their own subjective distress. Ethical issues may come into play when tensions exist among desired outcomes by different players.

Mental health practitioners sometimes think of assessment as the initial diagnostic and assessment visit. But assessment is also an ongoing effort throughout one's professional relationship with a client. Similarly, Medicare (the federal program that pays for the lion's share of health and mental health care for older adults and younger disabled people) requires an initial assessment to determine "medical necessity" to pay for mental health services but also an ongoing determination of whether the Medicare recipient is responding to psychotherapy or other therapeutic efforts (Norris, 2015). If an older client is not making therapeutic progress or is worsening, it is highly desirable for the practitioner to think about why and consider what other therapeutic options might lead to improvement. Client satisfaction counts too. I find that some older adults will stop coming for psychotherapy because they are reluctant to tell the therapist that they don't find sessions helpful; that they have gotten out of therapy what they wanted; or that they don't feel their investment of time, effort, or and money is worth what they are getting out of therapy. Setting therapy goals and periodically reevaluating them with the client is desirable. In a highly publicized article about a study conducted by *Consumer Reports* ("Mental Health: Does Therapy Help?," 1995; *Consumer Reports* is the magazine produced by the Consumers Union that includes, among its many activities, product testing), the study found that most "consumers" of psychotherapy services felt that they substantially benefited from it. The article led to much discussion about the importance of the consumer's perspective on psychotherapy as well as the contemporary utility of the tripartite model of assessing psychotherapy outcomes (Strupp, 1996).

PRAGMATICS OF PRACTICE: THE AGING-SERVICE NETWORK, MEDICARE, AND MEDICAID

Aging-related supportive services exist throughout the country (O'Shaughnessy, 2011), and the range and availability of those services vary by locale. A network of federally supported Area Agencies on Aging serves people 60 years of age and older and their families. Some agencies serve one large city; some, regions; and others, the entire state. It can be helpful to become familiar with services and programs for older adults in the area where you practice. Sometimes I feel the best thing I did for a client was to connect him or her to a service program. And I believe that a practitioner with contemporary and broad knowledge of local social services programs for older people is worth his or her weight in gold.

Almost all older adults have Medicare and receive Social Security (Kotlikoff, Moeller, & Solman, 2016; Moeller, 2016). Because these two programs are important in the lives of older people, it is advantageous for the practitioner to have broad familiarity with them because sometimes older clients may look to the practitioner for guidance. Medicare is the federal program of health insurance for people 65 years of age and older as well as younger disabled individuals. The managed care version of Medicare is called Medicare Advantage Plans (sometimes called "Part C"), which about one-third of adults choose in contrast to what is variously called "original," "fee-for-service," or "regular" Medicare, which is not managed. Some of my mental health colleagues refer to the Medicare managed care program as "Medicare Disadvantage" because of limitations in access to mental health and others services (Norris, 2015). Many older adults with regular (i.e., non-managed) Medicare have secondary policies (sometimes called "Medigap") to cover costs not covered by Medicare. Some older adults with Medicare also qualify for Medicaid, which is a federal–state program for low-income people. Older adults with both Medicare and Medicaid are sometimes as referred to as "dual eligible." Social Security is the federal program that provides income for eligible older adults and younger adults with disabilities. Many aspects of these programs are confusing, and sometimes older adults make choices and decisions about them and end up not appreciating the consequences of those decisions. Two excellent books on Medicare and Social Security are listed in Appendix A.

If you work as an employee of an institution, you may not be aware of many of the issues associated with getting paid for the mental health services you provide that are reimbursed by Medicare (or, for that matter, by other insurance carriers; Hartman-Stein & Georgoulakis, 2008; Hinrichsen, 2010). You see the client, and your institution bills. For those in independent practice, knowledge of the rules that govern what mental health services are eligible to be paid by Medicare and the processes of doing that is important. The truth is that signing up to be a Medicare provider and initially billing Medicare are often frustrating. It can be useful to have a colleague who bills Medicare explain how it all works. Of course, you can find instructions about this process on Medicare websites, but, frankly, they are not easy to understand. Some professional organizations provide individual guidance and workshops on the how-tos of Medicare. Also rules and fees differ among psychiatry, nursing, social work, and psychology. To make things more confusing, Medicare claims are administered through different organizations that are contracted to do this work (called "Medicare administrative contractors"). Rules vary among the contractor organizations about which mental health services are eligible for reimbursement (called "local coverage decisions"; Norris, 2015). The Medicare contractor organization to which you are assigned is based on geography. The amount that Medicare pays for different services fluctuates each year and varies according to geographic region (high-expense regions of the country generally have higher reimbursement rates) and professional discipline. For older adults with both Medicare and

Medicaid (adults who are dual eligible), a few states choose to pay that portion of the outpatient Medicare fee for which the client is responsible; most secondary Medigap policies will pay for the client's responsible portion of the fee (which is usually 20% for outpatient visits). Therefore, a visit may require billing two organizations. Some independent practitioners do their own billing and have become quite adept at it. When I had an independent practice for a while, I hired a billing agency—and am grateful that I chose to do that.

Once you're over the hurdle of signing up for Medicare and establishing a system for submitting bills, I've found that all goes relatively smoothly. Medicare pays promptly, and its fees for mental health services—relative to other insurance carriers—are competitive. For those who provide services to Medicare clients who are in managed care Advantage programs, the rules are quite variable, and practitioners often are paid a lesser fee than regular Medicare. Some of my independent practice colleagues will not see Medicare Advantage clients because of what they consider to be unattractive fees and required paperwork. All of this information and more are summarized in an article by Norris (2015), which is listed in Appendix A as an article worth reading.

Clinical social workers who see older adults in long-term care facilities cannot independently bill in these facilities because social work services are considered to be part of bundled services provided in those settings. Some psychologists work as independent providers of psychological services in long-term care settings. Others work for organizations (sometimes called "nursing home groups") that have established relationships with one or more long-term care settings and manage all the paperwork and billing— a sort of go-between. The disadvantage is that nursing home groups often pay practitioners less than what they would make if they were independent providers and not employees of the group.

SUMMARY

Providing treatment to an older adult encompasses a wide range of issues. Geropsychologist Bob Knight's CALTAP model (Knight & Pachana, 2015) nicely knits together several of them, including the impact of developmental forces, common late-life challenges, the social context in which older lives are lived, and the influence of generational and cultural issues. His model encompasses many of the issues that are discussed in Chapter 2. Common challenges often reflect a late-life version of issues that younger adults contend with, such as life transitions, disputes with others, and social isolation or loneliness. A challenge much more common to older adults is grief because, with advancing years, one is more likely to lose a spouse or partner, friends, and other important people.

Many practitioners possess therapeutic skills that can be of benefit to older adults because most treatments that have been found effective for younger adults are effective with older adults. The physical environment often plays a more important role in the social and emotional well-being of older people than younger adults because some older people have cognitive or physical limitations that circumscribe their lives. When thinking about making therapeutic recommendations, it is helpful for the practitioner to take stock of that. Settings in which older adults obtain mental health services are more varied than younger adults, reflecting, in part, that services are provided to older people in medical or health care settings, where they obtain services more frequently than younger people. Other factors come into play in the treatment of older people, including the importance of coordination of care, ongoing assessment of treatment progress, and familiarity with ethical issues that frequently arise. Finally, familiarity with the social services landscape of aging, Medicare, and Medicaid makes it likely that the practitioner can capably guide the older client to aging supportive services and that providers, including the mental health care practitioner, will be paid for them.

5

ASSESSMENT AND TREATMENT OF DEPRESSION AND ANXIETY

This chapter reviews foundational issues in the presentation, assessment, and treatment of depression and anxiety. The chapter also discusses the case of Mabel Brown, briefly introduced in Chapter 1, including the details of her assessment and treatment for major depression. A second case, Linda Jackson, summarizes her treatment for chronic insomnia and generalized anxiety disorder (GAD).

This chapter covers the Council of Professional Geropsychology Training Programs' recommended foundational knowledge competencies with respect to (a) clinical practice with older adults; (b) assessment of older adults; and (c) intervention, consultation, and other service provision (Hinrichsen, Emery-Tiburcio, Gooblar, & Molinari, 2018). Material in this chapter reflects content from the Pikes Peak model for training in professional geropsychology (Knight, Karel, Hinrichsen, Qualls, & Duffy, 2009), including II. Knowledge Base, B. Foundations of Clinical Practice With Older Adults; C. Foundations of Assessment of Older Adults; and D. Foundations of Intervention, Consultation, and Other Service Provision. It also addresses content from "Guidelines for Psychological Practice with Older Adults"

http://dx.doi.org/10.1037/0000146-006
Assessment and Treatment of Older Adults: A Guide for Mental Health Professionals,
by Gregory A. Hinrichsen

(American Psychological Association, 2014), including Guideline 8 (Psychologists strive to understand the functional capacity of older adults in the social and physical environment), Guideline 9 (Psychologists strive to be knowledgeable about psychopathology within the aging population and cognizant of the prevalence and nature of that psychopathology when providing services to older adults), Guideline 10 (Psychologists strive to be familiar with the theory, research, and practice of various methods of assessment with older adults, and knowledgeable of assessment instruments that are culturally and psychometrically suitable for use with them), Guideline 13 (Psychologists strive to be familiar with the theory, research, and practice of various methods of intervention with older adults, particularly with current research evidence about their efficacy with this age group), and Guideline 14 (Psychologists strive to be familiar with and develop skill in applying culturally sensitive, specific psychotherapeutic interventions and environmental modification with older adults and their families, including adapting interventions for use with this age group).

DEPRESSION

What Clinicians Need to Know About Depression in Older Adults

Diagnosable Disorders and Symptoms

Among older adults seen in mental health clinical practice, depressive disorders and depressive symptoms are common. In my clinical practice, a week does not go by without seeing an older adult with a diagnosable depression or depressive symptoms. Within the *Diagnostic and Statistical Manual of Mental Disorders* (fifth ed. [*DSM–5*]; American Psychiatric Association, 2013), psychiatric diagnostic system, major depressive disorder (MDD), persistent depressive disorder (formerly called dysthymia), and adjustment disorder (with depressive symptoms or depressive symptoms mixed with anxiety and functional impairment) are the most frequent diagnoses I encounter in clinical practice with older people. It is worth noting that depression symptoms (that do not meet criteria for a disorder) are estimated to be about 15% in the community (Blazer, 2003). For some older adults, treatment of depressive symptoms (that some have characterized as "subsyndromal") is appropriate and useful (Grabovich, Lu, Tang, Tu, & Lyness, 2010).

Depression in Older Versus Younger Adults

Early in the history of psychiatry, the term *involutional melancholia* was proposed to characterize a distinct kind of depression of middle age and older adults. (The word *involution* refers to shrinkage of an organ in old age—a somewhat odd way of thinking of later life!) This diagnostic classification was abandoned long ago but reflected an early question of whether depression looked different in older versus younger persons (Weissman, 1979). Some researchers believe that older adults are more likely than others to have subsyndromal depression, and they advocated for another diagnostic classification within the *DSM* ("minor depression") to capture this state, although the diagnosis was never adopted. I believe it is generally agreed among researchers that symptoms of depressive disorders are not that different in older versus younger persons, but some differences have been reported often. Older adults may be more likely to say they lack interest or pleasure in daily activities (*anhedonia*) than to say they have depressed mood when compared with younger people. Some researchers have found that older adults are more likely to have concerns about sleep, fatigue, being slowed down, hopelessness, and memory problems than younger adults (Fiske, Wetherell, & Gatz, 2009). The larger issue is that depression in later life is more likely to occur along with medical illness— and it may be difficult to sort out what is a medical symptom from a symptom of depression—a situation that can lead to over- and underdiagnoses of depression. In some medical conditions, depression is common and may be biologically caused by the medical condition, a medication prescribed for the condition, a psychological reaction to the condition, or combinations. Depression is increasingly common among people with cardiovascular disease, stroke, diabetes, Parkinson's disease, and dementia (Arnold, 2008; Edelstein, Bamonti, Gregg, & Gerolimatos, 2015).

Some older adults have contended with depression since adolescence and young adulthood; for others, the onset was in later life. Early life onset of depression (and other mental disorders) likely has a substantive genetic component compared with later onset. For about half of older adults, depression appears for the first time in later life. Some have suggested that late-onset depression may indicate cerebrovascular (brain) changes that increase vulnerability to depression and later dementia—what has been called the *vascular hypothesis*. Indeed, people with late-onset depression evidence changes in certain regions of the brain and are at increased risk of dementia compared with others (Edelstein et al., 2015).

Risk Factors for Depression in Later Life

As noted, some older adults have biological or genetic risk factors for depression and are likely to have had onset of depression in earlier life. For others, medical, social, and psychological factors—and their combination—are the chief reasons for depression. Also, as noted previously, certain medical problems and certain medications may biologically trigger depression (Arnold, 2008). Sleep problems, most notably, insomnia, increase risk for depression (McCrae, Roth, Zamora, Dautovich, & Lichstein, 2015). Life stressors (including onset or exacerbation of medical problems), interpersonal conflict, and social isolation increase risk for depression. Certain personality characteristics increase risk for depression in older adults, including those high on "neuroticism" (i.e., are prone to experience negative emotions) and those who are low in mastery (i.e., don't feel in control of their lives). In clinical practice, a common focus of psychotherapy with older adults is related to many of these risk factors and is discussed later in this chapter.

Depression, Health, and Functioning

Depression can have serious functional and health consequences that have not been fully appreciated within the health and mental health communities until recently. Depression increases the risk for medical problems and makes recovery from them more difficult. It can impair the immune system, heart functioning, bone density, and the brain, and it leads to increased use of medical services. Depression is tied with problems with functioning and increased disability. It also increases the risk for death. The ties between mind and body are clear: Successful treatment of depression often leads to improvements in many of these areas (Blazer, 2003; Fiske et al., 2009). The take-home message for practitioners is that treatment of depression in older adults can not only result in improvement in mood and functioning but also reduce the risk for health problems and even mortality.

Depression and Suicide

It comes as a surprise even to mental health professionals that older adults have the highest risk of suicide than any other age group. That fact seems like a paradox: Although older adults have the lowest rates of depression, they also have the highest rates of suicide. What might be going on?

First, a few definitions: *Suicidal ideation* varies along a continuum of severity from thoughts that, for example, life is not worth living to a concrete plan to end one's life. *Suicidal behavior* also exists on a continuum of overt or covert efforts to harm oneself with varying degrees of intention to death by suicide (or sometimes referred to as "die by suicide" or "completed suicide").

Although the highest rate of death by suicide is among older adults, that fact is somewhat misleading. This high rate of suicide is chiefly among

White men 85 years of age and older; their rate is more than 3 times that of the overall population. Older women and other older people from racial or ethnic groups have much lower rates of death by suicide. Past history of suicide attempts and depression are major risk factors for suicidal behavior. Almost every older adult who has died by suicide was depressed. Other factors that increase the risk for suicidal behavior are a high need for independence and control, rigidity, lack of openness to experience, onset or exacerbation of health problems, disability, pain, poor sleep quality, lack of social connectedness, relationship conflict, feeling that one is a burden on others, and hopelessness. Protective factors against suicide include contact with family and friends, religious practices, and active interests (Canadian Coalition for Seniors' Mental Health, 2006; Conwell, Van Orden, & Caine, 2011; Fiske, Smith, & Price, 2015). Older adults are much more likely to die from suicidal behavioral than younger adults. Likely reasons include a greater intention to die (versus a "suicide gesture") and less physical resilience to survive an attempt than younger individuals. Access to lethal means—particularly firearms—increases risk.

Of considerable interest is that most older adults who engaged in suicidal behavior had seen a health care professional in the month before the attempt (Luoma, Martin, & Pearson, 2002). Concern exists for the now aging baby boomers who, in their young and middle years, have had relatively high rates of suicide and who likely will have higher rates of suicide in their later years compared with the current cohort of older people (Conwell et al., 2011). For practitioners who work with older adults, the practical import of these facts about suicide and older adults is that among the minority of older adults who are depressed, a subgroup of them—White men—are vulnerable to suicide. Therefore, practitioners need to be alert to the risk of suicide—especially among older White men—and appropriately evaluate and, as needed, therapeutically address depression and the life issues associated with suicidal ideation and behavior.

Assessment

It bears repeating that in the assessment of older adults, the task can get complicated by the presence of cognitive impairment and coexisting medical problems. Cognitively impaired older adults may be unable to give an accurate report of their symptoms and concerns. Depression can sometimes be a symptom of a medical problem (e.g., endocrine disorder) that, when addressed, will lead to a reduction in or disappearance of the depression (Snowdon & Almeida, 2013).

Self-Report

It is often observed that some older adults do not subjectively experience being "depressed" but report other symptoms of depression, including loss of interest and pleasure in daily activities (i.e., anhedonia; Fiske et al., 2009). I have also found this to be the case. Generational understanding of subjective mood states, stigma, and assigned meaning to the word *depression* (e.g., weak, crazy), or changes in emotional regulation tied to aging (Carstensen et al., 2011) may explain this phenomenon. In the highly urbanized area where I have practiced, I find that many clients are familiar with the nature of and name for depression—especially those who have been depressed previously. Client self-report is one piece of the diagnostic puzzle. Another issue is that some older clients find it difficult to describe the onset of depression. It can be helpful to offer guideposts like: "Was it before you went into the hospital in June?" "This is 2019. Do you think it started this year?"

Clinician Observation

Diagnostic interviews include the practitioner's observations of the client that usually are characterized as part of the mental status exam. For example, the practitioner might note behaviors that sometimes are evident in depression: unkempt appearance, psychomotor slowing, slowness of speech, depressed and constricted affect, and difficulties with concentration. In the back of my mind during the interview, I'm attending to symptoms that would be consistent with a *DSM* depressive disorder and use follow-up questions to clarify the nature, severity, and duration of the symptoms.

Assessment Instruments

Depression assessment instruments are used with older adults, but it is important to keep in mind that many instruments have not been developed or normed for this population. Appendix B contains a list of depression evaluation instruments often recommended by geropsychologists and information on where to get them. These depression assessment instruments fall into two categories: client self-report and clinician rating scales.

Client-Self Report. One client self-report measure is the Beck Depression Inventory—Second Edition (BDI–II; Beck, Steer, & Brown, 1996), which is well regarded and has good psychometric properties with older adults. It asks the client to respond to 21 questions that cover cognitive and somatic–affective aspects of depression. Scores are categorized on a continuum from minimal depression to severe depression. There are two challenges in using the BDI–II: You must pay for each form, and some older adults find the response format difficult to understand. The Center for Epidemiological Studies Depression Scale (Radloff, 1977) has been used in many studies of depression. It is 20 items with four subscales (Depressed Mood, Psychomotor Retardation, Lack of Well-Being, and Interpersonal Difficulties). It has good psychometric properties, has been translated into languages other than English, and has support for use with older people in varied cultures. One critique of the CES-D is that some older adults (especially those with cognitive problems) find the response format hard to follow. Despite the strengths of this measure, my impression is that it is not widely used in clinical settings. The Geriatric Depression Scale (GDS; Yesavage et al., 1982–1983) was developed for older adults. Its original version contains 30 items, but briefer versions have been developed. It does not include somatic symptoms that are sometimes evident in depression (e.g., fatigue, appetite changes). Because health problems are common in older adults, an assumption that somatic symptoms are part of depression rather than medical problems may overdiagnose depressive disorders. Psychometric properties are good for this measure. The response format of the measure is yes or no, which makes it easier for some older people to answer than, for example, a continuum of responses (Likert measures). The Patient Health Questionnaire 9-Item Depression Scale (PHQ-9; Kroenke, Spitzer, & Williams, 2001) contains nine items that reflect the *DSM* criteria for major depressive episode. Clients are asked to recall how frequently they have experienced each of the symptoms in the past 2 weeks (from 0 [*not at all*] to 3 [*nearly every day*]). The PHQ-9 is an efficient way to review the symptoms tied to making a diagnosis of major depression. The measure has good psychometric properties with older clients and has been used with a wide range of populations, including primary care clients, community-residing older people, and residents of nursing homes. It has versions other than English. One practical problem is that clients may have difficulty characterizing the frequency of each of the symptoms for a 2-week period. Some medically ill older adults may endorse somatic symptoms measured by the PHQ-9 (i.e., anergia, psychomotor slowing, sleep problems) that are medical and are not a direct result of depression, which may artificially inflate the score.

Clinician Rating Scales. One clinician-administered rating scale is the Cornell Scale for Depression in Dementia (Alexopoulos, Abrams, Young, & Shamoian, 1988). The measure was developed to assess depression in persons with dementia who often have difficulty giving accurate self-report of depression-relevant symptoms. The 19 items of the Cornell Scale for Depression in Dementia are administered to an informant (e.g., family member, nursing home staff) as well as to the client. Four domains are covered: mood-related signs, behavioral disturbance, physical signs and cyclic functions (e.g., variations in mood, sleep), and ideational disturbance (e.g., suicidal thoughts, pessimism, delusions). One downside of the measure is that it takes about 30 minutes to administer. The Hamilton Depression Rating Scale (Hamilton, 1960) has been the workhorse of depression treatment studies for 50 years. The original version contained 17 items, but 6-, 2-, and 24-item versions exist. Despite its widespread use, it has been criticized for poor psychometric properties, and little research has addressed its utility in older adults. Nonetheless, it is mentioned here because of its popularity. The Geriatric Suicide Ideation Scale (GSIS; Heisel & Flett, 2006) is one of the few suicide measures developed specifically for older adults. It comprises 28 items with four subscales (Suicide Ideation, Death Ideation, Loss of Personal and Social Worth, and Perceived Meaning of Life). Its psychometric properties are good. The length of the measure might be an impediment for some older adults.

Over the years, I have used the BDI–II (Beck et al., 1996), GDS (Yesavage et al., 1982–1983), the PHQ-9 (Kroenke et al., 2001), and the Hamilton Rating Scale for Depression (Hamilton, 1960). In my current work in a geriatric primary care medical clinic, I use the PHQ-9, as do other clinicians in this setting. I also regularly use the GDS, which I find helpful with medically ill clients, in addition to the PHQ-9. For those interested in more details about the advantages and disadvantages of assessment instruments for depression and other mental disorders, see reviews by Edelstein et al. (2007; "Older Adult Psychological Assessment: Current Instrument Status and Related Considerations") and Edelstein et al. (2015; "Depression in Later Life").

Report of Others

Report of others can be a useful source of information. Geriatricians who refer clients to me have often known them for many months or years and can judge changes in behavior that concern them (e.g., "Mrs. Jones was always so upbeat. She seems so dispirited these days. I think something is going on"; "Mr. Rios continues to complain of lack of energy and interest in things, yet we don't find anything medical going on. Might he be depressed?"). For those who work in long-term care institutions, some staff may know the resident well and note changes in behavior that they suspect might be evidence of depression. Family members or friends of older clients can often be a good source of confirmatory observations.

Some have suggested that depression in older adults is best thought of on a continuum of severity (Edelstein, Drozdick, & Ciliberti, 2010). Indeed, some older adults evidence symptoms of depression that are not severe enough to meet criteria for a *DSM* diagnosis (e.g., subsyndromal depression), others have enough symptoms that meet criteria for the diagnostic category adjustment disorder (with depressive symptoms), and others meet criteria for MDD. Of course, there are individuals who have persistent depressive disorder in addition to a current episode of MDD (sometimes called "double depression"; Keller & Shapiro, 1982). One other diagnostic challenge is if the individual is bereaved because it may be hard to disentangle symptoms of bereavement from symptoms of depression. Current *DSM–5* criteria permit the diagnosis of MDD concurrent with bereavement even if the bereavement is of relatively recent origin. To me, the most substantive clinical issue is whether the individual evidences complicated grief with such symptoms as yearning and preoccupation for the dead person; loneliness; avoidance of reminders of the dead person; and purposelessness, which can then be a focus of psychotherapy (Prigerson et al., 2009). Sometimes at the end of an assessment, I feel I need more information, which I then obtain from others or from a follow-up assessment with the client.

Obstacles to and Tools for Assessing Depression and Suicide
The biggest obstacle to assessment of suicide in older adults may be practitioners themselves. As the reader may recall, I have had good-hearted and competent colleagues who don't professionally work with older people who have made casual remarks about their own plans to end of their lives if they had serious health problems in old age. Others have commented about seriously ill and depressed older adults: "What do they have to live for?" If a practitioner has underlying beliefs that late-life suicide is a viable option, he or she is less likely to carefully query it with the client. One study found that 45% of people who died by suicide had seen their primary care physician within a month of their deaths (Luoma et al., 2002). Sometimes health care providers do not feel competent to assess and treat suicide, so they do not ask (Graham, Rudd, & Bryan, 2011). Given that a subgroup of older adults—White men—have some of the highest suicide rates, it is critical to make an assessment. Keep in mind the factors—discussed earlier—that increase risk for suicide in older adults: depression, past history of suicide, need for control, onset or exacerbation of health problems, hopelessness, and lack of interpersonal connectedness or conflict as well as protective factors: social connectedness, religious practice, and active interests (Fiske et al., 2015).

Different practitioners and institutions have their own protocols for evaluating and, if necessary, taking next steps to assure client safety. The

Geriatric Suicide Ideation Scale (Heisel & Flett, 2006) was developed for older adults and is included in Appendix B. In an initial assessment with older clients, I conduct the PHQ-9; item 9 of this instrument asks about suicide-related thoughts. I find it's a good initial screen that, when answered in the affirmative, is a launching point for further discussion. Although not developed specifically for older adults, the safety planning intervention to mitigate suicide risk (Stanley & Brown, 2012) is worth reviewing. It offers a series of concrete actions that the client can take to cope with suicidal thoughts and feelings and to engage the support of others to reduce the likelihood of suicidal behavior. The approach has been adopted in U.S. Department of Veterans Affairs (VA) health care settings with good success.

Over the years, I have worked with many older adults with suicidal thoughts, the content of which ranged from "life is not worth living" to active plans to end their lives. Managing suicide risk is one of the more stressful things with which mental health practitioners must contend. I am struck by how serious depression can fundamentally alter an older adult's view of the world to the extent that suicide seems like viable option. I was referred an older woman who planned her own death for almost a year in an eerily methodological way. The plan failed when she didn't take into account that the opioid medication she used to attempt suicide was long past expired. After many months of psychotherapy, her mood significantly improved. For years after we ended psychotherapy, she would drop a note each year to thank me for working with her during the "darkest hours" and "saving my life." Recently, her son contacted me to advise that his mother had died of health problems in her nineties and thanked me for what I had done years earlier. Those notes were so meaningful.

Treatment

In treating late-life depression, the following treatments have been identified as effective with older adults: behavior therapy, cognitive behavior therapy (CBT), cognitive bibliotherapy, problem-solving therapy, brief psychodynamic psychotherapy, and reminiscence therapy. Interpersonal psychotherapy (IPT)—a modality I often use—has been identified as a promising treatment because, as the authors have noted, additional evidence for its efficacy with older adults is warranted (Shah, Scogin, & Floyd, 2012). Optimally, a practitioner might have well-developed skills in several psychotherapeutic modalities. In reality, practitioners have a preferred modality based on prior training, or they blend different perspectives. If you possess different psychotherapeutic skill sets, you might want to talk with the older client about what approach he or she prefers. In my experience, some depressed older adults love the structure of CBT, but, for others, the format is confusing and frustrating. Sometimes I change the therapeutic approach if the one I am using does not seem like a good fit for the depressed client. Among treatments for depression, I use these (in order of frequency): IPT, CBT, and supportive psychotherapy informed by psychodynamic principles.

Some older adults referred to me for psychotherapy are on antidepressant medications. Antidepressant medications are useful for the treatment of depression, although some surveys have shown that older adults prefer psychotherapy to medication (Gum et al., 2006). Antidepressant medications have been found to be equally effective when compared with others (although some older adults respond much better to a particular class), but they have varied side effects. Some older adults do not want to add an antidepressant to an already sizable medication regimen, and there are risks of interactions among medications, sometimes referred to as "polypharmacy" (Arnold, 2008). Older adults with long-standing depression appear to benefit most by a combination of medication and psychotherapy, whereas those with shorter term depression benefit less from antidepressants and may prefer psychotherapy alone (Edelstein et al., 2015). Some older adults with serious depression that has not responded to multiple medications, psychotherapy, or the combination can be good candidates for electroconvulsive therapy (ECT), which has been found to be effective (Edelstein et al., 2015). This form of therapy has cognitive side effects, and although most studies have indicated that these effects are short term (e.g., McDonald & Vahabzadeh, 2013), I have former clients who subjectively felt there were longer term, subtle changes in the clarity of thinking following ECT. Given the dramatic improvement in depression that many people experience, most former clients say they have few regrets about receiving ECT.

Among the four domains of problems (see Chapter 4, this volume) that are a common focus of psychotherapy with older adults, life transitions are most often tied to depression. When I worked in an outpatient geriatric mental health clinic, providing care to a spouse with health or cognitive problems was the modal issue associated with depression. In the geriatric primary care medical clinic where I work, onset or exacerbation of medical problems is the modal issue. But a full range of issues is evident among depressed older people, including life transitions (e.g., onset of medical problems, care for an older relative, residential move, chosen or forced retirement, onset of financial problems), disputes (e.g., with spouse, adult child, institution), grief (e.g., following the death of a spouse, an adult child, a close friend), and social isolation or loneliness (long-standing or more recent).

CASE EXAMPLE OF MABEL BROWN: PART 3

Assessment

Mrs. Brown was introduced in Chapter 1 and briefly mentioned in Chapter 2. Here, I return to that case example to walk the reader through the stages of referral, assessment, and treatment.

Referral

This 85-year-old White, widowed, Catholic woman with two children was referred to me by a geriatrician who had been her primary medical care provider for 5 years. The geriatrician advised that in the past year, Mrs. Brown had grown depressed, which seemed to be tied to increasing medical problems. The geriatrician had offered Mrs. Brown a prescription for an antidepressant medication on several occasions, but she refused it. She also refused a referral to a mental health clinic. Her daughter, Carol, expressed concern to the geriatrician about her mother's change in outlook ("She used to be so upbeat"), withdrawal from church and other social activities, and apparent poor compliance with her diabetes medical regimen. Carol told the geriatrician that she said to her mother. "You have no choice. You have to see someone." When the geriatrician assured Mrs. Brown that she knew and liked the referred psychologist, she reluctantly agreed to set up a first appointment.

Assessment Environment

Mrs. Brown was seen in an outpatient medical setting that was disability friendly—it had no stairs and the bathroom had grab bars. I met Mrs. Brown in the waiting room, and her daughter assumed that she would be part of the appointment. I told Carol that I would be meeting with her mother alone for most of the appointment but would touch base with her at the end of it.

At the beginning of the appointment, Mrs. Brown remarked, "I wasn't always this way." I asked her what she meant. She said that she did not need to use a walker until the preceding year. "Now, look at me," she said. I oriented her to the plan for our visit: "I'm going to meet with you for about an hour today and ask you a lot of questions. I'm going to be a bit businesslike. I appreciate your patience with that." I then added that her daughter had accompanied her to the appointment and seemed to want to join us at some point. "Would that be OK with you or not?" I asked. She replied, "Yes. I would like her to be here at the end, but I want to tell you what I think about all this first."

General Inquiry

I asked her why she had come to see me. "My daughter told me I had to come. And my doctor told me that too," she said. I asked, "Why did they tell you, you had to come?" Mrs. Brown replied, "They say I'm depressed. Oh, yes, and my daughter thinks I can't remember things." "What do you say?" I asked. "They are probably right—but not about everything," Mrs. Brown replied.

I asked her to briefly tell me when things began to get more difficult for her. She explained that in the past year, she had increasing health problems. About a year earlier, she had undergone back surgery; after that, it was more difficult for her to walk, and she reported becoming increasingly "negative" and less interested in seeing people. "I used to be a positive person, believe it or not," Mrs. Brown said.

Basic Background

I learned from Mrs. Brown that she was of European ancestry ("English" and "Irish"); had graduated from college; had worked as a high school teacher much of her life, retiring at age 62; and had been widowed 10 years earlier. She had a son (John) and daughter (Carol) who lived locally as well as several grandchildren. She expressed appreciation for Carol's "helping me" and annoyance at her "nagging." Mrs. Brown said that she and her son, John, got along well but was disappointed by his infrequent visits. She had a brother who lived elsewhere and one deceased brother. "Can I presume you're heterosexual?" I asked. "Yes, you can," she said, adding, "My granddaughter is married to a woman. I don't have problems with that."

Physical Health

I reviewed the information about Mrs. Brown's physical health that had been provided to me: Type 2 diabetes, high blood pressure, a back surgery, and problems with sight. "What kind of seeing problems do you have?" I asked. Mrs. Brown said, "They think I might have macular degeneration, but I can see well enough to read. I need glasses, though." I asked why she used the walker. She replied, "Ever since the back surgery, I needed the walker. They said after surgery, my back would be better, but it's worse."

She explained that she had undergone the back surgery for "disc problems." After reviewing with her the list of her prescribed medications, she added that she had been taking an over-the counter pill for insomnia. "I've been having problems with sleep."

Mental Health History

Mrs. Brown gave no history of past mental health treatment or episodes of depression or anxiety. "I told you I was a positive person," she said. When asked about mental health problems in her family, she paused and sighed: "When he was young, my little brother had drug problems and died from an overdose." She explained that family members felt he used drugs because he had problems with depression. "But I don't believe that. I think he got caught up with the wrong people."

She reported that she did not drink alcohol, had never smoked, drank two cups of coffee in the morning, and had never had alcohol or drug problems. "Seeing what happened to my brother convinced me to never use drugs—not even marijuana." She had no history of physical abuse, sexual abuse, or domestic violence. She did not express concerns that might indicate abuse or neglect. "I can take care of myself," she said. "I'm not sure that Carol believes that."

Life History

Mrs. Brown was born in New York City and raised by two parents along with two brothers Her father worked in a factory and her mother worked as a nursing aide after the children were older. Both her parents were Catholic and active members of their church. Mrs. Brown attended and then graduated from Catholic school, worked briefly as a secretary, and then went to college and obtained a teaching degree. While she was in college, her brother died of the drug overdose. "My parents were devastated, and so was I," she said.

She met her future husband at the same school where she worked. They married and had two children. "My mother helped with the kids so that I could continue to teach." Both she and her husband had successful careers in teaching. After retiring, she and her husband took leadership roles in their church. When he had died, Mrs. Brown said, "Of course, it was a shock. I was lucky to have been with such a great guy. I know he's in heaven, and I will see him again." Until the past year or so, she had continued to be active in her church. "I don't know what happened to me then. I stopped going to my church groups. I even have to push myself to go to mass on Sundays."

Assessment Instruments

I administered both the PHQ-9 (Kroenke et al., 2001) and Generalized Anxiety Disorder 7-item (GAD-7; Spitzer, Kroenke, Williams, & Lowe, 2006) to Mrs. Brown. On the PHQ-9 depression screening measure, she evidenced anhedonia, depressed mood, fatigue, self-critical behavior, concentration problems, and psychomotor slowing. She also complained of sleep problems—falling and staying asleep—for which she began to take an over-the-counter sleep aide. "It helped at first, but not so much now," she had reported. Notably, she did not indicate any thoughts of self-harm or suicide. "I would never do something like that." Her PHQ-9 score was 16, indicating "moderately severe depression." On the GAD-7 anxiety screen, she evidenced symptoms of nervousness, worry, problems relaxing, restlessness, and irritability. The GAD-7 score was 12, which indicates "moderate anxiety." The anxiety symptoms developed around the same time she began to become depressed. General inquiries didn't indicate the presence of other notable mental health symptoms. I administered the Montreal Cognitive Assessment (Nasreddine et al., 2005), a brief cognitive screening measure. She had a score of 27/30 with some difficulties in concentration and word recall, but nothing that would indicate substantive cognitive problems.

Clinical Observation

Mrs. Brown was well dressed and well groomed, cooperative, and spoke at a normal rate and tone. She evidenced moderate psychomotor slowing. Her affect was moderately depressed and mild to moderately anxious. Her mood was moderately depressed and anxious. Her thought processes were goal directed. She was alert and oriented and evidenced mild concentration and short-term memory deficits. There was no evidence of suicidal or homicidal ideation or psychotic symptoms. She experienced fatigue, some restlessness, and possibly some increase in appetite with weight gain in the past year. She had initial and middle insomnia of at least several months' duration. Her intelligence appeared to be above average. Her judgment and insight were intact.

DSM Diagnosis

Mrs. Brown met diagnostic criteria for MDD, single episode, moderate severity. She had notable symptoms of anxiety, but based on history and presentation, these did not appear consistent with a diagnosis of GAD.

Feedback to the Client

"I have asked you a lot of questions. Do you have questions for me?" I asked. She in turn asked, "Do you think this can get better?" "Yes," I replied, "I do think things will get better." "Why do you think that?" she asked. "You have a depression that seems connected to your health problems," I answered. "Depression is a treatable condition and I'm confident that you can feel much less depressed and anxious. Do you see that you're both anxious and depressed? It's common for people who are depressed to also have anxiety." She responded, "I think of it as being scared." "That makes sense," I said. "Often if people feel anxious, they also feel scared." She asked, "What about my memory? Is there a problem?" I replied, "You have some minor difficulties that are common among people with depression. I expect they will improve as your depression improves."

I then asked, "It's your choice whether you want to see me or not. If you did, what would you want to get out of it?" "To be less negative and less scared," Mrs. Brown replied. "Those seem like reasonable goals," I said, adding, "I also want to tell you that antidepressant medication is also an effective treatment for depression." "I told the doctor that I am not going to take an antidepressant medication," replied Mrs. Brown. "What is your concern?" I asked. She said, "I don't want to take any more medications." I responded, "I appreciate that. Psychotherapy—the kind of meetings we would have—has been found helpful for most people with depression. If you change your mind, medication is always an option."

I asked her again about whether she wanted her daughter to join us and whether there were things she did not want me to share with her daughter. "You can tell her anything," she replied. "I trust her."

Report of Others

Mrs. Brown's daughter joined us. She expressed concern about her mother's mood, negativity, withdrawal from social activities, failure to fully comply with recommendations for managing diabetes (e.g., diet, exercise), and excessive worry. "She's so different. At times, I don't recognize her," said the daughter. I told Carol what I had conveyed to Mrs. Brown: that she had a depression (along with a lot of anxiety), which appeared to be connected to her health problems, and that I was proposing a course of psychotherapy and expected that Mrs. Brown would improve. "Even without medication?" asked Carol. Mrs. Brown exclaimed, "Carol, I told you—I'm not taking antidepressant medication." I told Carol that I expected her mother would improve with psychotherapy alone—but that medication was an option if Mrs. Brown decided later that she wanted to take it.

Follow-Up

Mrs. Brown agreed to come for weekly psychotherapy. Her daughter said she would transport her mother to those visits. With the client's consent,

I contacted the geriatrician who had referred Mrs. Brown and advised of the plan.

Treatment

Treatment Modality

Mrs. Brown was treated with IPT for depression. Interpersonal psychotherapy is typically conducted over 16 sessions in three phases of treatment: initial sessions, intermediate sessions, and termination. In IPT, the focus is on one or two interpersonally relevant problems areas: role transitions (i.e., life changes), interpersonal disputes (i.e., conflict with another person), grief (i.e., complicated bereavement), and interpersonal deficits (i.e., social isolation or loneliness). This treatment modality has consistently been found to be effective in the treatment of depression in adults and, in a small number of studies, with older adults (van Hees, Rotter, Ellermann, & Evers, 2013). I chose IPT as the treatment modality because I and others have found it especially well suited to the problems of older adults (Hinrichsen, 2008; Hinrichsen & Clougherty, 2006). Within the IPT framework, Mrs. Brown's health problems would be characterized as role transitions (i.e., transitioning from someone with health problems to someone having more and more functionally impairing health problems than she previously had experienced).

Initial Sessions (Weeks 1–3)

When Mrs. Brown returned for her first psychotherapy session, I reviewed with her the issues that we had discussed in the intake. I discussed the symptoms associated with her depression and how they had made it much harder for her to function. She blamed herself for not taking care of her home the way she used to, for not being more active in her church, and for not following the diet that was required for her diabetes. "What's wrong with me?" she asked. I advised that problems with functioning as well as self-blame were symptoms of depression, and I asked if, in the short-run, she could take some pressure off of herself to reduce some of her usual responsibilities until she was feeling less depressed. I said, "If you had the flu, you wouldn't expect that you'd do everything you normally did until you were feeling better. So, for now, it is okay to let some things go. Does the house really need to be 100% right now?" She said she'd think about it. We talked more about the onset of the depression, which was tied to back surgery that did not go the way she had hoped. I restated that depression was a treatable condition and that I expected she would be less depressed at the end of our treatment. "How do you know that?" she asked. "Because," I replied, "most people with depression who are treated with this approach show meaningful improvement. Not everyone, but most people." I noted that hopelessness that things could change was another symptom of depression.

In the second psychotherapy session, I conducted a broad but brief review of important relationships in her life—what is called the *interpersonal inventory* in IPT. The inventory underscored that she had generally good relationships with others, found meaning in them, and could view relationships in a balanced way—that is, see that relationships had both satisfying and unsatisfying aspects. Another theme that emerged was how important being independent was to her and that she be treated with respect. "You probably don't remember, but I was one of the first group of women of my era who felt they had a right to a career along with being a mother," she said. "My husband appreciated that, but not everyone."

In the third initial session, I provided feedback to Mrs. Brown (in IPT, the *interpersonal formulation*). I restated that she had a depression along with anxiety that appeared to start after the back surgery she had undergone about 1 year earlier. Although she was used to managing health problems—including diabetes—she now was dealing with a new set of problems, including a back that was worse and not better after surgery, and needed a walker. As she grew more depressed, she did less: stopped going to church groups, did not take care of her house as she had before, and had neglected the diabetic diet. Neglect of the diet had led to weight gain and poorer diabetes blood test results, which made her feel more depressed and self-critical. She also had symptoms of anxiety. Her relationship with her daughter, Carol, was becoming strained as Carol began to "take charge," which made Mrs. Brown feel resentful and disempowered. Mrs. Brown concurred with this assessment. "So what are you going to do about it?" asked Mrs. Brown. "I think the better question is, What you are going to do about it?" I responded. "In the end, it's your life. I'm here to support you and provide some guidance." We agreed that the focus of psychotherapy would be in helping her to get a better handle on her health problems with the goal of decreased depression and anxiety. She said she was skeptical but would try.

Intermediate Sessions (Weeks 4–14)

At the beginning of each of the intermediate sessions, I asked Mrs. Brown to rate her depression on a scale of 1 (*not at all depressed*) to 10 (*most depressed*). I also asked her how the past week had been for her. I looked for the opportunity to point out the connection between her mood and events of the prior week, as is done in IPT.

In the first few weeks of these sessions, Mrs. Brown was highly critical of herself. She said that her house was a "mess" and that she did little. Of most concern was that she was neglecting management of her diabetes.

She didn't prepare diabetic-friendly meals, continued to put on weight, and did not take a walk each day as her doctor had recommended. Blood tests related to diabetes worsened. "How could I be doing this to myself?" She recounted that her father had died of diabetic complications, and she vowed that would never happen to her. I continued to underscore that problems with functioning, difficulty with following medical regimens, and self-blame were all common in depression. I told her that at this point, she was doing the best she could, but as her depression improved, she would do better. She was also preoccupied with a pile of winter clothes sitting in a spare bedroom and how she had not put them away. Each week she criticized herself for not doing this task. Friends were coming for a visit, and she felt some urgency to take care of this task. She eventually felt she would try to put away a few pieces of clothing. She returned to tell me—to her surprise—that she had put away half of the clothing. The next week, she put away all the clothing before the visit with her friends. She was a little encouraged with her efforts but still self-critical.

I engaged her in a discussion of how things had been before the back surgery. Before, she didn't need a walker, keep her home tidy, attended church gatherings, managed her diabetic diet, and went for daily walks and regular outings with her daughter and friends. "Things weren't perfect, but I had a good life," she had said. Things all changed with the back surgery, which the surgeon had said would improve her mobility. "But it didn't," said Mrs. Brown. "It was worse." I engaged Mrs. Brown in a discussion of how she had come to make the decision to have the back surgery. "I didn't want to do it, but the doctor pushed me, and so did my daughter." Further discussion of this issue revealed that Mrs. Brown had experienced serious concerns about the surgery but went along anyway. "I hated myself for saying *yes* when I wanted to say *no*. Now look at me," she said. Mrs. Brown didn't tell her daughter but, in part, she blamed Carol for pushing her to have the surgery. This discussion appeared to relieve some of Mrs. Brown's depression and distress. We clarified that part of Mrs. Brown's refusal to accept an antidepressant or initially take part in psychotherapy was her way of taking control of her health care and "not being told what to do."

Mrs. Brown's depression and anxiety slowly improved as well as some of her functioning. She felt her home was a little bit more tidy, got out to walk once a week, and went shopping with her daughter. "I had to sit down a lot, but it was okay." One week, Mrs. Brown mentioned that her eye doctor said she needed to have surgery on both eyes. I engaged her in a discussion of what she wanted to do. "I don't want to have both eyes done at once. What if there is a problem?" I asked if she had communicated her concern to the eye doctor. She had not. She said that, initially, she didn't know what to say, and then the appointment was over. We discussed what she was willing to do with regard to the eye surgery and how to communicate that to the eye doctor. She then had another appointment; the eye doctor said that he would operate on one eye and later the other eye. But when she met with me again, she told me that she didn't want her "good eye" operated on first, which the surgeon had recommended. "What if something goes wrong? That's my good eye," she said. She set up another appointment with the eye doctor and told him she was willing to have her "bad eye" operated on first but not the "good eye." The doctor said he preferred operating on her good eye first. Mrs. Brown said she would not take part in the surgery if that was the case. The doctor relented. Mrs. Brown was notably less depressed.

By session 10, her PHQ-9 (Kroenke et al., 2001) was 8, which indicates "mild depression"—and a 50% reduction in her depressive symptoms. Reduction on the GAD-7 (Spitzer et al., 2006) measure of anxiety was comparable. Notably, she was sleeping much better. This news further heartened Mrs. Brown who said that, indeed, she was feeling better.

Mrs. Brown's eye surgery went well. She was relieved but also proud that she had taken an active voice in deciding how she would have the eye surgery. Her functioning continued to improve, including return to one of her church clubs, where she was greeted warmly. "I wondered about how strong my faith was when I was feeling so depressed. I was always the one who cheered people up and then nobody could cheer me up," she said. "How strong could my faith have been? Now that I'm seeing my church friends, I feel more confident of my faith."

Termination

The last two sessions focused on review of treatment and looking to the future. Mrs. Brown's PHQ-9 (Kroenke et al., 2001) was 3, which indicates "minimal depression," at the end of psychotherapy. The GAD-7 measure of anxiety was 4, which indicates "mild anxiety." She said she had been skeptical that her depression would improve. "You said it would get better, and I guess you were right," she told me. She said that she was glad she didn't take an antidepressant medication. I asked why. "Because it would have been doing one more thing that other people told me to do that I didn't want to." She also said that she had been wary of drugs since her brother had died from a drug overdose.

We reviewed improvement in depressive symptoms and the status of the problems that brought her into therapy. She said she felt she was doing better, even though she needed to use a walker, which made getting to appointments and social events more difficult. Mrs. Brown still felt she needed to lose weight and do better with the diabetic diet, but said that she was cooking for herself, which made that effort easier. I asked her to look to the future and what might be possible triggers for return of depressive symptoms. She responded, "If I had more medical problems—but I think I now can say *no* if I don't want a medical procedure." She said she would know she was getting depressed if she felt discouraged and had less interest in going to church events. "If that happens, I could always talk to my daughter and church friends; and if that didn't work, see you again."

In the last appointment, her daughter, Carol, joined the session. Carol said, "She's dramatically better. You did such a nice job with my mom." I replied, "She did such a great job for herself."

Case Commentary

Mrs. Brown was a highly independent woman who prided herself on that trait. As she said, she was of an early generation of women who forged a life of being a mother and having a career. She had successfully contended with health problems as she got older but ran into trouble when a back surgery was unsuccessful. In my view, it was not so much the outcome of the back surgery but feelings of disempowerment about it because she had agreed to surgery when she did not want to do it. The opportunity to address another medical decision-making issue presented itself during the course of psychotherapy when eye surgery was proposed. She clarified what she wanted, better communicated with the eye surgeon about her wishes, and had her wishes honored.

During psychotherapy, she better understood that physical, emotional, and behavioral changes from the preceding year were not so much evidence of her personal failures or lack of religious faith but symptoms of depression. "Small" efforts on her part to increase functioning at home slowly built some hopefulness, relieved some depression, and laid the foundation for further efforts. I think this case is a cautionary tale about how health care providers—as well as family members—need to engage older adults in medical decision making, including the decision to take an antidepressant medication.

ANXIETY

What Clinicians Need to Know About Anxiety in Older Adults

Diagnosable Disorders and Symptoms

As noted in Chapter 3, about 8% of older adults have an anxiety disorder. Although this rate is much lower than for younger adults, among late-life mental disorders, it is much more common than others, including depression. Yet we know much less about anxiety in older adults than we do about depression or dementia. It is highly likely that anxiety disorders are more common among older adults living in long-term care facilities compared with those who are community residing (Seitz, Purandare, & Conn, 2010). Within the *DSM–5* diagnostic system, anxiety disorders relevant to older adults chiefly encompass GAD, specific phobia, social anxiety disorder, agoraphobia, and panic disorder. Anxiety disorders due to medications and medical issues are also included among anxiety disorders. (*Note:* In the *DSM–5*, posttraumatic stress disorder [PTSD] and other stressor disorders as well as obsessive–compulsive disorder [OCD] were removed from the anxiety disorders category and placed in other categories. Therefore, past epidemiological survey results overstate the percentage of older adults with the now newly defined set of anxiety disorders [Sachdev, Mohan, Taylor, & Jeste, 2015].)

I focus on GAD because, among the anxiety disorders, it is most commonly seen in clinical practice with older adults and because there is relatively little research on the other anxiety disorders in older adults. Also panic disorder, agoraphobia, and OCD are rare in community populations: Estimates are less than 1% (Gum, King-Kallimanis, & Kohn, 2009). I also discuss a few issues related to PTSD, even though it is not now classified in the *DSM–5* as an anxiety disorder. I hasten to add that adjustment disorders (now classified in the *DSM–5* as trauma and stressor-related disorders) are commonly seen among older adults in clinical practice and often are accompanied by anxiety as well as depression. Anxiety symptoms often co-occur with other mental disorders, including depression. One study found that more than one-third of older adults with anxiety disorders had an MDD, and that half of those with depression had a coexisting anxiety disorder (Bower, Wetherell, Mon, & Lenze, 2015). In a presentation to a community group of older adults, I characterized depression and anxiety as "close cousins." One older member of the audience who said she had experienced problems with depression and anxiety during her life remarked, "I'd say they were more like brother and sister."

One anxiety-related disorder that is much more common among older than younger adults is phobia tied to fear of falling. In the field of geriatric medicine, falls are an ongoing concern for older adults (Tinetti, 2003). Some older adults who have fallen become phobic of it happening again and may paradoxically limit their activities to avoid the possibility of falling—which increases the risk of falls because the person becomes physically deconditioned (Zijlstra et al., 2009). Major medical centers often have "fall clinics" in which older people are evaluated, provided guidance on how to prevent falls, and offered treatment to reduce fear of falling.

Anxiety in Older Versus Younger Adults

Older adults may be less likely to report anxiety and more likely to characterize symptoms as a "concern" than a "worry" compared with younger adults. The ways that older people characterize or experience anxiety symptoms may reflect differences in generational labeling of emotions and that older adults experience less arousal and better regulation of emotions than younger individuals (Carstensen et al., 2011). The content of worry for anxious older adults tends to be about loved ones and the state of the world in contrast to younger people for whom the focus of worry is on work or school (Bower & Wetherell, 2015). Anxiety is more common among older adults with physical health problems, and, yet, it may be difficult to disentangle medical symptoms from somatic symptoms of anxiety (e.g., fatigue, restlessness, muscle tension, sleep changes). Furthermore, some older adults experience anxiety symptoms that are a direct result of medical problems or medications.

In my current clinical practice, geriatricians refer clients to me who are experiencing anxiety—often GAD—related to their health problems. Despite evidence to the contrary, some clients are convinced that their anxiety symptoms are a result of acute health problems for which they may have sought numerous second medical opinions and made emergency room visits. Or, conversely, medical providers may misidentify anxiety symptoms for medical symptoms, treat those symptoms medically, and fail to refer for mental health services.

Risk Factors and Anxiety and PTSD

In clinical practice, some older adults will characterize themselves as "lifelong worriers" and report a waxing and waning of symptoms consistent with GAD throughout their lives. For others, symptoms of anxiety (which may or may not meet criteria for GAD) appeared later in life and are associated with medical problems or other late-life stressors. Women, those with lower education and income, a family history of anxiety, and early childhood abuse are associated with greater risk for anxiety disorders in older adulthood (Bower & Wetherell, 2015). Chronic health problems, cognitive impairment, restricted coping strategies, and lack of self-efficacy are also tied to anxiety disorders and symptoms in older people (Gonçalves, Pachana, & Byrne, 2011). Some research has suggested that older people with anxiety may be at increased risk for dementia and that individuals with dementia often experience anxiety (Beaudreau & O'Hara, 2008; Petkus et al., 2016). Anxiety disorders are more likely to appear earlier in life than depressive disorders. Medical problems—chiefly chronic pain, diabetes, lung problems, gastrointestinal problems, cardiovascular disease, and hyperthyroidism—increase the risk for anxiety symptoms or GAD. Older adults who have fallen are at risk for developing a phobia of falling. Some medical providers may see a self-restriction of activities among older adults who have fallen as prudent behavior on their part, yet fail to see that anxiety is the major driver of activity restriction rather than good judgment (Bower & Wetherell, 2015).

Some older adults who have experienced earlier life trauma may have delayed-onset of PTSD symptoms or reexperience them. Mental health care providers in the VA health care system have considerable experience with PTSD among both younger and older veterans, some of whom have contended with military service-related trauma (Karlin et al., 2010). Historical events can trigger reexperiencing of PTSD. After the September 11, 2001 attack on the World Trade Center complex in New York City, a number of VA colleagues observed a reemergence of PTSD symptoms in clients who were World War II veterans.

Anxiety, Health, and Functioning

Anxiety and GAD are tied to poorer quality of life, greater use of medications, overuse of health care, and functional impairment. Health care utilization that is driven by anxiety may lead to unnecessary medical procedures that may result in further health problems. Older adults with MDD and coexisting GAD have poorer clinical outcomes than those without GAD. GAD is also associated with increased risk of cardiac problems (Gonçalves et al., 2011).

A related complication can be the chronic use of sedating medications, most notably, benzodiazepines (e.g., Ativan, Klonopin, Valium, Xanax). Short-term use of these medications can be helpful, but long-term use is associated with physiological and psychological dependence, falling, cognitive impairment, and other problems (Tinetti, 2003). When I worked in an outpatient geriatric psychiatry program, we often saw older adults who were chronic users of benzodiazepines for anxiety (or even depressive disorders) prescribed by community physicians. It was often difficult for these older clients to reduce or stop use of these medications on which they had become dependent, and that in the long run had little therapeutic value.

Assessment

As is the case with depression, anxiety symptoms are often intertwined with late-life medical problems. Anxiety may be associated with a wide range of medical problems and medications (e.g., cardiac, endocrine, neurological, cancer, pulmonary disease; over-the-counter and prescription medications, caffeine, alcohol; Zarit & Zarit, 2007). Much less is known about anxiety disorders in older people than, for example, depression (Carmin & Ownby, 2010). Like depression, I think of anxiety on a continuum:

$$\text{Anxiety symptoms} \rightarrow \text{GAD}$$

and

$$\text{Adjustment disorder with anxiety symptoms} \rightarrow \text{PTSD or phobia}$$

Self-Report

Older adults are less likely to say they are anxious and may use language such as "concern" to convey what practitioners may characterize as anxiety. Furthermore, older adults are generally less likely to say they are worried and evidence more subsyndromal anxiety compared with younger adults (Carmin & Ownby, 2010). In clinical practice, I find that patients are referred to me by geriatricians because of the specialist's concern about the patient's anxiety more than the client's perception of an anxiety problem. When asked if they are anxious, clients may say no but describe a series of concerning life circumstances that strongly indicate that they are.

Clinician Observation

In view of these potential anxiety self-report issues, observation of client behavior during the interview can be especially important. Client complaints of somatic symptoms (e.g., muscle tension, stomach tightness, a feeling of restlessness, nondescript discomfort) may be indicative of anxiety. Observationally, some anxious older clients find it hard to stay on-task, find it difficult to give succinct responses, are preoccupied with describing physical symptoms in great detail, and evidence facial apprehension. As researchers have found, in interpersonal dyads, depressive symptoms in one person increase the likelihood of depression in another ("depressive contagion"; Joiner & Katz, 1999), I sometimes find myself feeling anxious after assessing an anxious client. It's as if I can "feel" the anxiety in the room.

Assessment Instruments

A wide variety of anxiety assessment instruments exists for anxiety, but most of them have been critiqued for not having been developed or normed with older adults (Bower & Wetherell, 2015; Edelstein et al., 2007). The chief problem is that many anxiety-screening instruments contain questions about physical symptoms of anxiety. Because older adults are much more likely than others to have medical problems, they are therefore more likely to have somatic symptoms of illness. But for many, these symptoms are a result of a health problem and are not necessarily reflective of anxiety or of uncertain origin. Appendix B lists some anxiety measures generally viewed as useful with older adults. For a comprehensive review and critique of anxiety assessment instruments for older adults, see Bower and Wetherell (2015).

The Geriatric Anxiety Inventory was created for older adults (Pachana et al., 2007). As originally developed, this measure has 20 items that are answered "Agree" or "Disagree." It has good psychometric properties and discriminates between those with and without *DSM* GAD. A five-item version of this measure is available and also has good psychometric properties (Byrne & Pachana, 2011). Some older adults will find the *yes* or *no* response format appealing (vs. a Likert format). The Geriatric Anxiety Scale (GAS; Segal, June, Payne, Coolidge, & Yochim, 2010) was also developed for older adults. Its original version is 30 items, which ask individuals to judge how often (from 0 [*not at all*] to 3 [*all of the time*]) they have experienced each symptom in the past week. Three subscales are Somatic Symptoms, Cognitive Symptoms, and Affective Symptoms. The GAS has good psychometric properties, and non-English versions of the measure are available. A 10-item version of this measure (Geriatric Anxiety Scale–10 Item Version; Mueller et al., 2015) exists and has good psychometric properties. The GAD-7 (Spitzer et al., 2006) is a brief assessment of whether the individual evidences symptoms that are part of the *DSM* criteria for GAD. In its development, older adults were included in the study sample in primary care, and it has good psychometric properties (Spitzer et al., 2006). One challenge in the use of this measure as well as its sister measure, the PHQ-9 (Kroenke et al., 2001), is that the individual is asked to judge the frequency of each symptom over the course of 2 weeks. Some individuals find recall over that period to be difficult, and for older people with cognitive impairment, such recall could be especially difficult. Furthermore, in the diagnosis of *DSM* GAD, symptoms must be present for 6 months, so further inquiry is needed to make the diagnosis. The PTSD Checklist for *DSM–5* (PCL-5; Blevins, Weathers, Davis, Witte, & Domino, 2015) is a 20-item self-report measure. The items correspond to the *DSM–5* symptoms for PTSD. The individual rates each symptom on a continuum of severity from 0 (*not at all*) to 4 (*extremely*). The measure can be especially useful as an initial screen for *DSM–5* PTSD symptoms. It is psychometrically sound, yet the validation sample did not include older adults.

Because GAD is a fairly common anxiety problem in older adults I see, I use the Generalized Anxiety Disorder–7 item screen (GAD-7; Spitzer et al., 2006) in all initial assessments. The GAD-7 is also used by many health care providers in my clinical setting so that we share a common metric. It also provides a quick review of anxiety-related symptoms and whether the older client meets criteria for GAD. Because I don't see that many clients with PTSD, I find the PTSD Checklist for *DSM–5* (Blevins et al., 2015) useful as an initial screen that, as needed, can be followed up with more detailed questioning.

Report of Others
Staff in long-term care facilities can be good observers of anxious behaviors in their residents, as are older clients' primary care physicians, family members, and friends. Sometimes family members will characterize the relative as a "lifelong worrier" but indicate that worry now dominates conversations and interactions in a way it hadn't previously.

Treatment

Research-supported treatments for anxiety with older people include CBT, cognitive therapy, relaxation training, supportive therapy, and bibliotherapy (Ghaed, Ayers, & Wetherell, 2012). Individual and group versions of some of these psychotherapies exist and have been studied and found effective. More recently, mindfulness-based stress reduction approaches for anxious as well as depressed older adults have been found to be helpful (Wetherell et al., 2017). Less is known about the treatment of anxiety than for depression in older adults. Furthermore, outcomes for the treatment of anxiety in older people are not as favorable as for younger adults (Wetherell et al., 2013). Nonetheless, these therapies are the best approaches to inform work with older people with anxiety problems. However, almost all older adults I have treated for anxiety have GAD or anxiety symptoms coexisting with depressive disorders. I am occasionally referred older people with compulsive hoarding, OCD, panic disorder, and PTSD (not currently classified in the *DSM–5* as an anxiety disorder), but I usually refer them to colleagues who have specialized expertise in the treatment of these problems.

Life problems that are commonly associated with anxiety in older adults are in the domain of life transitions and include onset or exacerbation of medical problems and care for a family member with health or cognitive problems. In the geriatric primary care medical clinic where I work, anxious clients are referred to me by primary care doctors—clients who chronically worry about health concerns, visit numerous doctors for the same condition, make frequent visits to emergency departments, or obsessively track indicators of health (e.g., taking blood pressure or pulse readings numerous times throughout the day, are highly vigilant about any perceived irregularities of heart rhythm). In my clinical work, I have found anxiety harder to treat than depression in older people: Reductions in anxiety symptoms are less dramatic than with depressive symptoms, and anxious older adults are not as easily engaged as depressed older adults. I often provide older clients with practical tools, such as relaxation protocols, psychoeducation handouts, and behavior- and thought-tracking worksheets. These approaches give older clients something practical they can do and increase awareness of the circumstances and thought patterns tied to anxiety.

Anxious older adults who are seen for psychotherapy are often prescribed medications for anxiety, including antidepressants and benzodiazepines. Both classes of medication have been found helpful for older people, but benzodiazepines and other sedating medications increase risk for falls, so long-term use is generally not advised in older adults (Bower & Wetherell, 2015; Tinetti, 2003). During the course of psychotherapy, the practitioner can engage the older client in their use (and possible misuse) of sedating medications and coordinate with the prescriber. Misuse of benzodiazepines and other sedating medication by older people is discussed in Chapter 6.

CASE EXAMPLE OF LINDA JACKSON: TREATMENT OF GENERALIZED ANXIETY DISORDER

Case Summary

Mrs. Jackson was a 75-year-old divorced, retired, African American woman with three grown daughters. She was diagnosed with thyroid problems, high blood pressure, and elevated cholesterol for which she was taking medication. She was referred to me by her primary care physician for insomnia and anxiety. The physician said that Mrs. Jackson was overly concerned about her health as evident by frequent phone calls about relatively minor symptoms and periodic requests for repeat of diagnostic tests, On the PHQ-9 (Kroenke et al., 2001), her score was 5, which indicates "mild depression," and on the GAD-7 (Spitzer et al., 2006), it was 15, which indicates "severe anxiety." Anxiety symptoms included anxiousness, worry, problems relaxing, and fears that something terrible might happen. Mrs. Jackson described these symptoms as "lifelong." She also reported long-standing insomnia with associated problems of falling asleep and staying asleep that had worsened in the past year or two. *DSM–5* diagnoses included insomnia disorder and GAD.

Treatment Modalities

Cognitive Behavior Therapy for Insomnia

Mrs. Jackson said that she first wanted to improve her sleep. I conducted a course of cognitive behavior therapy for insomnia (CBT-I). She said that she had previously been prescribed the sleep medication Ambien but discontinued taking it because it seemed to stop helping her. CBT-I is an effective treatment (Perlis, Jungquist, Smith, & Posner, 2008) that involves monitoring of sleep with diaries, restriction of sleep to the amount of time the client actually sleeps (vs. time in bed), direction to only use the bed for sleeping (and sex), information on good sleep regimen ("sleep hygiene"), and other techniques.

During the course of 8 weeks, her sleep significantly improved with some reduction in anxiety. Because Mrs. Jackson faithfully completed sleep diaries and followed through on recommendations for her sleep, I proposed to her that we work together with a protocol for the treatment of GAD that included readings and worksheets that would be completed throughout the approximately 12-week treatment. The protocol was based on cognitive behavior approaches for the treatment of anxiety, as outlined in a therapist manual (Zinbarg, Craske, & Barlow, 2006) and associated patient workbook (Craske & Barlow, 2006). She agreed but said that she first wanted to tell me "more about my life."

Brief, Exploratory Psychotherapy

For four sessions, Mrs. Jackson provided more history on her early life that she believed was relevant to her current problems. She was raised by two parents along with three siblings. Her family's economic situation was adequate, and both her parents worked. Her father worked in a factory and her mother worked as a domestic. When she was a child, her father had an automobile accident and was severely injured, could not work for months, and had a permanent disability. Her mother struggled to support the family and openly expressed fear about the family's becoming homeless if the father did not get another job. Fortunately, he obtained a clerical position, but each day was a struggle to get to work because of his disability. A few years later, Mrs. Jackson's sister became ill for a prolonged period, which financially strained the family as well as the relationship between her parents. To make matters worse, Mrs. Jackson herself became ill with a childhood illness when her sister was ill. At that time, her mother felt overwhelmed by the circumstances and did not show much affection or care for her. She recalled overhearing her mother say to her father about her, "If she had never been born, I wouldn't have to deal with this." Mrs. Jackson said that she felt "frightened and all alone in the world." She asked me whether these early life experience might contribute to her worries about health and associated anxiety. I said it made a lot of sense to me.

Cognitive Behavior Therapy for Generalized Anxiety Disorder

I used a protocol for the treatment of GAD. Mrs. Jackson found the initial discussion of the difference between normal versus abnormal anxiety helpful as well as learning that other older adults experienced anxiety problems. At the beginning, she began to complete a "worry record" through which she identified episodes of anxiety, likely triggers, and associated thoughts and behaviors. She also completed a daily summary sheet that characterized the nature and severity of her anxiety as well as a weekly summary of the frequency and severity of anxiety episodes. She grew to appreciate the physical, cognitive, and behavioral components of her anxiety. Not surprisingly, common triggers for anxiety episodes were health concerns. For example, if her arm was uncomfortable, she began to wonder what was "wrong" with her arm and possible reasons why: "I strained it when lifting a box," "A ligament was torn," "I might have an embolism in my arm." These concerns often led to Internet searches for diseases with the symptoms she was experiencing, which further raised her anxiety. Episodes of anxiety exhausted her, and she was less likely to leave her home to take part in daily activities. She would then criticize herself for not engaging in those activities. She understood that her health worries were tied to her anxiety but felt that she was being responsible by reviewing all possible causes for her physical symptoms and then seeking medical opinions about possible treatments for them. Other triggers for anxiety were the health of her former husband with whom she had regular contact as well as problems that came up with her daughters.

A progressive muscle relaxation protocol was introduced that she was asked to do several times a day. At first, she didn't feel it reduced her physical symptoms of anxiety, but as she completed written relaxation worksheets, she noted that symptoms eventually improved following relaxation efforts. She continued to complete daily worry records that included the introduction of a new concept: the real odds that an identified health worry was likely or not—on a scale of 0% (*not at all likely*) to 100% (*highly likely*). She noticed that the certainty of her thoughts about the cause of a physical symptom's being an identified illness was rarely 100% and was quite variable. On the worry sheets, she was now asked to generate alternative explanations for the symptoms she experienced. As she continued to complete worry sheets for several weeks, she noticed that episodes of anxiety were highly variable with respect to frequency, duration, and intensity.

In the coming weeks, she began to better understand how she was prone to engaging in catastrophic thinking. The daily worry sheets were further enriched by asking her to identify and try to engage in coping behaviors that were likely to reduce her anxiety—concurrent with the generation of alternative thoughts about an anxiety trigger and continued use of progressive muscle relaxation. Review of her weekly anxiety summary sheets indicated that the frequency and severity of anxiety were slowly but steadily declining.

Researchers have found that some individuals with anxiety experience brief, vivid images of possible events tied to anxiety. Ruminative thoughts reflect their "greatest fears" but also serve to distract the individual from the images. In this phase of the treatment, Mrs. Jackson was asked to imagine the "worst possible" outcomes of a focus of worry. For her, these were chiefly tied to her health. At first, she found this technique difficult to do, but with my encouragement, she identified several. Using behavioral principles of exposure, she was asked to imagine most feared events, which was followed by relaxation techniques and then reflection on the likelihood of the event's happening. This procedure was repeated many times. Her most vivid event included this scenario: "I am not feeling well at home, have a stroke and fall onto the floor. I cannot reach the phone to call for help and slowly die on the floor." I encouraged her to elaborate on this scenario so that it was even more vivid. She imagined the coldness of the floor, the feeling of desperation that no one would help her, the sense of loneliness, the inability to get to the bathroom and the discomfort of urinating on herself, and increasing hunger and thirst as the hours went by. She imagined her phone ringing and, later, a neighbor knocking at her door, but she was unable to speak. At first, these imagery exercises were highly anxiety provoking to her, but, as she repeated them, anxiety about them decreased. Notably, her overall weekly anxiety also continued to decrease as evident in the worry records she completed.

By the end of treatment, Mrs. Jackson's GAD-7 (Spitzer et al., 2006) score was 7, which indicates "mild to moderate anxiety"—about half of what it had been at the beginning of treatment. She had fewer episodes of worry, and when she did have an episode, she would respond with generating alternative explanations, judging the odds that a feared event might happen, and using relaxation procedures. She also found it helpful to remind herself that the reason she was prone to health concerns made good sense based on her early life experience of illness and illness in her family of origin. "I can see that what I imagined as the worst possible thing that could happen to me reflected my own childhood fears of being alone and not cared for."

Case Commentary

Geriatricians frequently refer clients to me for health-related concerns, including preoccupation with somatic symptoms. Some clients like Mrs. Jackson are willing to take part in a standardized protocol with accompanying homework and reading. Her active participation in CBT-I for insomnia was evidence that she could follow a clinical protocol. For older adults who are unwilling or unable to follow a clinical protocol for anxiety, I flexibly use different elements of CBT approaches for anxiety.

I was so glad that Mrs. Jackson wanted to talk about her early life before beginning of the GAD anxiety protocol. Essentially, she clarified for herself the historical reasons for why she was prone to anxiety about health issues—in the language of CBT therapists: getting to some "core schemas." Reflection on and understanding of childhood illness experiences were more tools she could use in managing health-related anxiety by telling herself that recurrent health concerns made perfect sense rather than, for example, blaming herself for being oversensitive or weak.

SUMMARY

Despite the relatively low prevalence of diagnosable depression in community-residing older adults, depressive disorders and symptoms are often seen in clinical practice as well as in long-term care settings. On the whole, depression has a presentation similar to that of younger adults, but some depressed older adults are more likely to experience it as anhedonia than as a subjective experience of depression. A variety of factors are tied to the risk of depression, and many of them are health related. Depression increases the risk of health problems and mortality in older people, including death by suicide. In the assessment of depression, multiple sources of information are useful, including depression screening instruments that have been validated for older people. Research has found that a wide range of treatments found effective in younger adults are also effective with older people.

Anxiety is another common problem seen in mental health practice with older adults. Anxiety disorders encompass a wide range of diagnoses, although in everyday clinical practice, GAD as well as anxiety symptoms concurrent with depression are the most frequently seen. Some people have long-standing anxiety problems, yet for others, anxiety problems appear in later life and are often tied to health issues. Anxiety is tied to poorer quality of life, greater use of medications, overuse of health care, and functional impairment. Some older adults chronically use sedating medications, such as benzodiazepines, on which they develop dependence and that increase the risk for falls. In the assessment of anxiety, coordination with medical care providers is important because some medical conditions and medications may trigger or exacerbate anxiety symptoms. Like depression, multiple sources of information are helpful in making an assessment, including the use of anxiety-screening instruments. Less is known about the treatment of anxiety than depression in older adults, yet a number of psychotherapies—notably, those informed by the principles of CBT—have been found useful.

6

ASSESSMENT AND TREATMENT OF COGNITIVE IMPAIRMENT, PROBLEM ALCOHOL USE, AND PRESCRIPTION DRUG MISUSE

In this chapter, I broadly review cognitive impairment and problem alcohol use and prescription drug misuse. This review provides definitions, recommendations for assessment, and a description of treatments. The clinical case example of Sarah Nadler illustrates the treatment of anxiety and depression associated with dementia caregiving. The case of Thomas White illustrates the treatment of problem alcohol use.

The content of this chapter covers the recommended foundational knowledge competencies of the Council of Professional Geropsychology Training Programs with respect to (a) clinical practice with older adults; (b) assessment of older adults; and (c) intervention, consultation, and other service provision (Hinrichsen, Emery-Tiburcio, Gooblar, & Molinari, 2018). Material in this chapter reflects content from the Pikes Peak model for training in professional geropsychology (Knight, Karel, Hinrichsen, Qualls, & Duffy, 2009), including II. Knowledge Base, B. Foundations of Clinical Practice With Older Adults; C. Foundations of Assessment of Older Adults; and D. Foundations of Intervention, Consultation, and Other Service Provision. It also addresses content from "Guidelines for Psychological Practice with Older Adults" (American

http://dx.doi.org/10.1037/0000146-007
Assessment and Treatment of Older Adults: A Guide for Mental Health Professionals,
by Gregory A. Hinrichsen

Psychological Association, 2014), including Guideline 7 (Psychologists strive to be familiar with cognitive changes in older adults), Guideline 8 (Psychologists strive to understand the functional capacity of older adults in the social and physical environment), Guideline 9 (Psychologists strive to be knowledgeable about psychopathology within the aging population and cognizant of the prevalence and nature of that psychopathology when providing services to older adults), Guideline 10 (Psychologists strive to be familiar with the theory, research, and practice of various methods of assessment with older adults, and knowledgeable of assessment instruments that are culturally and psychometrically suitable for use with them), Guideline 12 (Psychologists strive to develop skill at conducting and interpreting cognitive and functional ability evaluations), Guideline 13 (Psychologists strive to be familiar with the theory, research, and practice of various methods of intervention with older adults, particularly with current research evidence about their efficacy with this age group), and Guideline 14 (Psychologists strive to be familiar with and develop skill in applying culturally sensitive, specific psychotherapeutic interventions and environmental modifications with older adults and their families, including adapting interventions for use with this age group).

COGNITIVE IMPAIRMENT

I frequently give presentations to audiences of older adults in the community. People often ask, "Sometimes I can't remember the name of something. Does that mean I'm getting Alzheimer's disease?" Word-finding difficulty is a common experience for older adults and typically is not the hallmark of a serious cognitive problem; rather, it is part of the usual changes in brain functioning that come with age. Some older adults do have diagnosable cognitive problems, and older people are at increasing risk of dementia— almost one third of them contending with it by age 85.

Definitions and Diagnoses

I once met with an older woman whose husband was having memory problems. She remarked with some relief, "They told me he has dementia. I was grateful that it wasn't Alzheimer's disease." I explained to her that Alzheimer's disease is a type of dementia. She burst into tears and was despairing about what the future would hold. Often, the term *Alzheimer's* is used in a generic way that is not precise. Alzheimer's disease is a type of dementia of which there are several major types—in the same way that, for example, congestive heart failure is a type of cardiac problem of which there are many different types. People's confusion about the naming of late-life *cognitive impairment*—an even more inclusive term that reflects a continuum of problems with mental functioning, including dementia—likely reflects ongoing popular press coverage of Alzheimer's disease that uses that term synonymously with *dementia*. The clinician who diagnosed the husband of the older woman in the example just mentioned may not have provided good education to her about dementia, she may not have understood what the physician said, she may not have wanted to believe what she was told, or some combination. Studies have shown that many older adults with dementia and even their family members do not know of their own diagnosis of dementia (U.S. Office of Disease Prevention and Health Promotion, 2016). To add the confusion, in the *Diagnostic and Statistical Manual of Mental Disorders* (fifth ed. [*DSM–5*]; American Psychiatric Association, 2013), the terminology for cognitive impairment has changed.

I use the terms *mild cognitive impairment* (MCI; now "mild neurocognitive disorder" in the *DSM–5*) and *dementia* (now "major neurocognitive disorder" in the *DSM–5*) because health mental health care professionals commonly use those terms. It might be helpful to think of a continuum:

Normal, usual age-related cognitive changes → MCI → Dementia

Another important term to understand is *delirium* (sometimes known as an "acute confusional state"), which is fairly common among older adults in medical inpatient units and includes symptoms like problems focusing, disorganized thinking, disorientation, and altered levels of consciousness—symptoms that usually come on suddenly. I discuss delirium in more detail later. People can have both dementia and delirium.

Mild Cognitive Impairment (*DSM–5*: Mild Neurocognitive Disorder)
It is useful to recall from Chapter 2, this volume, that what Baltes (1993) called the hardware of the brain (*fluid intelligence*) works less efficiently over time than the software of the brain (*crystallized intelligence*) and that there are measurable decrements in select abilities over time (and, I hasten to add, variability in the presence and extent of those decrements). When some older adults say they have problems immediately "remembering" a word and then subsequently do, they are not so much having a memory problem as having a word retrieval problem that reflects the slowing of the process of accessing certain vocabulary at the speed they used to.

But some older people do have more than usual changes in cognition, and clinicians and researchers have wondered whether more than usual deficits in cognition might be the harbinger of dementia. In an earlier era, the term "benign senescent forgetfulness" was used to describe cognitive changes in older adults who did not have dementia (Heinik, 2010). During my career, people began to wonder whether some cognitive changes that were more than "usual" for older adults were not, in fact, "benign." The term *mild cognitive impairment* began to be used in the 1990s in an effort to better capture this phenomenon. Different ways of defining and describing MCI exist but generally include an observation by the client, a family member, friend, or health care provider that there has been some decrement in one or more mental abilities and usually include poorer memory. However, the older adult functions fairly independently, does not meet the criteria for dementia, and has good general intellectual functioning. Some have suggested that up to 22% of individuals 71 years and older have MCI (in addition to those with dementia; Plassman et al., 2008). People with MCI have an increased risk of developing dementia compared with those who do not; studies have found that anywhere from 5% to 20% of clients with MCI develop dementia in the following year. However, other studies have found that many (40%–70%) with MCI will not develop dementia over 10 years and that another group (15%–20%) will show improved cognitive abilities 1 to 2 years later (Langa & Levine, 2014). When making a diagnosis of mild neurocognitive disorder in the *DSM–5*, you are asked to specify the presumed cause (e.g., Alzheimer's disease, Lewy body, vascular disorder, frontotemporal degeneration), which I find difficult to do on an initial assessment because I usually do not have enough information to make that presumption.

Dementia (*DSM–5*: Major Neurocognitive Disorder)

Dementia is almost always a progressive decline in one or more mental abilities. Some dementias do not progress and some younger people have dementia, but those are rare occurrences. Dementia is one mental disorder for which older adults are at much higher risk than younger adults, and many older adults express fear that they might experience that condition in their later years. For older adults, four types of dementia are most commonly seen: Alzheimer's disease, Lewy body dementia, vascular dementia, and frontotemporal dementia. Some older adults have combinations of dementias. As these conditions progress, clients often have associated problems that may include behavioral agitation, psychotic symptoms and misinterpretations, depression, or apathy—problems discussed later in this chapter (Cohen-Mansfield, 2015).

Alzheimer's Disease. Alzheimer's disease is the most common of the dementias. This condition was first described by and is named after the 19th-century German psychiatrist and neuropathologist Alois Alzheimer. The cause is not really known, but many theories exist. Characteristic brain changes (seen on autopsy) distinguish it from other dementias, including the presence of amyloid plaques that interfere with the ability of brain cells to communicate with each other and neurofibrillary tangles that develop within and damage brain cells. Other brain changes are also evident. Interestingly, on autopsy, some people's brains contain plaques and tangles, yet they had not shown symptoms of dementia. A small percentage of people have an inheritable form of Alzheimer's disease that begins in their younger years. Scientists now believe that Alzheimer's disease begins many years before any symptoms appear and that, for some, MCI is one step in the progression to Alzheimer's disease. Some researchers have proposed stages of Alzheimer's disease progressing from Stage 1 "normal" through Stage 7 "severe dementia." As can be seen in Table 6.1, a slow, insidious onset of short-term memory loss is characteristic of Alzheimer's disease (Castro & Smith, 2015; Mast & Yochim, 2018).

Lewy Body Dementia. I evaluated an older man because his family thought he was depressed. During the evaluation in which I routinely assess for the presence of psychotic symptoms, I asked him, "Do you see things or

TABLE 6.1. Most Common Types of Dementia (Major Neurocognitive Disorder)

Type of dementia	Likely cause or associated with	Characteristic initial symptoms
Alzheimer's disease	Accumulation of amyloid plaques and neurofibrillary tangles	Short-term memory loss, gradual progression of the disease
Lewy body dementia	Related to Parkinson's disease with accumulation of Lewy cells	Fluctuating mental ability, visual hallucinations, motor symptoms, rapid eye movement sleep disorder
Vascular dementia	Accumulation of vascular damage in the brain	Symptoms vary, depending on the part of the brain that is affected; changes may be more sudden than other types of dementia
Frontotemporal dementia	Atrophy of frontal or temporal lobes	Socially inappropriate or other abnormal behaviors

Note. From *Alzheimer's Disease and Dementia* (pp. 17–28), by B. T. Mast and B. T. Yochim, 2018, Boston, MA: Hogrefe. Copyright 2018 by Hogrefe Publishing. Adapted with permission.

hear things that other people don't see or hear?" He said matter-of-factly, "I see elephants in the backyard every day." His family did not know he was seeing elephants, and he was later diagnosed with Lewy body dementia by a neurologist. On autopsy, people with Lewy body dementia have the accumulation of structures in parts of the brain that are named after the German neurologist Frederick Lewy, who first identified them. Parkinson's disease and Lewy body dementia are related: People with Parkinson's disease who have dementia have Lewy bodies in their brains. As noted in Table 6.1, characteristic symptoms of Lewy body dementia include visual hallucinations, motor problems similar to those of Parkinson's disease, disturbance of the rapid eye movement phase of sleep (as a result of which, people act as if dreams are real), and fluctuations in attention and alertness. Other symptoms develop as the disease progresses; death comes 8 to 12 years after the onset of the condition (Mast & Yochim, 2018; Sperling, Geneser, & Manning, 2015).

Vascular Dementia. Dementia due to vascular disease is the second most common type of dementia. When I was young, people would refer to older adults as having memory problems because of "hardening of the arteries," that is, arteriosclerosis. The role of compromised blood vessels as a cause of late-life cognitive impairment has been long presumed. Another earlier name was "multi-infarct dementia." The term *cerebrovascular disease* refers to a wide range of acute and chronic conditions that adversely impact the brain and brain functioning. Individuals may have acute strokes because of a lack of blood flow secondary to blockage or rupture of vessels. Others may have chronic accumulation of problems caused by blockage or rupture of very small blood vessels, such as lacunar strokes, white matter hyperintensities, microhemorrhages; or microinfarcts (Nyenhuis, 2015). Individuals with acute strokes have associated cognitive problems followed by chronic deterioration of mental abilities that are caused by further brain damage due to blockage of very small blood vessels. As noted in Table 6.1, cognitive problems from vascular disease vary, depending on which part of the brain is affected.

Frontotemporal Dementia. This is the general term for several types of dementia associated with atrophy of the frontal or temporal lobes, or both, of the brain. One variant of frontotemporal disease is associated with impairment of language and another variant, with personality or behavioral problems (e.g., apathy, disinhibition). Often, individuals with a personality or behavioral variant are referred to a psychiatrist because of marked changes in their behavior, such as neglect of self-care or life responsibilities, socially inappropriate behavior, or social withdrawal about which they have little or no insight. A client once told me that her husband with whom she said she had a "good marriage" of 40 years was diagnosed with the condition at the end of his life—only after he had left her for a much younger woman and spent much of their savings. This type of dementia is usually diagnosed in adults in middle age and late-middle age. The median survival time for people with frontotemporal dementia is only about 3 years (Mast & Yochim, 2018) compared with Alzheimer's disease, which is about 10 years. For almost half of individuals with this condition, there is a family history or genetic vulnerability (American Psychiatric Association, 2013).

Other Conditions That Cause Dementia. Individuals may have dementia for other less common reasons, including traumatic brain injury, infection with human immunodeficiency virus, Parkinson's disease, Huntington's disease, prion disease (e.g., "mad cow disease"), and other rare conditions. It is important to emphasize that often people have more than one type of dementia. Diagnostically disentangling one from the other is often difficult for the average practitioner.

Assessment

Basic issues in age-associated cognitive and intellectual functioning were discussed in Chapter 2. These issues are foundational knowledge on which clinical assessment of cognitive functioning rests. Because cognitive disorders are the one mental disorder for which the prevalence is higher in older compared with younger adults (Gum, King-Kallimanis, & Kohn, 2009), it is important that they be screened for by practitioners who see older adults. There is some controversy about whether older adults should be routinely screened for cognitive problems in primary care by virtue of age (Gerontological Society of America, 2017). I believe that mental health practitioners should conduct both a general inquiry of older people about whether they subjectively experience changes in cognition as well as a brief screening instrument. For most of us seeing older adults in mental health practice, our primary role is to make an initial determination of whether cognitive problems exist and, if so, make referral for further assessment. However, some geropsychologists possess skills to continue an evaluation that may include administration of neuropsychological instruments. I would like to highlight an especially helpful resource for practitioners interested in building their knowledge and skills in screening for cognitive impairment: the

KAER model, which was developed in collaboration with the Gerontological Society of America (2017). The acronym KAER stands for the four recommended steps in detecting possible cognitive problems in primary care: *K*ickstart the conversation about cognition, *A*ssess for the possible presence of cognitive problems, *E*valuate for cognitive impairment, and then *R*efer for further evaluation and resources related to cognition problems. Information on how to obtain the online KAER toolkit is in Appendix B.

KAER was developed as a resource for primary care medical personnel but can be used in other settings. Too often, older medical patients are not engaged in a discussion of cognitive health by providers, effectively assessed, or referred for community supports. When diagnosed with dementia, some patients—and family members—report that the diagnosis was not clearly communicated or they do not believe they were told they had dementia. Some health care providers are uncomfortable bringing up the topic of cognitive impairment, believe that their patients are similarly uncomfortable with a discussion, do not know the best way to bring up the topic, do not feel they have time to cover this issue in relatively brief appointments, or do not know how to assess for impairment. For practitioners who are unfamiliar with the terrain of cognition and cognitive impairment, the KAER model toolkit is be a faithful guide to the process. It is replete with numerous resources, including guidelines, handouts, recommended approaches, videos, assessment tools, and recommendations for locating local dementia-related support services.

Self Report

Some clients spontaneously mention concerns about cognitive functioning: "I can't seem to remember names of things like I used to" and "If I don't write things down, I won't remember to do them." Of course, it is important to help clarify the nature of those expressed concerns. I find that often individuals who raise memory concerns themselves are noting aging-related changes in the slowing of mental processes and acquisition of new information. If clients do not raise the issue themselves, a simple inquiry such as, "Do you have concerns about your memory?" is useful. The KAER model for kickstarting the conversation about cognition includes suggestions like: "Are you worried about your memory?" "Have you noticed a change in your memory that concerns you?" "During the past months, have you had increasing problems with your memory?" (Gerontological Society of America, 2017, p. 19). Among older adults with cognitive problems, a family member, other health care provider, or social services provider often raises the issue.

Clinician Observation

The KAER model (Gerontological Society of America, 2017, p. 22) lists symptoms that might indicate dementia. Among these warning signs are having problems remembering recent events or appointments, handling more complex tasks like paying bills or cooking a meal, dealing with daily tasks that require some planning ability, driving or finding one's way around familiar places, and understanding others or communicating clearly, as well as passivity and misinterpreting stimuli. Although some persons with significant cognitive impairment can do a pretty good job of covering that impairment, a good clinical interview will reveal evidence of problems. Typically, I find that older adults who appear to have cognitive problems (and have been or later are diagnosed with dementia) cannot remember important events, give vague responses, have difficulty following the structure of the interview, express annoyance or frustration with questions, refer me to family members for answers to questions, or a combination of all of these. These behaviors are usually evident on a cognitive screening instrument and are almost always confirmed by family or others who know the older adults.

Assessment Instruments

The topic of delirium was discussed in Chapter 4. As noted, delirium is different from dementia—but individuals can experience both. *Delirium* is characterized by an acute onset and fluctuating course, problems with attention (e.g., easily distracted, not being able to keep track of the conversation), disorganized thinking (e.g., rambling, changing topics frequently, not making a lot of sense), and altered consciousness (e.g., hyperalert, drowsy, or stuporous; Gerontological Society of America, 2017). Delirium is fairly common in medical settings: 10% to 31% among older adults being hospitalized and 11% to 42% during hospitalization (Siddiqi, House, & Holmes, 2006). People with delirium need immediate medical attention. As Lichtenberg (2010) cautioned, even in medical settings, some health care providers confuse delirium with dementia. The Confusion Assessment Method instrument (CAM; Inouye et al., 1990) includes a series of questions for the clinician about evidence of problems in these four areas: acute onset or fluctuating course, inattention, disorganized thinking, and altered level of consciousness. The CAM has good psychometric properties and has been translated into languages other than English. See Appendix B for this and other recommended measures.

The Mini-Cog (Borson, Scanlan, Chen, & Ganguli, 2003) is a 3-minute cognitive screen that involves two tasks: Draw a clock and try to remember three words. It measures memory, executive function, and constructional praxis. Its brevity is especially useful for primary medical care settings. It has solid psychometric properties and was developed to be free of racial, cultural, and educational biases. It has even been found to be more sensitive than physicians in detecting cognitive impairment in some populations. The Montreal Cognitive Assessment (Nasreddine et al., 2005) is another brief cognitive screen and takes about 10 minutes to complete. It assesses executive abilities, memory, orientation, abstraction, language, attention, and constructional praxis. Psychometric properties are very good, and it is available in many languages. It is superior in its ability to identify milder forms of cognitive impairment compared with the still widely used Mini-Mental State Examination (MMSE; Folstein, Folstein, & McHugh, 1975). For reviews of screening instruments and brief batteries for dementia, see Mast and Gerstenecker (2010) and Mast and Yochim (2018).

I administer a brief cognitive screen with all older adults who are referred to me. Many cognitive screening instruments exist, and each has advantages and disadvantages. For many years, providers, including me, used the MMSE (Folstein et al., 1975). An advantage of the MMSE is that a lot of psychometric information exists for the instrument, and many health care providers are familiar with the content and the scoring. A practical issue is that the instrument is now copyrighted and requires payment of a fee (Stewart, O'Riley, Edelstein, & Gould, 2012). I use the Montreal Cognitive Assessment (Nasreddine et al., 2005). A caution in using these instruments is that educational attainment and certain cultural factors may influence scoring (e.g., those with less education may score lower on the measures). Some measures make score adjustments based on education. It is important to remember that screening instruments are not diagnostic of dementia. Some symptoms of depression may be the same as symptoms of cognitive impairment (e.g., problems with concentration and associated memory difficulties).

In outpatient clinical practice, I have rarely seen an older adult referred to me who was delirious. However, in long-term care settings, practitioners are much more likely to encounter delirium and, of course, should bring it to the attention of medical staff. For those of us who see older adults, it can be helpful to have a copy of the CAM (Inouye et al., 1990) handy (or be broadly familiar with symptoms of delirium) in the event that a referred older adult might be delirious. Later in this section, I outline recommendations for next steps when an individual evidences cognitive impairment based one of these instruments and other information.

Although it is beyond the scope of this introductory book, I would like to bring the reader's attention to the issue of capacity assessment in older adults. Sometimes mental health practitioners are asked to make a judgment about the older adult's ability to function in one or more domains. Can the older person drive safely? Manage finances? Handle taking medications alone? Make medical or financial decisions? Make a will? Live independently? For more information about capacity assessment, I refer the reader to a publication by the American Bar Association and the American Psychological Association (2008): *Assessment of Older Adults With Diminished Capacity: A Handbook for Psychologists* (see Appendix A for a link to this publication).

Report of Others

In outpatient settings, older adults with cognitive problems are often accompanied by someone, typically a spouse or adult child. Some adult children assume that they will be part of the whole diagnostic interview. It may be evident from the initial encounter with the older adult (or from the person who made the referral) that the older client is cognitively impaired. Nonetheless, it is important to see the older person alone for some part of the interview. I have sometimes found that family members try to help by prompting the older adult to answer questions that the older adult may not know. That being said, family members often provide useful information about changes in the older person's cognitive functioning. For older people with severe cognitive impairment—and with the client's permission—I will see the accompanying family member separately to gather further information. Physical health care providers are also an important source of information. In long-term care settings, staff can be a good source of information about changes in the older resident's cognitive functioning.

Next Steps in the Assessment Process

For older individuals who evidence cognitive impairment, the next steps recommended by major medical and aging organizations are critical. Most tasks are performed by physicians and some by neurologists. However, practitioners in primary care medical practice frequently do not take all of these steps (Gerontological Society of America, 2017). Therefore, it is helpful for the mental health practitioner to be aware of whether a client with dementia has received recommended diagnostic care. In addition to a brief cognitive assessment, the following are recommended as part of a comprehensive diagnostic evaluation for dementia for relevant professionals: a complete medical history; an assessment of activities of daily living or instrumental activities of daily living, or both; physical and neurological examination; relevant laboratory tests; neuropsychological testing; neuroimaging; and, as needed, referral to a specialist in the area of cognitive impairment (Gerontological Society of America, 2017). Some older adults may evidence cognitive impairment because of an underlying medical condition that could be remediated or improved.

As is discussed later, family members are usually involved in the care of individuals with dementia and often experiences high levels of stress. They can benefit by referral to social services, dementia support organizations, and other resources. Also, older adults with cognitive impairment can benefit from supportive counseling to assist in coming to emotional terms with cognitive loss and ways to practically cope with limitations to enhance their quality of life.

Treatment

Contending with cognitive impairment, including dementia, has practical and emotional ramifications not only for the older individual but also for the caregivers. Providing care to an older adult with dementia is associated with depression, subjective distress, anger, and anxiety. Associated issues include contending with behavioral disturbances, the absence of adequate social support, little relief from responsibilities, the juggling of multiple roles, and financial stresses (Coon, Keaveny, Valverde, Dadvar, & Gallagher-Thompson, 2012).

In my view, dementia caregiving is one of the most difficult life situations a family member will face. Little was known about this area when I entered the mental health field, and now there are thousands of articles; many major studies of dementia; a myriad of service and advocacy organizations; and numerous federal, state, and local initiatives to provide support to family members caring for individuals with dementia and other health conditions. From a practitioner's perspective, basic questions (Gerontological Society of America, 2017; Mast & Yochim, 2018) include: What can be done for a client who complains of memory problems? What can be done for a client who has a diagnosis of dementia? What can be done for family members who are providing care to an older relative with dementia? Most research has focused on how to reduce family caregivers' distress and improve their ability to handle the many evolving issues tied to the older relative with dementia. Little work has focused on assisting the older client with the beginning stages of dementia to emotionally and practically come to terms with those circumstances, which I think of as a life transition (from someone with intact cognitive ability to someone who is losing cognitive ability). Research relevant to treatment for cognitive impairment roughly falls into four areas: improving memory function, providing support to the person with dementia, reducing distress in family member caregivers of older adults, and reducing behavioral disturbances of older people with dementia.

Improving Memory Function

Despite the popularity of online courses and games to enhance mental functioning or reduce the likelihood of dementia, limited evidence supports their usefulness. Teaching older adults with normal cognitive functioning some strategies to enhance select aspects of mental abilities has been found helpful; for those with MCI, results have been inconclusive; and for those with dementia, there is no evidence that substantive cognitive improvement can be made using varied training approaches (Rebok et al., 2012) Although medications exist to treat dementia (e.g., donepezil, rivastigmine, galantamine, memantine), they have a relatively modest effect in delaying the progression of loss of mental abilities (Mast & Yochim, 2018).

Providing Support to the Person With Dementia

Unfortunately, many newly diagnosed persons with dementia implicitly or explicitly get the message from health care providers that nothing can be done. However, cardiovascular risk management, diet, exercise, cognitive engagement, and social engagement may slow the dementia process (Mast & Yochim, 2018). Encouragement of these efforts may yield an enhanced sense of mastery and reduced distress. Providing an opportunity for the newly diagnosed client with an opportunity to frankly discuss the topic and related concerns may be beneficial. A useful model for psychotherapy with cognitively impaired older adults is an adaptation of interpersonal psychotherapy (IPT; Miller, 2009).

Reducing Distress in Family Caregivers

Psychoeducational programs that build caregiver knowledge and enhance the ability to problem solve practical issues and manage mood have been found effective for caregivers of persons with cognitive and physical health problems (Coon et al., 2012). In addition, psychotherapy or counseling (particularly with a cognitive behavior therapy [CBT] focus) and multi-component programs—those that combine two or more approaches (e.g., respite care, family counseling, and a support group)—have been found to be effective.

Reducing Behavioral Disturbance in People With Dementia

Behavioral problems are common among individuals with dementia and present practical challenges for family caregivers and professional caregivers in residential settings, notably, long-term care institutions. Problem behaviors have been generally characterized as verbal agitation (e.g., repeated questioning, crying out), physically nonaggressive behaviors (e.g., wandering, restlessness, stealing, pacing), and verbal and physically aggressive behaviors (e.g., hurting self or others; Cohen-Mansfield, 2015). Often, the older person with dementia evidences more than one type of behavior, and the nature of problem behaviors often changes over the course of the dementia.

In the past, and unfortunately today, although to a lesser extent, institutions overused sedating medications to manage behavioral problems. However, sedating older adults with dementia has not been found to be effective and, in more recent years, some of these medications (notably, antipsychotic medications) have been found to have serious side effects, including the risk of death (Crystal, Olfson, Huang, Pincus, & Gerhard, 2009). Although there are appropriate uses of sedating medication, federal regulations generally prohibit use of them to control behavioral problems in long-term care facilities, but regulations are not always followed. Behavioral approaches in the management of disruptive behaviors in older adults are highly recommended, yet they rarely are taught to staff in a systematic way or used in a standardized and coordinated manner in most long-term care institutions. U.S. Department of Veterans Affairs health care facilities are an exception: They have tried systematically to integrate these approaches into their long-term care residences (Karel, Teri, McConnell, Visnic, & Karlin, 2016).

Three commonly recognized approaches to assessing and responding to disruptive behaviors are learning behavior, person–environment fit, and need-driven models, all of which have evidence for their usefulness (Curyto, Trevino, Ogland-Hand, & Lichtenberg, 2012). *Learning behavior* approaches posit that there are often behavioral triggers for problem behaviors, and response to those behaviors makes it more or less likely that they will continue. *Person–environment fit* approaches emphasize the degree to which the immediate environment may increase or decrease the likelihood that problem behaviors will be triggered. The *need-driven* approach is based on the idea that problem behaviors are efforts by an older adult with dementia to fulfill a need. For example, a person might be verbally agitated because of pain, may need stimulation, may be emotionally distressed, or may be upset over the behavior of another resident.

Familiarity with these approaches can be especially useful in working with family members of older adults with dementia or with long-term care staff.

Some work has found that teaching behavioral strategies to family members of persons with dementia is helpful. The use of more optimal behavioral strategies reduces problems and distress in older persons with dementia but also improves emotional well-being of the family member. That is because the family member who has learned more effective behavioral management strategies feels more capable and has fewer daily problems with which to contend (Teri, McCurry, Logsdon, & Gibbons, 2005). In the domain of mental health, aging, and the family, the preponderance of work and studies has been focused on caregiving issues. As noted in Chapter 2, there is a lot of research—much of it sociological—on late-life families. There is hardly any research on family therapy with older families. However, geropsychologist Sara Honn Qualls has written extensively on psychological approaches to late-life families, including a highly recommended book listed in Appendix A. Also, little published literature exists on psychotherapeutic approaches to helping a newly diagnosed older person with dementia come to emotional and practical terms with this fact (Miller, 2009). I have found clinically that many older adults appreciate an opportunity to discuss the diagnosis of cognitive impairment; options to maximize opportunities for meaningful engagement in life now; options to plan for the future when cognitive problems may worsen; and feelings of sadness, fear, and mourning tied to cognitive loss.

In my own clinical work, I have seen many family members of older adults with dementia and other health problems who themselves require care. For some, an important issue is emotionally coming to terms with the reality that their relative has dementia, which often includes contending with feelings of fear, sadness, and mourning for a "lost future" with the older person. Psychoeducation about cognitive loss is helpful; too often, family members have not been provided enough information about cognitive loss or, if told, were not emotionally prepared to absorb it (Gallagher-Thompson & Steffen, 1994). Guidance on planning for the future is critical, including consulting a lawyer while the person with dementia has the cognitive ability to execute legal documents (e.g., will, advance directives, durable power of attorney) and think through the potential financial consequences of progressive cognitive loss, which, for many, eventually includes moving to a long-term care residence. Information about dementia support and advocacy organizations (of which there are many) is useful (Gerontological Society of America, 2017). If the family member is dealing with behavioral or emotional distress in the older adult to whom they are providing care, exploration of options on how to better contend with that distress using some of the approaches previously discussed is helpful.

CASE EXAMPLE OF SARAH NADLER: TREATMENT OF DEPRESSION AND ANXIETY IN DEMENTIA CAREGIVING

Case Summary

Mrs. Nadler was a 78-year-old White, married, Jewish woman and retired bank manager with two adult children. She was referred to me because of increasing depression and anxiety associated with the care of husband with vascular dementia. It appeared that depressive and anxiety symptoms had markedly worsened in the past 4 months. When asked why she agreed to see a psychologist, she said, "My daughter thinks I'm depressed. I don't know what to think."

Initial Evaluation

Medical problems included hypertension, arthritis, and glaucoma for which she was receiving medications. She had experienced a prior episode of depression in early life that appeared postpartum for which she received no treatment. The PHQ-9 (Kroenke, Spitzer, & Williams, 2001) measure of depression was 18, which indicates "moderately severe depression," with depressed mood, anhedonia, middle insomnia, fatigue, self-criticism, and passive suicidal ideation. The Generalized Anxiety Disorder 7-item (Spitzer, Kroenke, Williams, & Lowe, 2006) measure of anxiety was 14, which indicates "moderate to severe anxiety," with symptoms of worry, fearfulness, and irritability. She did not evidence any cognitive impairment. Mrs. Nadler met the *DSM–5* criteria for major depressive episode, moderate, recurrent.

Treatment

Initial Sessions

I summarized with Mrs. Nadler what I had learned in my initial evaluation of her: that she had been depressed and anxious for some considerable period, but these symptoms had worsened in the past months and appeared tied to the care of her husband with vascular dementia. She said this was accurate. I asked her what was going on in her life 4 months ago. "My husband, Joe, just started getting worse, and so did I," she answered. She explained that she had provided increasing support to her husband since he had been diagnosed with vascular dementia 7 years earlier. In the past year, his cognitive abilities worsened, and he began to have behavioral problems. "One day, he just walked out of the house, and the police had to bring him back."

I noted that providing caregiving to a family member with dementia was very stressful for many people, but now she had another problem. "What's that?" she asked. "You have a depression that only makes it more difficult for you to provide care to your husband as well as everything else you must do," I answered. "In addition, you have a lot of anxiety. Until you are feeling better, might it be possible to get some help with care of your husband?" She said this wasn't possible, and even if her daughters wanted to help, she would not ask them because they had families. I asked her to think about it. I advised that depression and anxiety were treatable and that she should anticipate that she would improve with psychotherapy. "My doctor said I should take an antidepressant. I am willing to do that," she said. "Both antidepressant medication and psychotherapy are helpful for depression and anxiety too," I noted.

In the next session, I completed an inventory of past and current relationships that revealed a solid history of interpersonal functioning yet lessened engagement with others over the years she cared for her husband. The relationship with her daughters, Rachel and Jane, was reasonably good, but in recent years, Jane had been "a never-ending source of unsolicited advice about how I should care for her father. I think I can take care of him and myself."

In the third session, I proposed to Mrs. Nadler that she take part in a course of IPT and noted that it has been found helpful in the treatment of depression in both younger and older adults. She had begun an antidepressant medication prescribed by her primary care doctor, which I restated should also help improve the depression and anxiety symptoms. I indicated that the total number of planned sessions would be 16—with the twin goals of reducing her depressive symptoms and anxiety as well as finding ways to better manage her caregiving responsibilities. She concurred with the plan.

Intermediate Sessions

Mrs. Nadler described a reasonably good relationship with her husband during most of their marriage. In retirement, they had both planned to travel, spend more time with their children and grandchildren, and become more active in their synagogue. "We had a few good years, then he began to have ministrokes and memory problems." With medical treatment, his condition seemed to stabilize, but then came more problems. "As the years went on," she said, "he continued to forget things, and then, one day, I realized he was having problems writing checks. Can you believe it? He was an accountant." She assumed more and more responsibility. "But I handled all of it pretty well. I'm a very organized person, you know."

Each week, I would ask Mrs. Nadler to rate her depression and anxiety on a scale of 1 (*not at all*) to 10 (*the most depressed/anxious*). These ratings fluctuated. One week, both depression and anxiety were quite high. I asked her about the events of the prior week. She said that her husband had repeatedly asked her the same question, and at some point, she shouted at him, "Shut up!" He began to cry, and then she began to cry. I engaged her in discussion of other incidents in which she had grown highly frustrated with her husband. With some reluctance, she told me that several months earlier, she had slapped her husband because of his repetitive questioning. "I hated myself for that. What kind of person am I?" I asked her if the incident occurred around the time she had become more depressed and anxious. She said yes. I told her that along with depression and anxiety, anger was often part of the mix of emotions experienced by family caregivers. I said that, in my view, her role as caregiver transitioned about 6 months earlier when her husband began to have more behavioral problems—repetitive questions, agitation, wandering—which taxed her abilities to manage those problems. She then remarked, "But I didn't tell you this: At times now, he forgets who I am. That's devastating to me." She talked sadly about their many years together, how he was always supportive to her as she forged a career as a woman, and what a "fine man" he was. "He's disappearing," she said.

In the next sessions, we discussed options to better enable Mrs. Nadler to more capably handle care for her husband and reduce her own stress. She generated a number of ideas, as well as their perceived advantages and disadvantages. Some of these included: get more help from her daughters (advantage: get more help with care of husband vs. disadvantage: run the risk of being "ordered around"), go to a dementia support group (learn better ways to handle husband's behavioral problems vs. have to listen to other people's problems), hire someone to be with her husband part time (have more time for myself vs. have a "stranger" in my house), and rejoin a bridge club at the synagogue (see my friends again vs. find time to play bridge and reintegrate into the group).

In our next meeting, Mrs. Nader said that her daughter Jane had asked if she could join in our next psychotherapy session. I asked Mrs. Nadler if that is what she wanted, and she said yes. Jane joined our next session, during which she shared her perspectives on her mother. Jane said she admired her mother for all of her accomplishments and independence. She also felt that her mother had done a great job in caring for her father, but that she needed help now. Mrs. Nadler acknowledged the need for help but said that Jane already had enough to do with her job and family. Jane said she wanted to help but also respected her mother's wishes. At the end of the session, they worked out a plan for Jane to spend part of each Saturday with her father so that her mother could go to the synagogue and reestablish relationships with her friends.

Friends at the synagogue welcomed Mrs. Nadler back, and a woman said that she knew of an "excellent" home health aide. Despite some reluctance, Mrs. Nadler arranged for the aide to care for her husband three mornings a week. With help from her daughter, some respite from the aide, and reconnection to friends, she felt less depressed, anxious, and angry. Her weekly depression and anxiety self-ratings reduced from 8 to 4. By session 10, the PHQ-9 (Kroenke et al., 2001) rating was 9, which indicates "mild depression." As she felt emotionally better, there seemed to be fewer problems with her husband. Furthermore, her husband enjoyed the company of the aide, who appeared especially skillful in engaging him in pleasurable activities.

Termination

The last two sessions focused on ending treatment. Mrs. Nadler said that she felt sad about ending: "This was more helpful than I thought it would be." I conducted a final PHQ-9 (Kroenke et al., 2001), which was 7, indicating "mild depression," and Generalized Anxiety Disorder 7-item (Spitzer et al., 2006), which was 7, indicating "mild anxiety." The *DSM–5* diagnostic criteria indicated that the major depression was in remission. I reviewed efforts she had made that were tied to improvement, including coming for therapy, taking an antidepressant medication, thinking through the issues tied to care of her husband, and then taking steps to get additional help and support. We discussed future issues that could potentially trigger an increase in symptoms of depression and anxiety that she identified as worsening of her husband's cognitive and behavioral problems. She also said that she learned that getting additional help to contend with those problems made it easier for her husband as well as herself.

Case Commentary

Providing long-term care to a relative with dementia or other health problems is stressful for many individuals. From an IPT perspective, the role of caregiving encompasses many tasks for which the individual may not be well-prepared. Mrs. Nadler had done an admirable job of providing care to her husband, but when those responsibilities evolved to responsibility for the management of her husband's behavioral problems, she unexpectedly became angry with him and with herself and then became more depressed and anxious. It was difficult for this highly independent woman to accept or ask for her.

In therapy, however, she more realistically reckoned with her current circumstances, generated options to get practical and emotional support, and took action. Mrs. Nadler also had an opportunity to mourn the loss of the relationship she had with her husband in earlier years and the life they had envisioned for the later years. Interpersonal psychotherapy was a good modality to frame psychotherapy and establish goals—and was informed by a broader understanding of stresses and the rewards of caregiving; the common presence of depressive, anxiety, and anger symptoms among caregivers; and the benefits of support from others.

PROBLEM ALCOHOL USE AND PRESCRIPTION DRUG MISUSE

Problems with alcohol is not among the stereotypes of older adults. Indeed, the vast majority of older people do not have alcohol problems, but mental health providers are more likely to see those who do (Gum et al., 2009). Holding an overly benign view that, by virtue of age, older people do not overconsume alcohol or have problems with drugs can do a disservice to clients who do. I know that earlier in my career, I could have done a better job in screening for alcohol and prescription drug problems in my older clients. I do a pretty good job now. Recently, in an initial diagnostic and evaluation intake, I asked a woman in her late seventies, "How much alcohol do you drink?" "Oh, a couple of glasses of wine with dinner," she casually replied. Now I know that a "couple" could likely mean more than two, and I asked further follow-up questions. In the end, we agreed that she was likely drinking 25 glasses of wine per week (at least), which is almost 4 times the amount recommended in healthy drinking guidelines for older people.

When I worked at an outpatient geriatric mental health clinic, I learned to screen for problems with sedating drugs like benzodiazepines. In that setting, we often saw older adults who had developed dependence on benzodiazepines that they sometimes had taken for many years (valium seemed to be a favorite in the 1980s) and were prescribed by community primary care doctors. Along with alcohol problems, prescription drug use and misuse are the most common substance use issues seen by mental health care professionals.

Definitions and Diagnoses

Perhaps a good place to start is what constitutes a "standard" drink. The following have the equivalent amount of alcohol: 12 ounces of beer, 5 ounces of wine, 1.5 ounces of spirits (e.g., whiskey, gin, vodka), and 4 ounces of liqueur or aperitif (e.g., vermouth, sherry, schnapps; Blow & Barry, 2012). Size matters. I recall a client from long ago who said that he only had one drink a day; by his definition, that meant one glass into which he poured drinks throughout the day. The National Institute on Alcohol Abuse and Alcoholism (NIAAA) guidelines indicate that people 65 years of age and older should have no more than seven standard drinks in 1 week and no more than three drinks at a time (NIAAA, n.d.). Understanding what constitutes an alcohol problem has always been a bit of a challenge for me. Terms like "problem drinker," "heavy drinker," "binge drinker," "at-risk drinker," "nonhealthy drinker," and other designations seem to be defined differently by different authors–and the prior *DSM* criteria for alcohol abuse and dependence seemed so strict that clients who clearly had problems with alcohol didn't meet those criteria. To complicate things, the *DSM* criteria for alcohol-related diagnoses changed with the fifth edition. *DSM–5* includes only one substance-relevant diagnosis—substance use disorder—which essentially says that substance use leads to distress or impairment, or both, and is associated with other specific problems. I find this *DSM* diagnostic category more useful and flexible than the previous ones. The framework that I like best for alcohol is a continuum: low-risk use (generally does not lead to problems), at-risk use (no current problems, but current pattern of use could lead to problems), problem use (current behavior has adverse negative consequences), and substance use disorder (continued use despite negative consequences and that are diagnosable within the *DSM* system; Blow & Barry, 2012).

Because many older adults take one or more medications, including those for anxiety, sleep, and pain, these medications can be misused. "Misuse of prescription medication can include using others' medication, taking a lower or higher dose than prescribed, using medication for a longer duration than prescribed, or using medication for recreational or nonmedical purposes" (Satre & Wolf, 2015, p. 122). Older adults may unintentionally misuse prescribed medication because they have not been given clear directions by health care providers, did not understand those directions, or were incapable of following directions because of cognitive deficits. Use of illicit drugs (e.g., marijuana, opioids, cocaine) is rare among older adults, but occasionally I have had clients who use them. In some settings, mental health practitioners frequently see older adults who use illicit drugs.

Prevalence of Problem Alcohol Use and Prescription Drug Misuse

Onset of new substance abuse by older adults is quite rare (but different studies define *abuse* in different ways). About 40% of older adults drink alcohol (NIAAA, n.d.), and about one-tenth of older women and one-third of older men drink above NIAAA recommendations for health drinking for older people. Satre and Wolf (2015) have summarized findings about alcohol use in older people: Overall, 10% to 15% of older people in the general population drink more than NIAAA guidelines, and 9% exceed 30 or more drinks per month or four or more drinks in any single day in the past month. In reviewing alcohol problems in late life, Barry and Blow (2016) have summarized others' findings: 9.1% of people 65 and older "binge drink" (five or more drinks on one occasion), 10% to 15% of older people in primary care evidence "at risk" or "problem drinking," but only 0.5% of older people meet the criteria for the *Diagnostic and Statistical Manual of Mental Disorders* (fourth ed. [*DSM–IV*]; American Psychiatric Association, 1994) diagnosis of alcohol dependence. The astute reader will note that these percentages are much higher than those indicated in Table 3.1 for substance abuse in Chapter 3. I believe this is because much of problematic drinking and prescription drug misuse has not been captured by prior *DSM* criteria. Furthermore, the data in Table 3.1 do not include prevalence of substance dependence. Consistent with my own observations, studies have found that most older adults who appear to be drinking too much do not meet the criteria for the *DSM–IV* definition of alcohol abuse or dependence (Barry & Blow, 2016). My take-away message from reading reviews of this area is that many older people drink alcohol without problem but that roughly 10% of those drink too much or so much that it does or will have negative health or mental health consequences and should be addressed by health or mental health care professionals. These rates may change as the baby boomer generation continues to enter later adulthood, and rates of substance use problems are higher for baby boomers during their lifetimes compared with generations that preceded them (Kuerbis, Sacco, Blazer, & Moore, 2014).

The prevalence of misuse of psychoactive medications by older adults is not well studied, but for those of us who work with older adults, it is an ongoing issue of concern. Older adults are prescribed psychoactive medications for anxiety, sleep problems, and pain, most of which have potential for misuse or abuse. One study found that one-quarter of older adults received medications that have the potential for abuse (Simoni-Wastila & Yang, 2006). Benzodiazepines, as well as sleep medications, are commonly prescribed to older people, despite cautions about their long-term use with this age group (Kuerbis et al., 2014). It is not well understood how many older adults use alcohol and psychoactive drugs in combination, which can create serious problems for them. Tobacco use is a problem for some older adults. One study found that 14% of older people used tobacco in the prior year, and a smaller number both smoked tobacco and drank alcohol (Moore et al., 2009).

Factors Tied to Substance Use

Studies have found that different factors are tied to increased risk for alcohol problems in later life and also use or misuse of other psychoactive substances. A recent review of this area nicely summarized the risk factors—physical, mental health, and social—associated with substance use in later life (Kuerbis et al., 2014):

- Physical risk factors were being male, White, life transitions, health-related problems (poor health, multiple concurrent health problems, chronic pain, reduced mobility and physical disability), and use of many medications concurrently ("polypharmacy");

- mental health relevant factors were history of alcohol problems, previous or concurrent substance use disorder, prior or current mental health problems; and

- social risk factors were being affluent, social isolation, grief, and unplanned or forced retirement.

Another risk factor for substance use problems in later life is being a member of the baby boomer generation. In an interesting study of older adults who drink (most of whom currently had or had experienced problems with alcohol), participants were asked about their reasons for drinking. These qualitative findings were similar to the aforementioned factors based on quantitative research studies. Reasons for drinking included lifelong drinking, enjoyment or socializing, self-medication (for mental health problems, physical health problems, or insomnia), bereavement, retirement or loss of work, social isolation, boredom or loneliness, and homelessness (Haighton, 2016). For practitioners, general knowledge of these risk factors may result in a more careful assessment of the potential for substance use problems, especially among those older adults who have multiple risk factors.

Potential Consequences of Substance Use or Misuse

Older adults are much more susceptible than younger adults to the adverse effects of alcohol, prescribed psychoactive medications, and illicit drugs. The reason is because aging is associated with physical changes, including reduced lean body mass and increased fat body mass, less resilient physiological processes than younger people, and other factors. Alcohol use in older people is tied to increased risk for physical health problems, including diabetes, hypertension, liver disease, cancer, nutritional deficiency, adverse interactions with prescribed medications, falls (and associated emergency department visits), and functional impairment. Alcohol overuse increases the risk for depression, suicide, cognitive impairment, and nonadherence to medical regimens. Older people who overuse alcohol also are at risk for social isolation (Barry & Blow, 2016; Blow & Barry, 2012; Kuerbis et al., 2014; Satre & Wolf, 2015).

Combining alcohol and sedating medications (e.g., benzodiazepines, sleep medications) creates even further problems because the combination can increase the effects of one or both. Although increasingly accepted, marijuana is tied to physiological changes (e.g., increased rates of heart and respiration, higher blood pressure) which can be problematic for some older people (Kuerbis et al., 2014). In my experience, older adults who have used alcohol throughout their lives are often unaware that with increasing age, they should use less and talk with health care providers about the wisdom of continued use if they have certain medical conditions or are taking certain medications.

Assessment

In this section, I focus on the screening of problem alcohol use and prescription drug misuse because they are the most common substance use issues with older adults. I hasten to add that some older adults use nonprescribed and illicit drugs, and there is concern that the baby boomer generation is at higher risk than earlier generations of problems with nonprescribed and illicit drugs (Administration for Community Living, 2017; Kuerbis et al., 2014).

I recently gave a continuing education presentation on mental health and older adults to a group of mental health providers in southern California. One audience member asked, "How do you handle meth problems in your older population?" I said that I had never seen an older adult in New York with meth problems. I then asked the audience, "How many of you have older clients with meth problems?" Eight hands went up. Audience members explained that there were meth labs in their vicinity and that older people were not immune to using this drug or becoming addicted to it.

Self-Report

I cannot recall that I have ever evaluated an older adult who spontaneously said to me that he or she had an alcohol or substance misuse problem. It is important to inquire because many health care providers do not do a good job in asking older people about this topic (Kuerbis et al., 2014). Many people who do drink too much are embarrassed about it. Taking a supportive, matter-of-fact position can help ease their discomfort. Or sometimes older adults do not understand that they are engaging in at-risk drinking. Furthermore, embedding a discussion of alcohol and substance misuse in a series of questions about caffeine and tobacco use can lessen the client's apprehension. I ask, "How much alcohol do you drink?" If the person indicates he or she drinks alcohol, I then ask how much. Vague answers ("sometimes," "at dinner," "in the evening") are clarified. Others suggest asking questions such as "Do you sometimes drink beer, wine, or other alcoholic beverages?" If the answer is yes, then ask, "How many times in the past year have you had four or more drinks in a day?" If yes, ask, "On average, how many days a week do you have an alcoholic drink?" and "On a typical day, how many drinks do you have?" (Moore, Kuerbis, Sacco, Chen, & Garcia, 2016, p. 172). It helps to indicate what a standard drink is, as defined earlier. (Some clinicians have visual representations of different types of alcoholic beverages and associated alcohol content.)

I also ask, "Are you taking anything not prescribed by a doctor or taking more of a prescribed medication than the doctor recommended?" If a client is taking sedating medications like benzodiazepines or opiate drugs, I ask specifically about any problems with taking them in a non-prescribed manner. For clients who both drink and take sedating or pain medications, I ask if they are taken together. Clinicians often assume that clients underreport alcohol use, but research has not found that to be the case (Blow & Barry, 2012). In the context of a supportive inquiry, I find that most older adults will give a pretty accurate portrayal of their use of alcohol. I don't think the issue is so much client underreporting but rather health care provider "underasking."

Clinician Observation

Barry and Blow (2010) provided a great summary of behavioral warning signs of alcohol and medication misuse problems in older adults. Warning signs for alcohol problems they have outlined include mood swings, falls or bruises, headaches, sleep problems, memory difficulties, poor hygiene, poor nutrition, and social isolation. Warning signs for medication misuse include strong preferences for certain kinds of sedating or pain-relieving medications and unusually detailed knowledge about them, complaints about physicians who won't give them medications they want, anxiety about when a medication prescription runs out or whether they will have enough medication to last, poor hygiene or grooming, and withdrawal from others. I had a client who was referred to me who was never asked by her medical provider if she drank alcohol until she had experienced two falls that resulted in a broken wrist and shoulder. It turns out that she did drink—a lot.

Assessment Instruments

It can be useful to administer an alcohol screening instrument to older adults who appear to have alcohol use problems. Appendix B contains commonly recommended screening instruments. The CAGE (Ewing, 1984) is a widely used screening instrument. The four items that compose its name are: wanting to *C*ut down on alcohol use; felt people were *A*nnoyed or critical of drinking; felt bad or *G*uilty about drinking; and drank first thing in the morning, sometimes referred to as an *E*ye-opener (Moore et al., 2016). Despite its widespread use, CAGE has been criticized for not focusing on current drinking, including the amount and binge drinking. Studies have found variable psychometric properties (Barry & Blow, 2010). An adapted version of the CAGE adds "drug use" to the drinking questions (CAGE-AID; Brown & Rounds, 1995), but it has been critiqued on psychometric grounds (Moore et al., 2016).

I have been unable to find a recommended screening instrument for prescription drug misuse in older adults, so clinical inquiry is important. There are better alcohol screens for older adults than the CAGE, but some have suggested its use in conjunction with others. One often recommended measure is the AUDIT (Babor, de la Fuente, Saunders, & Grant, 1992); the letters stand for Alcohol Use Disorders Identification Test. The AUDIT Alcohol Consumption Questions (AUDIT-C; Bush, Kivlahan, McDonell, Fihn, & Bradley, 1998) is a brief version of that measure. The AUDIT has a clinician interview and client self-report version. The 10 alcohol questions ask the client about alcohol use in the past year. It has good psychometric properties in adults and older adults. Another alcohol screening tool is the Michigan Alcoholism Screening Test—Geriatric Version (MAST–G; Blow et al., 1992) and its brief form, The Short Michigan Alcoholism Screening Test—Geriatric Version (SMAST–G; Blow, Gillespie, Barry, Mudd, & Hill, 1998), both of which were developed for older adults. The MAST–G has 24 questions to which the client responds *yes* or *no* compared with the SMAST–G, which has 10 questions. Both have good psychometric properties. I recommend the SMAST–G because of its brevity.

Report of Others
Sometimes family members and others are not aware that the older person is drinking too much or may think, "It's one thing they enjoy. Why take it away from them?" (Kuerbis et al., 2014). Some physicians do not do a good job in assessing excess alcohol use. Sometimes after an assessment, I contact the primary care physician to advise that the older adult drinks too much or meets criteria for a substance use disorder. That news often is met with surprise.

Treatment

In comparison with other mental health problems, much less evidence exists about the effectiveness of treatments for alcohol among older adults than for other mental health conditions, and few studies address prescription drug misuse (Barry & Blow, 2016; Kuerbis et al., 2014). The good news is that older adults who take part in alcohol and, to some extent, substance abuse treatment programs are much more likely than younger adults to engage in and complete those programs. Use of CBT and other approaches have generally favorable outcomes with older people (Kuerbis et al., 2014; Satre & Wolf, 2015). Alcohol problems in later life include those older people who have had long-standing difficulties as well as a sizable number of older people for whom alcohol became a problem in later years. Those with late-onset alcohol problems have a generally favorable prognosis when treated (Satre & Wolf, 2015). A continuum of approaches for the treatment of alcohol and substance use problems exists from brief counseling to inpatient treatment programs. I chiefly discuss how to address overuse of alcohol among older adults seen in outpatient mental health practice.

For older adults who are engaging in what has variously been called "at risk," "nonhealthy," and "problem" drinking, short-term alcohol counseling is the preferred approach. Some older adults also overuse or misuse psychoactive prescription drugs. One brief, time-limited approach for both alcohol and prescription drug overuse includes the following eight steps:

1. Find out what the older adult values and what his or her existing life goals are.

2. Identify the current pattern of unhealthy drinking or use of potentially harmful substances.

3. Provide education on what is a standard drink, healthy drinking, and prudent use of prescription medications.

4. Discuss the downside of overuse of alcohol or misuse of prescriptions.

5. Discuss the advantages of reducing problematic use.

6. Make a plan for limiting use or misuse.

7. Make a plan for responding to life circumstances that could trigger alcohol use or prescription drug misuse (e.g., loneliness, boredom, pain, problems with family).

8. At the end of the course of brief treatment, summarize what has been covered, including gains the older adult has made. (Substance Abuse and Mental Health Services Administration, 2012)

The most important first step is to ask an older client about use of alcohol and other substances. In clinical practice, I have found that many older clients who overuse alcohol will reduce the amount used with the kind of brief intervention just described. If done in a nonjudgmental, supportive, and matter-of-fact way, many older clients are relieved that they can talk about their alcohol use and—most important—make a plan for reducing it.

For older clients who appear to be misusing prescription medications—in my experience, benzodiazepines and sleep medications—close coordination with the professional who is prescribing the medication is critical. Among the older adults referred to me by primary care physicians because of chronic use of sedating medications for sleep, I have found that the vast majority will stop when the medications are tapered by the physician and the clients are concurrently provided with CBT for insomnia (Perlis, Jungquist, Smith, & Posner, 2008). I find it more difficult to engage older adults with chronic use of benzodiazepines that were prescribed for anxiety. Older adults who do not respond to brief treatment or have more serious problems with drugs or alcohol are referred to specialty substance use programs, which include programs designed for older adults. However, many regions do not have specialized programs for older people, and some older adults may find participation in programs with a preponderance of younger adults uncomfortable (Kuerbis et al., 2014).

CASE EXAMPLE OF THOMAS WHITE: TREATMENT OF PROBLEM ALCOHOL USE

Case Summary

Mr. White was an 82-year-old widowed, White man with two daughters. He was a retired advertising executive who had a variety of medical problems, including cardiac irregularities, hypertension, insomnia, and recent falls. His daughter strongly encouraged him to move to assisted living, which he reluctantly agreed to think about. His primary care physician referred him to me for depression, sleep problems, difficulty adjusting to medical problems, and because of the death of Mr. White's wife.

Initial Evaluation

Mr. White had never received mental health services in the past and was "amused" that his physician had suggested he see a psychologist. He acknowledged that the past 2 years had been difficult with the loss of his wife, increasing health problems, falling, and contemplation of moving to assisted living. When asked about his alcohol use, he said he had always been "a two-martinis-a-day kind of guy" but drank less as he got older. He said he usually had wine with dinner "but not always" and estimated that he probably had a total of 12 drinks per week. On the SMAST–G (Blow et al., 1998), he said yes to these questions: "Do you drink to take your mind off your problems?" and "When you feel lonely, does having a drink help?" I talked with him about healthy drinking guidelines and said that he exceeded the limit of seven drinks per week. He laughed, "So you think I'm an alcoholic?!" I said, "No, but it would be helpful if you drank less." I was mindful that older adults with alcohol problems are at increased risk of falls, but he affirmed that falls were not associated with alcohol use.

He had a diagnosis of adjustment disorder with depressed mood. His sleep problems were reportedly intermittent and did not meet the criteria for an insomnia disorder. We agreed that the focus of treatment would be on more successfully contending with current life stressors with a reduction in depressive symptoms but also on monitoring his alcohol use. My initial impression was that Mr. White tended to minimize difficulty coping with his current circumstances, including their emotional impact on him. I suspected he also might be minimizing report of alcohol use.

Treatment

In the initial sessions of psychotherapy, I asked Mr. White how things were going with alcohol use. He said that he had made an effort to cut down and would continue to try. I sensed his unease with the discussion and emphasized that alcohol had many pleasurable aspects, but—like anything—it could become a problem. I advised that there was information about alcohol use and older adults on a National Institute of Aging website that he might want to check out. The next week he said, "I have not been entirely candid with you or with myself about how much alcohol I use." He continued, "When I looked at the website, I began to see that I had some of the problems it mentioned that can go along with alcohol overuse." He went on to say that he drank in the evening out of loneliness and boredom. He decided to keep a diary of his alcohol use that week and was distressed to see that he was drinking more than he thought. "Some nights, I have a martini, then a glass of wine dinner, and then another glass after that." I thanked him for his efforts, restated that alcohol can become a problem for some older people, and that I thought we could work together so that alcohol was less of a problem.

He continued to keep his diary in which he recorded about 15 to 20 standard drinks per week. "I know that's too much. I'm going stop drinking martinis." And he did. I asked him about how his sleep had been. "Better. I wonder why?" he asked. I talked with him about the impact of alcohol on disruption of sleep. "Alcohol will get you to sleep, but you won't stay asleep," I noted. In the following week, he began to keep track of the relationship between how much he drank and his sleep—and found that he rarely had sleep problems when he only had one glass of wine earlier in the evening.

As we continued to work on ways to better adapt to health and life issues, Mr. White began to be less depressed. As he felt better, he felt less need to drink alcohol. He also felt much better in the morning and more likely to go out of his home. Over the course of 2 months, he significantly reduced his alcohol use. "I only have one glass of wine with dinner. That's it. And some nights, I don't drink at all." He said he felt relief and some pride in how he had reduced his alcohol intake. After I completed psychotherapy with Mr. White, his geriatrician remarked that he seemed much better and said, "He told me how much alcohol he used to drink. I wish I had asked more questions about that. I strongly suspect alcohol contributed to his past falls."

Case Commentary

It can be hard for older adults to reckon with the possibility that they have a drinking problem, especially if they believe that means they are an *alcoholic*—a person unable to function and who is out of control. For older adults who take pride in having had successful lives as a spouse, parent, and primary wage earner, being an alcoholic doesn't fit. Thinking of alcohol use on a continuum from healthy drinking to problem drinking makes more sense to them.

Approaching problem drinking in a supportive, matter-of-fact, hopeful, and nonstigmatizing way makes it increasingly likely that the person will be more forthcoming. I have found that physicians with whom I work are grateful that I ask about the presence of alcohol problems in their older patients and, for those who have a problem, try to engage them to address the problem.

SUMMARY

Late cognitive changes exist on a continuum from normal, expectable changes (notably, slowing of mental processes or fluid intelligence) to dementia, now known as major neurocognitive disorder. The four major causes of dementia are Alzheimer's disease, Lewy body, vascular disease, and frontotemporal degeneration. Each has a somewhat different initial manifestation, yet all share a progressive and functionally impairing course. In assessment, MCI and dementia reports from the client and family are useful as well as the practitioner's clinical observations and use of assessment screens. Clients suspected of dementia require further follow-up for which there are recommended components, including medical and neurological evaluations. Individuals with a diagnosis of dementia can benefit by supportive counseling. Family caregivers of persons with dementia can benefit by efforts to help manage their own distress and learn more effective strategies to manage problem behaviors in the person with dementia.

Some older adults have problems with alcohol and misuse of prescription medications that have the potential for abuse. Both can have negative health, cognitive, social, and emotional consequences. Late-life stressors can increase the likelihood of these problems. A critical step is asking older people about their use of alcohol and misuse of prescriptions that have the potential for abuse. A number of screening instruments have been found to be appropriate and useful. For some older adults, psychoeducation about healthy drinking guidelines results in reduced use. For others, engagement in a nonjudgmental and supportive plan for reduction in problem alcohol or prescription drug misuse can result in improvement. For those who have not responded to these initial efforts, referral to a substance abuse specialist is prudent.

7 SUMMARY AND NEXT STEPS

"I wasn't always this way," remarked Mabel Brown on her first visit with me. She wanted to convey to me that I should not take a narrow view of her as only an old woman struggling with health problems and depression. She knew she was so much more than that, and she believed that I should know that too. As a geropsychologist, I did understand that she wasn't always the way she appeared on the day I first saw her. I also understood that things could be different for her now. Armed with a broad understanding of aging, skillful assessment, and experience in the treatment of late-life depression, I and other practitioners could reasonably expect she would become less depressed, more hopeful, and more capable of handling her current life circumstances.

SUMMARY OF KEY CONCEPTS

In this section, I briefly summarize key issues and concepts discussed in earlier chapters. Remarkable in human history, most people now make it to old age. In a little more than 10 years, older adults will constitute 20% of the U.S. population. The field of aging has not drawn a lot of professionals into its ranks, in part, I believe, because many do not see older adults as an interesting or meaningful area of practice given widely held negative expectations about aging and their own aging. There will never be enough geriatric specialists in any professional field to serve the older adult population. Increasing numbers of older people will be seeking health and mental health services from providers, most of whom who have little or no training related to aging. Therefore, existing practitioners can benefit by obtaining foundational knowledge about older adults that should enhance their ability to work more effectively with this population. Many conscientious and good-hearted mental health practitioners want to do the best for both their older and younger clients, and professional ethics (American Psychological Association, 2017) indicate that can best be done by continuing to build knowledge and skills relevant to the type of clients they see.

Research clearly demonstrates that the general public and professionals alike possess factually inaccurate information about aging and often hold notions of older adults that skew toward the negative. Older adults themselves often hold negative and self-limiting views about their own aging that are reinforced by the behavior of others toward them, negative media images, and public policy discourse that sees older adults as a drain on resources and a problem to be solved. The reality is the aging population is enormously diverse, including diversity that is reflective of life experience, gender, culture, ethnicity, race, place of residence, socioeconomic circumstances, religion and spirituality, sexual orientation, and other factors. This diversity stands in stark contrast to simplistic views of older adults as one homogenous group that is often called "the elderly."

Physical aging is evident throughout the lifespan and is most personally witnessed in changes in the physical appearance of ourselves and others. Older adults have increasing health problems and decline in sensory functions. Despite these changes, most older people view themselves as being in reasonably good physical health and function fairly well in day-to-day life. Lifespan developmental researchers and others have documented continuity and change throughout the adult lifespan that involves both losses and gains to which most individuals actively respond to maintain emotional and social stability. These processes are influenced by the historical circumstances tied each age cohort. Each generation of older adults is different than the prior one. Late life usually involves regulation and management of loss; optimal aging involves maximizing gains and minimizing losses. Those who study the lifespan have tried to methodologically disentangle factors that influence the aging process, including those that can be attributable to age per se, cohort or generational factors, and recent "period" influences. Mental abilities change over the lifespan: Cognitive functioning gradually slows (fluid intelligence) while people continue to build knowledge and experience throughout their lives (crystallized intelligence). Contrary to common stereotypes, older adults are generally happier in their later years than younger adults. There is relative stability of personality throughout the adult and older adult years. Older adults have generally meaningful and durable social connections with family, friends, and community that are actively reshaped by the older person to best meet social and emotional needs. For those who have worked in competitive employment, people generally make a relatively smooth and sometimes gradual transition out of work. Although few older adults are in abject poverty, some face financial stressors as late-life economic security in the United States has been gradually shifted from the society as a whole (e.g., pensions) to individuals who are required to save and invest for a postretirement that may last as long as 40 years. Women, minorities, and low-wage workers often face the greatest economic challenges in the later years.

With the exception of dementia, older adults have almost half the rates of mental disorders than do younger adults. Mental disorders are more common among older people in residential care (e.g., nursing homes). Rates of mental disorders may change as a new generation of people enters later adulthood—reflecting the cohort or generation influence on emotional well-being and risk for mental disorders. Depression, anxiety, cognitive disorders, and problem alcohol use and prescription drug misuse are seen in clinical practice with older people. Depression may look somewhat different in older versus younger adults (e.g., older adults are more likely to report anhedonia than a subjective experience of depression) and can significantly impair people's ability to function. A subgroup of older people—older White men—have rates of suicide that are much higher than younger adults. Anxiety disorders are more common among older adults than depressive disorders in part because a wide variety of conditions are classified under that diagnostic umbrella. Cognitive disorders become increasingly common in later life. They are broadly classified as mild neurocognitive disorder (also known as mild cognitive impairment) and major neurocognitive disorder (also known as dementia). The most common subtypes of dementia are Alzheimer's disease, Lewy body dementia, vascular dementia, and frontotemporal dementia. Although these conditions have some symptoms in common (notably loss of memory), each subtype has its own characteristic presentation, although some older people have more than one subtype.

Probably about 10% of older adults who drink alcohol do so in a way that is problematic. Older adults are prescribed psychoactive medications (for sleep, anxiety, pain) that can become a problem for some because those medications have the potential to be overused or misused. Overuse of alcohol and prescription drugs increases the risk for a variety of health, cognitive, and mental health problems. Common life problems that are associated with depression, anxiety, and alcohol problems or prescription drug misuse are life transitions (e.g., medical problems, caregiving, job loss or retirement, financial stresses, parenting of grandchildren, residential move), interpersonal disputes (e.g., with spouse or partner, adult children, health care providers or institutions), grief (e.g., death of spouse, adult child, sibling, friend), and social isolation or loneliness.

The diagnostic and assessment intake of an older client is a critical first step. Intakes look similar to those of younger adults, but more primacy is placed on assessment of cognitive function, presence of medical problems and medications, and the possibility of elder abuse and neglect. Furthermore, clarification of the reasons for referral, attention to possible sensory deficits (e.g., sight, hearing) that may impede information-gathering, and establishment of a sensitive interpersonal environment are helpful. A variety of screening instruments can aid in the process of making an initial assessment, yet practitioners need to be mindful that some instruments have not been developed or normed on older adults, so they must use them with caution. Placing present problems in the context of the older adult's larger life history is beneficial. Multiple sources of information in making an evaluation are helpful, including practitioner observation or assessment, client self-report, and report of others. A solid assessment of suicidal thoughts and behaviors is critical, especially in view of the high rates of suicide in older White men. Typically during the assessment, the clinician begins to determine which life problems appear connected to mental health symptoms.

Psychotherapy with older adults is informed by an understanding of developmental forces in the life of the older client, common late-life challenges or problems, the social context and environment, the influence of cohort or generational experiences and perspectives, and cultural factors. Older adults receive mental health services across a range of residential, community program, mental health services, and physical health services settings. Interdisciplinary collaboration with other providers yields better care. A number of ethical issues come into play in work with older people, especially balancing safety with autonomy. Most psychotherapeutic modalities that are used with younger adults are helpful for older adults.

Those working with older adults with cognitive deficits and their family caregivers benefit from familiarity with approaches that seek to maximize functioning and enhance well-being among cognitively impaired older people and to provide practical and emotional support to family members who provide care. Professional practice with older people is informed by a broad knowledge of available aging-related services, Medicare and Medicaid that pay for the lion's share of mental health care, and associated requirements of these insurance programs.

NEXT STEPS

Some readers with an interest in further expanding knowledge and skills about mental health and aging may wonder what might be next steps after reading this book. For those who have read this book, completion of the Pikes Peak Geropsychology Knowledge and Skills Assessment Tool (Karel, Holley, et al., 2012; see Appendix A for a link to this tool) will hopefully reveal how much the reader has learned and will identify additional areas for learning. Further reading would be beneficial. Reading another book on mental health and aging will help to consolidate and deepen information that has been gleaned from this book. I recommend books in Appendix A; that list is far from exhaustive, but the geropsychology books are ones with which I am familiar and are written by respected authors.

I also recommend that the reader learn more about adult development and aging, including the lifespan developmental perspective. A number of excellent introductory textbooks cover this topic and are often used in undergraduate or graduate classes. Also, a free, online, 6-hour series of presentations on lifespan developmental psychology is available from the Adult Development and Aging Division of the American Psychological Association, which developed the series (see Appendix A for a link). It is a sort of minicourse on this topic. I have recommended books and other resources on specific topics throughout this book. It may be helpful to read one or more books that relate to the setting in which you provide care or would like to provide care to older people. For example, if that setting is residential long-term care, a number of books are available and listed in Appendix A.

Continuing education (CE) courses related to aging are another option. Often CE courses are 1-day, in-person workshops or online offerings. The practical problem is where to find them. Professional organizations offer CE courses in various formats, including at annual professional meetings. State or regional professional organizations often offer intermittent

CE workshops. A number of national CE organizations offer in-person and web-based training relevant to the practice of mental health. Sometimes these organizations have aging-relevant offerings. However, CE offerings often do not build knowledge incrementally. This book hopes to remedy that situation a bit because the content of this book is shaped by recommendations from the Council of Professional Geropsychology Training Programs on what it regards as foundational knowledge in geropsychology from the Pikes Peak model for training in professional geropsychology (Hinrichsen, Emery-Tiburcio, Gooblar, & Molinari, 2018; Knight, Karel, Hinrichsen, Qualls, & Duffy, 2009). As of this writing, geropsychology colleagues and I are working on an initiative to create in-person and web-based training that map onto the Council's recommended foundational knowledge competencies in geropsychology. Also, as noted in the "Introduction," other professional organizations have published their own recommendations for what they regard as fundamental aging-relevant knowledge competencies for the respective discipline.

The thorniest issue is how to develop and refine skills relevant to providing mental health services to older adults. Acquiring or refining professional practice skills for postlicensure professionals is a challenge for all professions. Consultation with a colleague with expertise in aging in your discipline is highly beneficial. How do you find such a person? I would try an individual with substantive professional experience in aging as evident by formal preparation in the mental health and aging field or evident by extensive experience with older adults that has been guided by a contemporary understanding of practice with this population. For example, the American Board of Professional Psychology (ABPP) has a formal process for evaluating and recognizing individuals who wish to receive board certification in geropsychology. An ABPP in geropsychology would be evidence of recognized expertise. The challenge is that there is not a large number of geropsychology or other specialists in aging. A good place to start might be locally: Inquire about individuals by reputation who are known to demonstrate expertise relevant to mental health and aging. National, state, and regional professional organizations may provide guidance on those individuals regarded as having substantive experience with older adults. Typically, individuals providing such consultation on your professional work with older adults are paid for their time. If you have little experience in aging, it is highly beneficial to have ongoing consultation on your work with older adults for some period. Such consultation may be critical for cases that are especially complicated. In Appendix A within the "On My Favorite Links Tab" section, I have included a list of professional organizations and interest groups within them that are relevant to aging and mental health. It might be worth reaching out to one or several of them to see if any of their members might be interested in providing ongoing consultation. I am aware that devotion of time and money to the development or refinement of new professional skills is not an easy decision for a practitioner who works full-time. But I think it is worth considering, especially if you see a lot of older adults in practice.

FINAL THOUGHTS

We all share the fact that we will age as will our family, friends, and colleagues. Aging is personal. I end this book by sharing my experience of the aging of my own mother—Katherine Berndt Hinrichsen—from whom I learned a lot during her last years.

My mother was born in 1919 and grew into maturity during the great economic depression in the United States. Her family struggled economically during the Depression, which was made worse when her sister contracted a childhood disease and died at age 13. My mother was part of a generation that valued hard work and independence. When she finished high school, she took a course and became a beautician. In her early 20s, she started her own beauty shop. As we grew up, my mother told my siblings and me many stories of her beauty shop customers. Some were refugees from Europe, and a few were Holocaust survivors. As a kid living in the rural Midwest, those stories expanded my understanding of the world beyond its relatively confined geographical limits. While running her beauty business, she went to college and graduated with honors. My mother loved her life as an independent woman. The truth is, she looked on those years as her most treasured.

At age 29, she married and shortly thereafter had six children in 7 years. She probably felt marriage was as much a social obligation as it was a choice. To makes things more complicated, she didn't use birth control because of her Catholic faith and had more children than she had planned. During my childhood, my mother would sometimes remark that motherhood didn't come naturally to her as it did for others. "I've made a thousand mistakes raising you children," she'd say.

In her 80s, my then widowed mother had increasing health problems. With the help of family and friends, she managed these problems pretty well, lived at home, and continued to be involved in community organizations to which she and my father had meaningfully contributed, including the founding of a local historical museum. But her health problems worsened, and she needed to spend time in the local nursing home until she was better. She knew that particular nursing home well because, as a younger woman, she had volunteered there to cut the hair of its older residents—while raising her six children. As a beautician, she felt that looking good was part of feeling good. After visits to the nursing home, she told us loving stories of nursing home residents; those stories made them seem interesting and heroic.

What was intended as a brief nursing home stay became extended as her health problems worsened. There were many conversations with my siblings about my mother's health, and I decided to travel to her rural community to take stock of things. As a lifelong geropsychologist, I felt well prepared to enter into the world of doctors and a long-term care setting. Driving up to the nursing home that sat on a hill overlooking fields of corn, I thought about my mother's stories of the older residents whose hair she had cut many years earlier. When I entered my mother's nursing home room, I saw her sitting patiently, waiting for me. She had put on her nicest dress and had carefully prepared her hair to look the best for her son. I was struck by how frail she looked and quite unexpectedly burst into tears. "Oh, honey. It must be so hard to see your mother so old," she said softly. She was so right: She "hadn't always been that way." Nursing home staff confided that she wasn't doing so well. I called my siblings, and we gathered to talk with my mother together at the nursing home.

When my siblings arrived, I suggested to my mother that we all meet together in a common room. "Looks like we're having a meeting," she keenly observed. Pointing to me, she commented, "And it looks like you're the chairman." In the common room, I explained to my mother that the nursing home stay was supposed to be temporary but that her health had deteriorated, and we wanted to share our thoughts. "It's your choice, Mom," I said, "but we think you likely need to stay here." She closed her eyes, seeming to block out the reality of what was happening. We didn't know what she would say or do. My mother could speak her mind when she wanted and sometimes did so fiercely. After about a minute, my mother opened her eyes, looked around the room, and said, "You're right. I do need to stay here. I have wise children." Knowing that this was a sacred moment in the life of our family, my youngest brother—a person of religious faith—said that it was time for a prayer. So we held hands around the oak table where we sat and prayed the "Our Father" together. When we finished, my mother stood up and declared, "And I am going to be positive about this."

In the remaining months of her life, my mother became a sort of mayor of the nursing home. She busied herself with getting to know the other residents and their lives. On visits, she would introduce us to fellow residents and tell their stories. "Greg, I'd like you to meet Mary Johnson," she'd start. "Mrs. Johnson and her husband had that big farm on Route 92. Did you know that when Mary was 50, her husband died and she single handedly ran that farm and raised three children? Isn't that remarkable?" Like she had done as a younger woman volunteering time to cut the hair of an earlier generation of older residents, she continued to see her now fellow residents as individuals with life stories filled with challenges and triumph. She knew her fellow residents "hadn't always been that way." And I knew that my mother was not what she had been but, in certain respects, had always been the same: someone who regarded other people as individuals with the right to recognition and dignity.

After she died, my youngest brother said, "What an incredible legacy our mother has left to us in her old age. Mom was the very best at the end, and I'm so grateful." One day, I may need to reside in a nursing home. If so, I hope that I will remember the image of my mother standing and forthrightly declaring, "I will be positive about this," as she decided, at the end of her life, that she would walk down the road of integrity and not despair.

Katherine Berndt Hinrichsen (1919–2005). Copyright by Olin Mills, Inc./Lifetouch, Inc. Reprinted with permission.

Appendix A

RESOURCES

Recommended resources in this appendix are organized by chapter. Books and other print materials are listed under the heading "On My Bookshelf"; links to materials or organizations, under "On My Favorite Links Tab"; and scholarly articles, under "An Article Worth Reading."

CHAPTER 1: THINKING ABOUT AGING AND WORK IN THE FIELD OF AGING

On My Bookshelf

The following is the second edition of this book by Todd Nelson. I read the first edition in its entirety and learned a lot. Some practitioners might find the book a bit academic, but for those interested in learning more about the topic of ageism, this is the go-to overview.

Nelson, T. D. (Ed.). (2017). *Ageism: Stereotyping and prejudice against older persons* (2nd ed.). Cambridge, MA: MIT Press.

This book draws on Ellen Langer's seminal counterclockwise experiment in which older men lived for a week in an environment that recreated the experience of living in 1959—a year when they were young men. After a week, Langer documented the physical, cognitive, and emotional improvement associated with that experience. This book testifies to the power of social expectancies on how people behave and think about themselves, including older adults.

Langer, E. J. (2009). *Counter clockwise: Mindful health and the power of possibility.* New York, NY: Ballantine Books.

On My Favorite Links Tab

Get a sense of your own aging-related perceptions by taking the Age Implicit Association Test (IAT). You can also explore your perceptions of others based on sexuality, gender, race, religion, weight, and other statuses. Go to https://implicit.harvard.edu/implicit and choose "Project Implicit Social Attitudes"; then, among the varied topics, choose "AGE IAT."

An Article Worth Reading

Elaine Brody was well known in the gerontology world for her work on the challenges women face providing care to older parents, including those women who are simultaneously raising children. She coined the term *women in the middle*. I ran into her at a gerontology meeting many years after she had retired and asked, "Has your long career in the field of aging prepared you for your own aging?" She replied, "Intellectually but not emotionally." She later gave an award lecture on her experience of being a "very, very old" gerontologist. which is the part of this article title:

Brody, E. M. (2010). On being very, very old: An insider's perspective. *Gerontologist,* *50,* 2–10. http://dx.doi.org/10.1093/geront/gnp143

CHAPTER 2: FACTS ABOUT AGING AND THE LIFESPAN DEVELOPMENTAL PERSPECTIVE

On My Bookshelf

Overview of Aging

Would you like a brief and very readable overview of key ideas in the field of aging that is written for the general public? This is your book:

Pachana, N. A. (2016). *Ageing: A very short introduction.* Oxford, England: Oxford University Press.

Overview of Adult Development and Aging

If you are interested in doing more in-depth reading about the topics in this chapter, I recommend this undergraduate textbook by John Cavanaugh and Fredda Blanchard-Fields. If you find this newest edition expensive (to me, textbooks seem awfully expensive these days), get a used eighth edition or even the seventh edition. You can also rent it online at a lower cost.

Cavanaugh, J. C., & Blanchard-Fields, F. (2018). *Adult development and aging* (8th ed.). Stamford, CT: Cengage Learning.

Overview of Public Policy and Aging

This is a terrific, well-written overview of public policy issues and aging authored by James Schulz and Robert Binstock, two of the foremost individuals in the field. The book is a little dated, but the issues are still contemporary.

Schultz, J. H., & Binstock, R. H. (2006). *Aging nation: The economics and politics of growing older in America.* Westport, CT: Praeger.

Sexuality and Later Life

This book by Jennifer Hillman draws together important issues relevant to sexuality and older adults that inform a practitioner's understanding of this topic and how to address common clinical issues:

Hillman, J. (2012). *Sexuality and aging: Clinical perspectives.* New York, NY: Springer. http://dx.doi.org/10.1007/978-1-4614-3399-6

The following work provides an excellent overview of this topic:

Kimmel, D., Rose, T., & David, S. (Eds.). (2006). *Lesbian, gay, bisexual, and transgender aging: Research and clinical perspectives.* New York, NY: Columbia University Press.

On My Favorite Links Tab

Facts About Aging

Older Americans 2016: Key Indicators of Well-Being. Are you interested in learning more about facts on aging? This terrific sourcebook is updated every couple of years. The current (seventh) version is for 2016 and uses data from many national sources to summarize facts on select topics. Graphs are downloadable in PowerPoint format for those who may want to use them for a presentation. Go to https://agingstats.gov/docs/LatestReport/Older-Americans-2016-Key-Indicators-of-WellBeing.pdf to order a hard copy of this sourcebook or download it.

Planning for Your Own Aging

Life Plan for the Life Span. Interested in learning more about what you can do at different stages of life to enhance your own aging? The American Psychological Association's Committee on Aging created this brochure to help the reader think about what can be done as a young, middle-age, and older adult to enhance late-life health or health care, financial or legal, work or retirement, and social well-being. Go to https://www.apa.org/pi/aging/lifespan.pdf

Overview of the Lifespan Developmental Perspective

45 Years of Influence of the Lifespan Developmental Approach: Past, Present, and Future. Learn more about the lifespan developmental perspective from leaders in the field. The American Psychological Association Division 20 (Adult Development and Aging) website contains almost 6 hours of a series of presentations recorded at the 2016 annual meeting. The presentations include three modules: (a) Theoretical and Conceptual Approaches; (b) Methodological Issues; and (c) Intervention, Modifiability, and Plasticity. The online recordings are free and essentially constitute a daylong workshop on this topic. Go to http://www.apadivisions.org/division-20/education/lifespan-developmental/index.aspx

Multicultural Competency in Aging

Multicultural Competency in Geropsychology. This report from the American Psychological Association's Committee on Aging emphasizes that age is one aspect of diversity and that within aging, multiple diversities exist (e.g., race, ethnicity, country of origin, religion, disability, gender, sexual orientation). The report offers 25 recommendations for education, training, practice, research, and policy. Go to http://www.apa.org/pi/aging/programs/pipeline/multicultural-competency.pdf

Health and Health Care of Multicultural Older Adults. Stanford University School of Medicine's website on ethno-specific geriatric care in the United States offers a series of training modules on the health status of and optimal health care for older adults of 13 cultural backgrounds. Go to https://geriatrics.stanford.edu

An Article Worth Reading

Review of Social and Emotional Aging

If you'd like a good, readable summary of research on social and emotional aging, I recommend this article by Susan Charles and Laura Carstensen. By the way, you can go to the National Institutes of Health public access site at https://publicaccess.nih.gov to get this and other articles for free. Research funded by the National Institutes of Health must be made available to the public 12 months after their publication; go to https://www.ncbi.nlm.nih.gov/pmc to find them through PubMed Central.

Charles, S. T., & Carstensen, L. L. (2010). Social and emotional aging. *Annual Review of Psychology, 61,* 383–409. http://dx.doi.org/10.1146/annurev.psych.093008.100448

Social Connections in Later Life and Their Impact on Health
This article is a readable, interesting review of positive and negative social ties in later life and their impact on health written by Karen Rook and Susan Charles, leading researchers in this area.

Rook, K. S., & Charles, S. T. (2017). Close social ties and health in later life: Strengths and vulnerabilities. *American Psychologist, 72,* 567–577. http://dx.doi.org/10.1037/amp0000104

CHAPTER 3: OVERVIEW OF ASSESSMENT

On My Bookshelf

Engagement and Assessment
In this reader-friendly book, Forrest Scogin, a well-known geropsychologist, provides recommendations for engagement and assessment of older adults who are seeking psychological services.

Scogin, F. R. (2000). *The first session with seniors: A step-by-step guide.* San Francisco, CA: Jossey-Bass.

Psychological Assessment
This is a terrific book for those who want an overview of the assessment of issues relevant to clinical practice with older adults. The book has four sections: psychopathology later in life, behavioral disorders, cognition, and everyday functioning.

Lichtenberg, P. A. (Ed.). (2010). *Handbook of assessment in clinical gerontology* (2nd ed.). San Diego, CA: Academic Press.

On My Favorite Links Tab

Enhancement of Communication With Older Adults
This publication offers 29 specific recommendation on how to maximize communication with older adults:

Gerontological Society of America. (2012). *Communicating with older adults: An evidence-based review of what really works.* Available at https://www.geron.org/publications/communicating-with-older-adults

Capacity Assessment
American Bar Association and American Psychological Association. This handbook was a joint project between the American Bar Association and the American Psychological Association's Committee on Aging. It bridges legal

and psychological concepts of capacity and discusses how different domains of capacity (e.g., medical, functional, sexual consent, financial, testamentary (will-making), independent living) can be understood and assessed. This booklet is one of a series of three; the others are for lawyers and judges.

American Bar Association, & American Psychological Association. (2008). *Assessment of older adults with diminished capacity: A handbook for psychologists.* Retrieved from the American Psychological Association website: http://www.apa.org/images/capacity-psychologist-handbook_tcm7-78003.pdf

Elder Abuse or Mistreatment

American Bar Association, Commission on Law and Aging. This commission does many projects related to law and aging. The website offers resources, including those related to elder abuse. Go to https://www.americanbar.org/groups/law_aging/resources.html

National Center on Elder Abuse. This is a program of the U.S. Administration on Aging. The website includes many resources, links to programs funded by the Administration on Aging, and publications. Go to https://ncea.acl.gov/index.html

U.S. Department of Health and Human Services. The "Elder Justice" web page discusses, among several topics, elder abuse, financial scams, and fraud prevention. Go to https://www.hhs.gov/aging/elder-justice/index.html

Mental Health and Aging Resources

SAMHSA-HRSA Center for Integrated Health Solutions: Older Adults. This is a U.S. government website with information about a wide range of mental health issues relevant to older adults, including behavioral health identification and treatment; screening and assessment tools; and evidence-based practices. Go to https://www.integration.samhsa.gov/integrated-care-models/older-adults

CHAPTER 4: OVERVIEW OF TREATMENT

On My Bookshelf

Ethics

If you want one place to review foundational ethical issues with older adults, this is your book. It includes many case examples in varied settings where older adults are served.

Bush, S. S., Allen, R. S., & Molinari, V. A. (2017). *Ethical practice in geropsychology.* Washington, DC: American Psychological Association.

Psychotherapy With Older Adults

I don't work in long-term care settings, so I asked a trusted colleague who works in these settings, "If there were one book you'd recommend for an overview of this topic, what would it be?" He said it was this book.

O'Shea Carney, K., & Norris, M. P. (2017). *Transforming long-term care: Expanded roles for mental health professionals.* Washington, DC: American Psychological Association.

This work by Deborah Frazer, Arthur Jongsma, Jr., and me is part of a larger series of psychotherapy treatment planners. We identify 30 clinical problems commonly treated in psychotherapy with older adults and provide an outline of treatment goals, objectives, and interventions for each. Evidence-based interventions are noted.

Frazer, D. W., Hinrichsen, G. A., & Jongsma, A. E., Jr. (2014). *The older adult psychotherapy treatment planner, with DSM–5 updates* (2nd ed.). New York, NY: Wiley.

This is a wonderful first book on how to do psychotherapy with older people. It is perhaps the most popular book on this topic—and for good reason.

Knight, B. G. (2004). *Psychotherapy with older adults* (3rd ed.). Thousand Oaks, CA: Sage.

This book by Kristen Sorocco and Sean Lauderdale discusses the use of cognitive–behavior therapy interventions with older adults in different settings—with a focus on mental disorders that are commonly treated with that form of psychotherapy.

Sorocco, K. H., & Lauderdale, S. (2011). *Implementing CBT with older adults.* New York, NY: Springer.

This book is rich with case material, commentary, and discussion of older adult clients who have varied mental health problems and are treated in different health care delivery settings. The book includes "reflective questions" about the cases.

Pachana, N. A., Laidlaw, K., & Knight, B. G. (2010). *Casebook of clinical geropsychology: International perspectives on practice.* Oxford, England: Oxford University Press.

If you are interested learning more about evidence-based treatment for older adults, this book by Forrest Scogin and Avani Shah is a good one. Topics include anxiety, depression, insomnia, memory problems, behavioral disturbances in long-term care, and distress in family caregivers. Chapters include clinical examples, resources, and implementation challenges.

Scogin, F., & Shah, A. (Eds.). (2012). *Making evidence-based psychological treatments work for older adults.* Washington, DC: American Psychological Association. http://dx.doi.org/10.1037/13753-000

Bereavement

George Bonanno provides an easily accessible and engaging summary of what we currently know about bereavement and how it challenges many of the assumptions that mental health professionals and the general public alike hold about this topic. A second edition of this book is in the publishing pipeline.

Bonanno, G. A. (2009). *The other side of sadness: What the new science of bereavement tells us about life after loss.* New York, NY: Basic Books.

Medicare and Social Security

These two books are by far the clearest and most helpful on Medicare and Social Security that I have found. As friends and family become eligible for these programs, I highly recommend these books to them. I also recommend them to some older clients. No one has been disappointed.

Kotlikoff, L. J., Moeller, P., & Solman, P. (2016). *Get what's yours: The secrets to maxing out your Social Security* (Rev. ed.). New York, NY: Simon & Schuster.

Moeller, P. (2016). *Get what's yours for Medicare: Maximize your coverage, minimize your costs.* Waterville, ME: Thorndike Press.

On My Favorite Links Tab

AARP

This is a recent report from AARP (formerly called the American Association for Retired Persons) that analyzes data on social connections and loneliness in American older adults:

AARP Foundation. (n.d.). *A profile of social connectedness in older adults.* Retrieved from https://connect2affect.org/wp-content/uploads/2017/03/A-Profile-of-Social-Connectedness.pdf

American Psychological Association

This resource guide includes a list of journal articles, books, book chapters, videos, and reports relevant to psychotherapy with older adults:

American Psychological Association. (2009). Psychotherapy & older adults: Resource guide. Retrieved from http://www.apa.org/pi/aging/resources/guides/psychotherapy.aspx

The following document provides numerous resources, including guidelines, reports, training manuals, and online resources, for mental health professionals who are interested in working in long-term care settings.

American Psychological Association, Office on Aging. (2013). Psychological services in long-term care: Resource guide. Retrieved from http://www.apa.org/pi/aging/resources/guides/long-term-care.pdf

American Psychological Association Practice Organization

This "Complete Guide to Medicare for Psychologists" is available to members of the American Psychological Association by using a login name and password. It will walk you through how to enroll in and bill through Medicare. Some of the material is available to non-American Psychological Association members. Go to https://www.apaservices.org/practice/medicare/index

National Association of Area Agencies on Aging

This website will direct you to your local Area Agency on Aging as well as to other aging-relevant programs and services. Go to https://www.n4a.org

An Article Worth Reading

This is by far the clearest and most comprehensive explanation of Medicare for practicing psychologists that I have found.

Norris, M. P. (2015). Evolutions and revolutions in Medicare policy and reimbursement of geropsychology services. In P. A. Lichtenberg, B. T. Mast, B. D. Carpenter, & J. Loebach Wetherell (Eds.), *APA handbook of clinical geropsychology: Vol. 1. History and status of the field and perspectives on aging* (pp. 45–69). Washington, DC: American Psychological Association. http://dx.doi.org/10.1037/14458-004

CHAPTER 5: ASSESSMENT AND TREATMENT OF DEPRESSION AND ANXIETY

On My Bookshelf

Treatment of Depression

For those interested in conducting cognitive behavior therapy (CBT) with depressed older adults, this is an excellent book to guide treatment. It is written by the foremost experts in CBT for older people. It provides a step-by-step approach for implementation. A companion workbook for clients is available that includes many useful handouts for psychoeducation and CBT homework.

Gallagher-Thompson, D., & Thompson, L. W. (2010). *Treating late-life depression: A cognitive–behavioral therapy approach (therapist guide).* New York, NY: Oxford University Press.

This is the clinical treatment manual for interpersonal psychotherapy with older people that was written by Kathleen Clougherty and me and based on our clinical work:

Hinrichsen, G. A., & Clougherty, K. F. (2006). *Interpersonal psychotherapy for depressed older adults.* Washington, DC: American Psychological Association.

Treatment of Anxiety

This therapist treatment manual for generalized anxiety disorder is not older adult specific but clearly outlines the CBT approach to the treatment of anxiety. I have used this treatment manual with older adults.

Zinbarg, R. E., Craske, M. G., & Barlow, D. H. (2006). *Mastery of your anxiety and worry: Therapist guide* (2nd ed.). New York, NY: Oxford University Press.

This companion workbook for clients includes helpful handouts and worksheets:

Craske, M. G., & Barlow, D. H. (2006). *Mastery of your anxiety and worry: Workbook* (2nd ed.). New York, NY: Oxford University Press.

On My Favorite Links Tab

You can get a DVD free of charge or download these series of booklets. This is an excellent resource that provides especially helpful guidance on evidence-based treatments for depression and associated programmatic and implementation issues.

Substance Abuse and Mental Health Services Administration. (2011). Treatment of Depression in Older Adults Evidence-Based Practices (EBP) Kit [CD-ROM/DVD]. Retrieved from http://store.samhsa.gov/product/ Treatment-of-Depression-in-Older-Adults-Evidence-Based-Practices-EBP-KIT/SMA11-4631CD-DVD

CHAPTER 6: ASSESSMENT AND TREATMENT OF COGNITIVE IMPAIRMENT, PROBLEM ALCOHOL USE, AND PRESCRIPTION DRUG MISUSE

On My Bookshelf

Benjamin Mast and Brian Yochim offer this brief, contemporary, readable summary of theories about, symptoms of, diagnostic steps for, and assessment and treatment of common types of dementia.

Mast, B. T., & Yochim, B. T. (2018). *Alzheimer's disease and dementia*. Boston, MA: Hogrefe.

If you know little about the topic of family care for older adults, this is the book to start with. It is written by authors with extensive experience working with families of older people. Their approach is caregiver family therapy; in my view, the approach incorporates the best of what we know about late-life families, a family systems perspective, and research on effective approaches to help caregivers.

Qualls, S. H., & Williams, A. A. (2013). *Caregiver family therapy: Empowering families to meet the challenges of aging*. Washington, DC: American Psychological Association.

On My Favorite Links Tab

American Bar Association and American Psychological Association

One of three handbooks (the others are for lawyers and judges), this work is an excellent review of important issues in the assessment of capacity. The project was a joint effort between the American Bar Association and the American Psychological Association's Committee on Aging.

American Bar Association, & American Psychological Association. (2008). *Assessment of older adults with diminished capacity: A handbook for psychologists*. Retrieved from the American Psychological Association website: http://www.apa.org/images/capacity-psychologist-handbook_tcm7-78003.pdf

Alzheimer's Association

This is the preeminent organization on Alzheimer's disease and related cognitive impairments. The website has many resources for professionals, family members, and persons with dementia, including ways to find local support groups. Go to http://www.alz.org

American Psychological Association, Office on Aging

The "caregiving briefcase" includes useful and practical information, tools, and resources about how caregiving affects all of us; facts about family caregiving; common caregiving problems; how to identify and reach caregivers; and roles psychologists can have in working with family caregivers. This website is a great place to get an overview of this topic. Links to other organizations and resources can be found here too.

American Psychological Association, Office on Aging. (2015). *Caregiver briefcase*. Retrieved from http://www.apa.org/pi/about/publications/caregivers/index.aspx

CHAPTER 7: SUMMARY AND NEXT STEPS

On My Bookshelf

The following are all excellent books written by leaders in the field. Note that book recommendations have been made on selected topics in earlier chapters.

Geropsychological Perspectives on Mental Health and Aging

Hyer, L. (Ed.). (2014). *Psychological treatment of older adults: A holistic model.* New York, NY: Springer.

Knight, B. G., & Pachana, N. A. (2015). *Psychological assessment and treatment with older adults.* Oxford, England: Oxford University Press. http://dx.doi.org/10.1093/med:psych/9780199652532.001.0001

Segal, D. L., Qualls, S. H., & Smyer, M. A. (2018). *Aging and mental health* (3rd ed.). Hoboken, NJ: Wiley Blackwell.

Social Work Perspectives on Mental Health and Aging

Galambos, C. M., Greene, R. R., Kropf, N. P., & Cohen, H. L. (2018). *Foundations of social work practice in the field of aging: A competency-based approach* (2nd ed.). Washington, DC: NASW Press.

Kropf, N., & Cummings, S. (2017). *Evidence-based treatment with older adults: Theory, practice, and research.* New York, NY: Oxford University Press.

Nursing Perspectives on Mental Health and Aging

Melillo, K. D., & Houde, S. C. (Eds.). (2011). *Geropsychiatric and mental health nursing* (2nd ed.). Sudbury, MA: Jones & Bartlett Learning.

Psychiatric Perspectives on Mental Health and Aging

Steffens, D., Blazer, D. G., & Thakur, M. (Eds.). (2015). *The American Psychiatric Publishing textbook of geriatric psychiatry* (5th ed.). Washington, DC: American Psychiatric Publishing.

Adult Development and Aging

Cavanaugh, J. C., & Blanchard-Fields, F. (2017). *Adult development and aging* (8th ed.). Boston, MA: Cengage Learning.

Moody, H. R., & Sasser, J. R. (2018). *Aging: Concepts and controversies* (9th ed.). Thousand Oaks, CA: Sage. [*Note:* This book emphasizes policy perspectives and aging.]

Whitbourne, S. K., & Whitbourne, S. B. (2017). *Adult development and aging: Biopsychosocial perspectives* (6th ed.). Hoboken, NJ: Wiley.

On My Favorite Links Tab

The following are professional mental health and aging organizations and websites worth knowing about.

American Psychological Association, Society of Clinical Geropsychology (Division 12, Section II)

The society is devoted to research, training, and the provision of psychological services for older adults (i.e., geropsychology). This site includes information on geropsychology training guidelines and training opportunities for students and professionals, including clinical psychology internships, postdoctoral fellowship opportunities, continuing education offerings, research funding and jobs. Go to https://www.geropsychology.org

American Psychological Association, Division of Adult Development and Aging (Division 20)

This division is the primary home for academic and research psychologists who study and teach adult development and aging. The website includes a directory of graduate programs in the psychology of adult development and aging, suggested readings, adult development and aging course syllabi, videos, and many other resources. Go to http://www.apadivisions.org/division-20/publications/index.aspx

American Psychological Association, Office on Aging

The Office on Aging is a coordination point for the American Psychological Association's activities pertaining to aging and geropsychology. The Office on Aging also supports the work of the Committee on Aging. This website is rich with resources. Go to https://www.apa.org/pi/aging/index.aspx

American Society on Aging

The organization offers professional education, publications, and online information and training resources related to aging. This is a multidisciplinary organization and include a sizable social work presence. Go to http://www.asaging.org

Council of Professional Geropsychology Training Programs

This is an international organization of graduate, internship, postdoctoral, and postlicensure individuals as well as programs that provide geropsychology training consistent with the Pikes Peak model for training in professional geropsychology. The website includes a copy of the Pikes Peak Geropsychology Knowledge and Skills Assessment Tool (Karel, Holley, et al., 2012). You can find the tool by clicking on "Resources" in the header's navigation menu (and then in the drop-down menu, select "Online Resources"). On the "Online Resources" web page, click on "Recommended Resources Associated with the Pikes Peak Model Competencies," which will take you to a page that includes suggested articles, books, and other materials relevant to each of the Pikes Peak model competencies. Go to http://copgtp.org

GeroCentral

This website is a collaborative effort among the American Psychological Association's Society of Clinical Geropsychology, Division of Adult Development and Aging, and Committee on Aging as well as the Council of Professional Geropsychology Training Programs and Psychologists in Long-Term Care to bring together available resources in one place for geropsychology training, service provision, policy, and research, online assessment of geropsychology competencies, and other content. Go to https://gerocentral.org

Psychologists in Long-Term Care

This network of psychologists and other professionals is dedicated to the enhancement of mental health and quality of life for those involved in long-term care through practice, research, and advocacy. Go to www.pltcweb.org/index.php

Appendix B

ASSESSMENT SCREENING INSTRUMENTS

Assessment screening instruments in this appendix are organized by the chapter—3, 5, or 6—to which they relate, and some of the instruments in this appendix are recommended in those chapters. Entries include information on how to obtain the instruments.

CHAPTER 3: OVERVIEW OF ASSESSMENT

Assessment Instruments: Websites

The Hartford Institute for Geriatric Nursing, New York University, College of Nursing (HIGN)

The institute website reviews a variety of assessment instruments for older adults, including those that are relevant to a mental health assessment. The "Try This Series" section summarizes a clinical topic; recommends the best tools for assessment; and provides psychometric properties, strengths or limitations, recommended readings, and a copy of the actual instruments. Use the search keywords box on the website to find the instrument you are interested in. Go to https://consultgeri.org/try-this/general-assessment

Assessment screening instruments for depression and anxiety available on this website are listed in this appendix (see the Chapter 5 section), and screening instruments for cognitive impairment and problem alcohol are also listed in this appendix (see the Chapter 6 section).

The following are specific instruments relevant to a mental health diagnostic and assessment intake on the HIGN website.

Functional Ability
- Katz Index of Independence of Activities of Daily Living (ADL) scale (Katz, Downs, Cash, & Grotz, 1970)
- Lawton Instrumental Activities of Daily Living (Lawton & Brody, 1969)

Pain
- Faces Pain Scale–Revised (Hicks, von Baeyer, Spafford, van Korlaar, & Goodenough, 2001)
- Numeric Rating Scale (Jacox, Carr, & Payne, 1994)

Sleep Problems
- Epworth Sleepiness Scale (Johns, 1991)

Sexuality
- Questions to Guide Sexuality Assessment Among Older Adults (Wallace, 2003)

Elder Abuse
- Elder Assessment Instrument (Fulmer, Paveza, Abraham, & Fairchild, 2000)

Hearing Loss
- Hearing Handicap Inventory for the Elderly Screening Version (Ventry & Weinstein, 1983)

CATCH-ON (Collaborative Action Team Training for Community Health–Older Adult Network)
The website for this federally funded program to Rush University Medical Center in Chicago, Illinois, offers many useful resources, including assessment tools. Go to http://catch-on.org/hp-home/hp-catch-on-community-health/measures

Alabama Research Institute on Aging (ARIA), University of Alabama
Among ARIA's many resources is a "Measurement Archive," which is described by the program as follows:

> Archived here is a collection of empirically supported measures intended to facilitate research and clinical work with older adults. Featured resources are diverse in their purposes and applications—ranging from measures of depression, caregiving, and attitudes toward sexuality to assessments of cognitive impairment, substance abuse, and mobility. In addition to the measure itself, available information about each measure's native literature(s), psychometric properties, and coding is also provided.

If you want access to the measures, click on "Members" in the header's navigation menu to request a password. You will be asked to send an e-mail to the administrator, who will then send a password to you. Go to http://aria.ua.edu

CHAPTER 5: ASSESSMENT AND TREATMENT OF DEPRESSION AND ANXIETY

Measures for Depression

The following are recommended measures for depression in older adults and information on where to find the measures. Some of these measures are available in a language other than English.

Self-Report Rating Scales

- Beck Depression Inventory—Second Edition (BDI–II; Beck, Steer, & Brown, 1996): A fee is charged for use of this instrument. Go to https://www.pearsonclinical.com/psychology/products/100000159/beck-depression-inventoryii-bdi-ii.html

- Center for Epidemiological Studies Depression Scale (CES-D; Radloff, 1977): Go to the Alabama Research Institute on Aging (ARIA), University of Alabama website at http://aria.ua.edu

- Geriatric Depression Scale (GDS; Yesavage et al., 1982–1983): Go to the ARIA website at http://aria.ua.edu or to The Hartford Institute for Geriatric Nursing, New York University, College of Nursing website at https://consultgeri.org/try-this/general-assessment

- Patient Health Questionnaire 9-item Depression Scale (PHQ-9; Kroenke, Spitzer, & Williams, 2001): Go to the CATCH-ON (Collaborative Action Team Training for Community Health–Older Adult Network) website at http://catch-on.org/hp-home/hp-catch-on-community-health/measures

Clinician Rating Scales
- Cornell Scale for Depression in Dementia (CSDD; Alexopoulos, Abrams, Young, & Shamoian, 1988): Go to the ARIA website at http://aria.ua.edu
- Geriatric Suicide Ideation Scale (GSIS; Heisel & Flett, 2006): Go to the ARIA website at http://aria.ua.edu
- Hamilton Depression Rating Scale (HDRS, also known as the HAM-D; Hamilton, 1960): Go to the ARIA website at http://aria.ua.edu

Measures for Anxiety

The following are recommended measures for anxiety in older adults and information on where to find the measures.

- Generalized Anxiety Disorder 7-item screen (GAD-7; Spitzer, Kroenke, Williams, & Lowe, 2006): Available on the CATCH-ON website at http://catch-on.org/hp-home/hp-catch-on-community-health/measures

- Geriatric Anxiety Inventory (GAI; Pachana et al., 2007): A free copy of this instrument is available for those in academic settings; otherwise, clinical use requires a licensing agreement with a small fee. See also the five-item version of this measure (Byrne & Pachana, 2011). Go to http://gai.net.au

- Geriatric Anxiety Scale (GAS; for the 30 item GAS, see Segal, June, Payne, Coolidge, & Yochim, 2010; for the Geriatric Anxiety Scale–10 Item Version, see Mueller et al., 2015): To obtain a copy of the instruments, contact the developer: Daniel L. Segal, PhD, Professor, Department of Psychology, University of Colorado at Colorado Springs, 1420 Austin Bluffs Parkway, Colorado Springs, CO 80918; e-mail: dsegal@uccs.edu. The 2013 (version 2) of the 30-item GAS measure is also available on the ARIA website at http://aria.ua.edu

- The PTSD Checklist for DSM–V (PCL-5; Blevins, Weathers, Davis, Witte, & Domino, 2015): Go to https://www.ptsd.va.gov/professional/assessment/adult-sr/ptsd-checklist.asp

CHAPTER 6: ASSESSMENT AND TREATMENT OF COGNITIVE IMPAIRMENT, PROBLEM ALCOHOL USE, AND PRESCRIPTION DRUG MISUSE

The following are recommended measures for cognitive screening for older adults and information on where to find the measures.

Delirium

- Confusion Assessment Method (CAM; Inouye et al., 1990): Go to The Hartford Institute for Geriatric Nursing, New York University, College of Nursing website at https://consultgeri.org/try-this/general-assessment or to the KAER website at https://www.geron.org/

programs-services/alliances-and-multi-stakeholder-collaborations/
cognitive-impairment-detection-and-earlier-diagnosis

Mild Cognitive Impairment and Dementia

KAER (Kickstart, Assess, Evaluate, Refer)

- KAER: The KAER toolkit is a highly recommended document by the Gerontological Society of America (2017) that was developed by a multidisciplinary group of professionals in conjunction with the society. It outlines a four-step model to evaluate and, if need be, refer older adults for further evaluation of cognitive problems. It is rich with screening instruments, family and client handouts, bibliographic references, and links to other resources. To access this toolkit online, go to https://www.geron.org/programs-services/alliances-and-multi-stakeholder-collaborations/cognitive-impairment-detection-and-earlier-diagnosis

- Mini-Cog (Borson, Scanlan, Chen, & Ganguli, 2003): Go to the Mini-Cog website at http://mini-cog.com, the HIGN website at https://consultgeri.org/try-this/general-assessment, or the KAER website at https://www.geron.org/programs-services/alliances-and-multi-stakeholder-collaborations/cognitive-impairment-detection-and-earlier-diagnosis

- Montreal Cognitive Assessment (MoCA; Nasreddine et al., 2005): Go to the MoCA website at https://www.mocatest.org, the HIGN website at https://consultgeri.org/try-this/general-assessment, or the KAER website at https://www.geron.org/programs-services/alliances-and-multi-stakeholder-collaborations/cognitive-impairment-detection-and-earlier-diagnosis

Problem Alcohol Use

The following are recommended measures for alcohol screening for older adults and information on where to find the measures.

- Alcohol Use Disorders Identification test (AUDIT; Babor, de la Fuente, Saunders, & Grant, 1992): Go to https://pubs.niaaa.nih.gov/publications/Audit.pdf or to the CATCH-ON (Collaborative Action Team Training for Community Health–Older Adult Network) website at http://catch-on.org/hp-home/hp-catch-on-community-health/measures

- The AUDIT Alcohol Consumption Questions (AUDIT-C; Bush, Kivlahan, McDonell, Fihn, & Bradley, 1998): Go to the CATCH-ON website at http://catch-on.org/hp-home/hp-catch-on-community-health/measures

- The CAGE (Ewing, 1984): Go to the Alabama Research Institute on Aging, University of Alabama, website at http://aria.ua.edu

- The Short Michigan Alcoholism Screening Test—Geriatric Version (SMAST–G; Blow, Gillespie, Barry, Mudd, & Hill, 1998): Go to the CATCH-ON website at http://catch-on.org/hp-home/hp-catch-on-community-health/measures or to the HIGN website at https://consultgeri.org/try-this/general-assessment

References

AARP. (2005, January). *Prescription drug use among midlife and older Americans.* Retrieved from https://assets.aarp.org/rgcenter/health/rx_midlife_plus.pdf

AARP Foundation. (n.d.). *A profile of social connectedness in older adults.* Retrieved from https://connect2affect.org/wp-content/uploads/2017/03/A-Profile-of-Social-Connectedness.pdf

Achenbaum, W. A. (1978). *Old age in the new land: The American experience since 1790.* Baltimore, MD: Johns Hopkins University Press.

Administration for Community Living. (2017, December). *The opioid emergency and older adults.* Retrieved from https://www.acl.gov/aging-and-disability-in-america/issue-briefings

Administration on Aging. (2016). *A profile of older Americans: 2016.* Retrieved from Administration for Community Living website: https://www.acl.gov/aging-and-disability-in-america/data-and-research/profile-older-americans

Alexopoulos, G. S., Abrams, R. C., Young, R. C., & Shamoian, C. A. (1988). Cornell Scale for Depression in Dementia. *Biological Psychiatry, 23,* 271–284. http://dx.doi.org/10.1016/0006-3223(88)90038-8

Alliance for Aging Research. (2003, March). *Ageism: How healthcare fails the elderly.* Retrieved from https://zdoc.site/ageismhow-healthcare-fails-the-elderlypdf-alliance-for-aging.html

American Association of Colleges of Nursing. (2016). *Adult-gerontology acute care and primary care NP competences.* Retrieved from http://www.aacnnursing.org/Portals/42/AcademicNursing/pdf/Adult-Gero-NP-Comp-2016.pdf?ver=2017-05-17-102558-277

American Bar Association, & American Psychological Association. (2008). *Assessment of older adults with diminished capacity: A handbook for psychologists.* Retrieved from American Psychological Association website: https://www.apa.org/images/capacity-psychologist-handbook_tcm7-78003.pdf

American Psychiatric Association. (1994). *Diagnostic and statistical manual of mental disorders* (4th ed.). Washington, DC: Author.

American Psychiatric Association. (2013). *Diagnostic and statistical manual of mental disorders* (5th ed.). Washington, DC: Author.

American Psychological Association. (2002). *Guidelines on multicultural education, training, research, practice, and organizational change for psychologists.* Retrieved from https://www.apa.org/about/policy/multicultural-guidelines-archived.pdf

American Psychological Association. (2014). Guidelines for psychological practice with older adults. *American Psychologist, 69,* 34–65. http://dx.doi.org/10.1037/a0035063

American Psychological Association. (2015). Guidelines for psychological practice with transgender and gender nonconforming people. *American Psychologist, 70,* 832–864. http://dx.doi.org/10.1037/a0039906

American Psychological Association. (2016). *APA Fact Sheet Series on Psychologist Supply and Demand Projections 2015–2030: Demand across age groups.* Washington, DC: Author.

American Psychological Association. (2017). *Ethical principles of psychologists and code of conduct* (2002, Amended June 1, 2010 and January 1, 2017). Retrieved from http://www.apa.org/ethics/code/index.aspx

American Psychological Association Committee on Aging. (2009). *Multicultural competency in geropsychology.* Washington, DC: American Psychological Association. Retrieved from http://www.apa.org/pi/aging/programs/pipeline/multicultural-competency.pdf

American Psychological Association Committee on Aging. (2018). *Life plan for the life span.* Retrieved from http://www.apa.org/pi/aging/lifespan.pdf

American Psychological Association Presidential Task Force on Integrated Health Care. (2007). *Blueprint for change: Achieving integrated health care for an aging population.* Retrieved from http://www.apa.org/pi/aging/programs/integrated/integrated-healthcare-report.pdf

American Psychological Association Task Force on Re-Envisioning the Multicultural Guidelines for the 21st Century. (2017). *Multicultural guidelines: An ecological approach to context, identity, and intersectionality.* Retrieved from http://www.apa.org/about/policy/multicultural-guidelines.pdf

Antonucci, T. C., Ajrouch, K. J., & Birditt, K. S. (2014). The convoy model: Explaining social relations from a multidisciplinary perspective. *Gerontologist, 54,* 82–92. http://dx.doi.org/10.1093/geront/gnt118

Areán, P. A., Alvidrez, J., Barrera, A., Robinson, G. S., & Hicks, S. (2002). Would older medical patients use psychological services? *Gerontologist, 42,* 392–398. http://dx.doi.org/10.1093/geront/42.3.392

Armento, M. E. A., & Stanley, M. A. (2014). Psychological interventions in non-mental health settings. In N. A. Pachana & K. Laidlaw (Eds.), *The Oxford handbook of clinical geropsychology* (pp. 911–926). Oxford, England: Oxford University Press.

Arnold, M. (2008). Polypharmacy and older adults: A role for psychology and psychologists. *Professional Psychology: Research and Practice, 39,* 283–289. http://dx.doi.org/10.1037/0735-7028.39.3.283

Association of Gerontology in Higher Education. (2014). *Gerontology competencies for undergraduate and graduate education.* Retrieved from https://www.aghe.org/images/aghe/competencies/gerontology_competencies.pdf

Atchley, R. C., & Barusch, A. S. (2004). *Social forces & aging: An introduction to social gerontology* (10th ed.). Belmont, CA: Thomson/Wadsworth.

Babor, T. F., de la Fuente, J. R., Saunders, J., & Grant, M. (1992). *AUDIT: The Alcohol Use Disorders Identification Test—Guidelines for use in primary health care* (Document No. WHO/PSA/92.4). Geneva, Switzerland: World Health Organization. Retrieved from http://citeseerx.ist.psu.edu/viewdoc/download?doi=10.1.1.505.4146&rep=rep1&type=pdf

Balsis, S., Zweig, R. A., & Molinari, V. (2015). Personality disorders in later life. In P. A. Lichtenberg, B. T. Mast, B. D. Carpenter, & J. Loebach Wetherell (Eds.), *APA handbook of clinical geropsychology: Vol. 2. Assessment, treatment, and issues of later life* (pp. 79–94). Washington, DC: American Psychological Association. http://dx.doi.org/10.1037/14459-003

Baltes, P. B. (1993). The aging mind: Potential and limits. *Gerontologist, 33,* 580–594. http://dx.doi.org/10.1093/geront/33.5.580

Baltes, P. B. (1997). On the incomplete architecture of human ontogeny: Selection, optimization, and compensation as foundation of developmental theory. *American Psychologist, 52,* 366–380. http://dx.doi.org/10.1037/0003-066X.52.4.366

Baltes, P. B., Lindenberger, U., & Staudinger, U. M. (2006). Life span theory in developmental psychology. In R. M. Lerner & W. Damon (Eds.), *Handbook of child psychology: Vol. 1. Theoretical models of human development* (6th ed., pp. 569–664). Hoboken, NJ: Wiley.

Barry, K. L., & Blow, F. C. (2010). Screening, assessing, and intervening for alcohol and medication misuse in older adults. In P. A. Lichtenberg (Ed.), *Handbook of assessment in clinical gerontology* (pp. 307–330). San Diego, CA: Elsevier. http://dx.doi.org/10.1016/B978-0-12-374961-1.10012-0

Barry, K. L., & Blow, F. C. (2016). Drinking over the lifespan: Focus on older adults. *Alcohol Research: Current Reviews, 38*(1), 115–120.

Beaudreau, S. A., & O'Hara, R. (2008). Late-life anxiety and cognitive impairment: A review. *American Journal of Geriatric Psychiatry, 16,* 790–803. http://dx.doi.org/10.1097/JGP.0b013e31817945c3

Beck, A. T., Steer, R. A., & Brown, G. K. (1996). *Manual for the Beck Depression Inventory* (2nd ed.). San Antonio, TX: Psychological Corporation.

Bélanger, L., LeBlanc, M., & Morin, C. M. (2012). Cognitive behavioral therapy for insomnia in older adults. *Cognitive and Behavioral Practice, 19,* 101–115. http://dx.doi.org/10.1016/j.cbpra.2010.10.003

Bengtson, V. L., Giarrusso, R., Mabry, J. B., & Silverstein, M. (2002). Solidarity, conflict, and ambivalence: Complementary or competing perspectives on intergenerational relationships. *Journal of Marriage and Family, 64,* 568–576. http://dx.doi.org/10.1111/j.1741-3737.2002.00568.x

Bergman, Y. S. (2017). Ageism in childhood. In T. D. Nelson (Ed.), *Ageism: Stereotyping and prejudice against older persons* (2nd ed., pp. 3–36). Cambridge, MA: MIT Press.

Blazer, D. G. (2003). Depression in late life: Review and commentary. *Journals of Gerontology: Series A. Biological Sciences and Medical Sciences, 58,* M249–M265. http://dx.doi.org/10.1093/gerona/58.3.M249

Blevins, C. A., Weathers, F. W., Davis, M. T., Witte, T. K., & Domino, J. L. (2015). The Posttraumatic Stress Disorder Checklist for *DSM–5* (PCL–5): Development and initial psychometric evaluation. *Journal of Traumatic Stress, 28,* 489–498. http://dx.doi.org/10.1002/jts.22059

Blieszner, R., & Roberto, K. A. (2012). Partners and friends in adulthood. In S. K. Whitbourne & J. J. Sliwinski (Eds.), *The Wiley-Blackwell handbook of adulthood and aging* (pp. 381–398). Chichester, England: Wiley-Blackwell. http://dx.doi.org/10.1002/9781118392966.ch19

Bloom, H. G., Ahmed, I., Alessi, C. A., Ancoli-Israel, S., Buysse, D. J., Kryger, M. H., . . . Zee, P. C. (2009). Evidence-based recommendations for the assessment and management of sleep disorders in older persons. *Journal of the American Geriatrics Society, 57,* 761–789. http://dx.doi.org/10.1111/j.1532-5415.2009.02220.x

Blow, F. C., & Barry, K. L. (2012). Alcohol and substance misuse in older adults. *Current Psychiatry Reports, 14,* 310–319. http://dx.doi.org/10.1007/s11920-012-0292-9

Blow, F. C., Brower, K. J., Schulenberg, J. E., Demo-Dananberg, L. M., Young, J. P., & Beresford, T. P. (1992). The Michigan Alcoholism Screening Test—Geriatric Version (MAST–G): A new elderly specific screening instrument. *Alcoholism: Clinical and Experimental Research, 16,* 372.

Blow, F. C., Gillespie, B. W., Barry, K. L., Mudd, S. A., & Hill, E. M. (1998). Brief screening for alcohol problems in elderly populations using the Short Michigan Alcoholism Screening Test—Geriatric Version (SMAST–G). *Alcoholism: Clinical and Experimental Research, 22,* 131A.

Bodner, E. (2017). Cross cultural differences in ageism. In T. D. Nelson (Ed.), *Ageism: Stereotyping and prejudice against older persons* (2nd ed., pp. 291–322). Cambridge, MA: MIT Press.

Bonanno, G. A. (2009). *The other side of sadness: What the new science of bereavement tells us about life after loss.* New York, NY: Basic Books.

Bonanno, G. A., Wortman, C. B., Lehman, D. R., Tweed, R. G., Haring, M., Sonnega, J., . . . Nesse, R. M. (2002). Resilience to loss and chronic grief: A prospective study from preloss to 18-months postloss. *Journal of Personality and Social Psychology, 83,* 1150–1164. http://dx.doi.org/10.1037/0022-3514.83.5.1150

Bonanno, G. A., Wortman, C. B., & Nesse, R. M. (2004). Prospective patterns of resilience and maladjustment during widowhood. *Psychology and Aging, 19,* 260–271. http://dx.doi.org/10.1037/0882-7974.19.2.260

Boron, J. B., Schaie, K. W., & Willis, S. L. (2010). The aging personality and self: Diversity and health issues. In H. M. Fillit, K. Rockwood, & K. Woodhouse (Eds.), *Brocklehurst's textbook of geriatric medicine and gerontology* (3rd ed., pp. 178–183). Philadelphia, PA: Elsevier. http://dx.doi.org/10.1016/B978-1-4160-6231-8.10029-7

Borson, S., Scanlan, J. M., Chen, P., & Ganguli, M. (2003). The Mini-Cog as a screen for dementia: Validation in a population-based sample. *Journal of the American Geriatrics Society, 51,* 1451–1454. http://dx.doi.org/10.1046/j.1532-5415.2003.51465.x

Bower, E. S., & Wetherell, J. L. (2015). Late-life anxiety disorders. In P. A. Lichtenberg, B. T. Mast, B. D. Carpenter, & J. Loebach Wetherell (Eds.), *APA handbook of clinical geropsychology: Vol. 2. Assessment, treatment, and issues of later life* (pp. 49–77). Washington, DC: American Psychological Association. http://dx.doi.org/10.1037/14459-002

Bower, E. S., Wetherell, J. L., Mon, T., & Lenze, E. J. (2015). Treating anxiety disorders in older adults: Current treatments and future directions. *Harvard Review of Psychiatry, 23,* 329–342. http://dx.doi.org/10.1097/hrp.0000000000000064

Bragg, E., & Hansen, J. C. (2010). A revelation of numbers: Will America's eldercare workforce be ready to care for an aging America? *Generations, 34*(4), 11–19.

Brokaw, T. (1999). *The greatest generation speaks.* New York, NY: Random House.

Brown, R. L., & Rounds, L. A. (1995). Conjoint screening questionnaires for alcohol and other drug abuse: Criterion validity in a primary care practice. *Wisconsin Medical Journal, 94,* 135–140.

Bush, K., Kivlahan, D. R., McDonell, M. B., Fihn, S. D., & Bradley, K. A. (1998). The AUDIT alcohol consumption questions (AUDIT-C): An effective brief screening test for problem drinking. *Archives of Internal Medicine, 158,* 1789–1795. http://dx.doi.org/10.1001/archinte.158.16.1789

Butler, R. N. (1969). Age-ism: Another form of bigotry. *Gerontologist, 9,* 243–246. http://dx.doi.org/10.1093/geront/9.4_Part_1.243

Butler, R. N. (1975). *Why survive? Being old in America.* New York, NY: Harper & Row.

Byrne, G. J., & Pachana, N. A. (2011). Development and validation of a short form of the Geriatric Anxiety Inventory—The GAI-SF. *International Psychogeriatrics, 23,* 125–131. http://dx.doi.org/10.1017/S1041610210001237

Canadian Coalition for Seniors' Mental Health. (2006). *National guidelines for seniors' mental health: The assessment of suicide risk and prevention of suicide.* Toronto, Ontario, Canada: Author.

Carmin, C., & Ownby, R. L. (2010). Assessment of anxiety in older adults. In P. A. Lichtenberg (Ed.), *Handbook of assessment in clinical gerontology* (pp. 45–60). San Diego, CA: Elsevier. http://dx.doi.org/10.1016/B978-0-12-374961-1. 10002-8

Carstensen, L. L., Isaacowitz, D. M., & Charles, S. T. (1999). Taking time seriously. A theory of socioemotional selectivity. *American Psychologist, 54*, 165–181. http://dx.doi.org/10.1037/0003-066X.54.3.165

Carstensen, L. L., Turan, B., Scheibe, S., Ram, N., Ersner-Hershfield, H., Samanez-Larkin, G. R., . . . Nesselroade, J. R. (2011). Emotional experience improves with age: Evidence based on over 10 years of experience sampling. *Psychology and Aging, 26*, 21–33. http://dx.doi.org/10.1037/a0021285

Castro, M., & Smith, G. E. (2015). Mild cognitive impairment and Alzheimer's disease. In P. A. Lichtenberg, B. T. Mast, B. D. Carpenter, & J. Loebach Wetherell (Eds.), *APA handbook of clinical geropsychology: Vol. 2. Assessment, treatment, and issues of later life* (pp. 173–207). Washington, DC: American Psychological Association. http://dx.doi.org/10.1037/14459-007

Cavanaugh, J. C., & Blanchard-Fields, F. (2015). *Adult development and aging* (7th ed.). Stamford, CT: Cengage Learning.

Cavanaugh, J. C., & Whitbourne, S. K. (2003). Research methods in adult development. In J. Demick & C. Andreoletti (Eds.), *Handbook of adult development* (pp. 85–100). New York, NY: Kluwer Academic/Plenum.

Chambless, D. L., Crits-Christoph, P., Wampold, B. E., Norcross, J. C., Lambert, M. J., Bohart, A. C., . . . Johannsen, B. E. (2006). What should be validated? In J. C. Norcross, L. E. Beutler, & R. F. Levant (Eds.), *Evidence-based practice in mental health: Debate and dialogue on the fundamental questions* (pp. 191–256). Washington, DC: American Psychological Association. http://dx.doi.org/10.1037/11265-005

Charles, S. T., & Carstensen, L. L. (2010). Social and emotional aging. *Annual Review of Psychology, 61*, 383–409. http://dx.doi.org/10.1146/annurev. psych.093008.100448

Cicirelli, V. G. (2009). Sibling death and death fear in relation to depressive symptomatology in older adults. *Journals of Gerontology: Series B. Psychological Sciences and Social Sciences, 64*, 24–32. http://dx.doi.org/10.1093/geronb/gbn024

Clark, G., Rouse, S., Spangler, H., & Moye, J. (2018). Providing mental health care for the complex older veteran: Implications for social work practice. *Health & Social Work, 43*, 7–14. http://dx.doi.org/10.1093/hsw/hlx046

Cohen, P., & Cohen, J. (1984). The clinician's illusion. *Archives of General Psychiatry, 41*, 1178–1182. http://dx.doi.org/10.1001/archpsyc.1984.01790230064010

Cohen-Mansfield, J. (2015). Behavioral and psychological symptoms of dementia. In P. A. Lichtenberg, B. T. Mast, B. D. Carpenter, & J. Loebach Wetherell (Eds.), *APA handbook of clinical geropsychology: Vol. 2. Assessment, treatment, and issues of later life* (pp. 271–317). Washington, DC: American Psychological Association.

Cole, T. R. (1984). The prophecy of senescence: G. Stanley Hall and the reconstruction of old age in America. *Gerontologist, 24,* 360–366. http://dx.doi.org/10.1093/geront/24.4.360

Cole, T. R. (1992). *The journey of life: A cultural history of aging in America.* New York, NY: Cambridge University Press.

Conwell, Y., Van Orden, K., & Caine, E. D. (2011). Suicide in older adults. *Psychiatric Clinics of North America, 34,* 451–468, ix. http://dx.doi.org/10.1016/j.psc.2011.02.002

Coon, D. W., Keaveny, M., Valverde, I. R., Dadvar, S., & Gallagher-Thompson, D. (2012). Evidence-based psychological treatments for distress in family caregivers of older adults. In F. Scogin & A. Shah (Eds.), *Making evidence-based psychological treatments work with older adults* (pp. 225–284). Washington, DC: American Psychological Association.

Craske, M. G., & Barlow, D. H. (2006). *Mastery of your anxiety and worry: Workbook* (2nd ed.). New York, NY: Oxford University Press.

Crystal, S., Olfson, M., Huang, C., Pincus, H., & Gerhard, T. (2009). Broadened use of atypical antipsychotics: Safety, effectiveness, and policy challenges. *Health Affairs, 28,* w770–w781. http://dx.doi.org/10.1377/hlthaff.28.5.w770

Cuddy, A. J. C., & Fiske, S. T. (2002). Doddering but dear: Process, content, and function in stereotyping of older persons. In T. D. Nelson (Ed.), *Ageism: Stereotyping and prejudice against older persons* (pp. 3–26). Cambridge, MA: MIT Press.

Cumming, E., & Henry, W. E. (1961). *Growing old: The process of disengagement.* New York, NY: Basic Books.

Curyto, K. J., Trevino, K. M., Ogland-Hand, S., & Lichtenberg, P. (2012). Evidence-based treatments for behavioral disturbances in long-term care. In F. Scogin & A. Shah (Eds.), *Making evidence-based psychological treatments work for older adults* (pp. 167–223). Washington, DC: American Psychological Association. http://dx.doi.org/10.1037/13753-006

Demos, V., & Jache, A. (1981). When you care enough: An analysis of attitudes toward aging in humorous birthday cards. *Gerontologist, 21,* 209–215. http://dx.doi.org/10.1093/geront/21.2.209

Depp, C. A., & Jeste, D. V. (2006). Definitions and predictors of successful aging: A comprehensive review of larger quantitative studies. *American Journal of Geriatric Psychiatry, 14,* 6–20. http://dx.doi.org/10.1097/01.JGP.0000192501.03069.bc

Depp, C. A., Vahia, I. V., & Jeste, D. V. (2012). Successful aging. In S. K. Whitbourne & M. J. Sliwinski (Eds.), *The Wiley-Blackwell handbook of adulthood and aging* (pp. 459–476). Chichester, England: Wiley-Blackwell. http://dx.doi.org/10.1002/9781118392966.ch23

De Vries, B., Davis, C. G., Wortman, C. B., & Lehman, D. R. (1997). Long-term psychological and somatic consequences of later life parental bereavement. *Omega—Journal of Death and Dying, 35,* 97–117. http://dx.doi.org/10.2190/39HG-YLKC-4CUV-NRAF

Edelstein, B. A., Bamonti, P. M., Gregg, J. J., & Gerolimatos, L. A. (2015). Depression in later life. In P. A. Lichtenberg, B. T. Mast, B. D. Carpenter, & J. Loebach Wetherell (Eds.), *APA handbook of clinical geropsychology: Vol. 2. Assessment, treatment, and issues of later life* (pp. 3–47). Washington, DC: American Psychological Association. http://dx.doi.org/10.1037/14459-001

Edelstein, B. A., Drozdick, L. W., & Ciliberti, C. M. (2010). Assessment of depression and bereavement in older adults. In P. A. Lichtenberg (Ed.), *Handbook of assessment in clinical gerontology* (2nd ed., pp. 3–43). San Diego, CA: Academic Press. http://dx.doi.org/10.1016/B978-0-12-374961-1.10001-6

Edelstein, B. A., Woodhead, E. L., Segal, D. L., Heisel, M. J., Bower, E. H., Lowery, A. J., & Stoner, S. S. (2007). Older adult psychological assessment: Current instrument status and related considerations. *Clinical Gerontologist, 31,* 1–35. http://dx.doi.org/10.1080/07317110802072108

Erikson, E. H. (1959). *Identity and the life cycle: Selected papers.* New York, NY: International Universities Press.

Erikson, E. H., & Erikson, J. M. (1998). *The life cycle completed.* New York, NY: Norton.

Ewing, J. A. (1984). Detecting alcoholism. The CAGE questionnaire. *JAMA, 252,* 1905–1907. http://dx.doi.org/10.1001/jama.1984.03350140051025

Federal Interagency Forum on Aging-Related Statistics. (n.d.). *Population aging in the United States: A global perspective.* Retrieved from https://agingstats.gov/images/olderamericans_agingpopulation.pdf

Federal Interagency Forum on Aging-Related Statistics. (2016). *Older Americans 2016: Key indicators of well-being.* Retrieved from https://agingstats.gov/docs/LatestReport/Older-Americans-2016-Key-Indicators-of-WellBeing.pdf

Fiske, A., Smith, M. D., & Price, E. C. (2015). Suicidal behavior in older adults. In P. A. Lichtenberg, B. T. Mast, B. D. Carpenter, J. Loebach Wetherell (Eds.), *APA handbook of clinical geropsychology: Vol. 2. Assessment, treatment, and issues of later life* (pp. 145–172). Washington, DC: American Psychological Association. http://dx.doi.org/10.1037/14459-006

Fiske, A., Wetherell, J. L., & Gatz, M. (2009). Depression in older adults. *Annual Review of Clinical Psychology, 5,* 363–389. http://dx.doi.org/10.1146/annurev.clinpsy.032408.153621

Folstein, M. F., Folstein, S. E., & McHugh, P. R. (1975). "Mini-mental state": A practical method for grading the cognitive state of patients for the clinician. *Journal of Psychiatric Research, 12,* 189–198. http://dx.doi.org/10.1016/0022-3956(75)90026-6

Freud, S. (1923). *Das Ich und das Es* [The ego and the id]. Vienna, Austria: Internationaler Psychoanalytischer Verlag.

Freund, A. M., & Baltes, P. B. (2002). The adaptiveness of selection, optimization, and compensation as strategies of life management: Evidence from a preference study on proverbs. *Journals of Gerontology: Series B. Psychological Sciences and Social Sciences, 57,* P426–P434. http://dx.doi.org/10.1093/geronb/57.5.P426

Fry, P. S. (1997). Grandparents' reactions to the death of a grandchild: An exploratory factor analysis. *Omega—Journal of Death and Dying, 35,* 119–140. http://dx.doi.org/10.2190/4FMB-ELX3-JUUD-2RU0

Fulmer, T., Paveza, G., Abraham, I., & Fairchild, S. (2000). Elder neglect assessment in the emergency department. *Journal of Emergency Nursing, 26,* 436–443. http://dx.doi.org/10.1067/men.2000.110621

Galambos, C. M., Greene, R. R., Kropf, N. P., & Cohen, H. L. (2018). *Foundations of social work practice in the field of aging: A competency-based approach* (2nd ed.). Washington, DC: NASW Press.

Gallagher-Thompson, D., & Steffen, A. M. (1994). Comparative effects of cognitive-behavioral and brief psychodynamic psychotherapies for depressed family caregivers. *Journal of Consulting and Clinical Psychology, 62,* 543–549. http://dx.doi.org/10.1037/0022-006X.62.3.543

Gatz, M., & Pearson, C. G. (1988). Ageism revised and the provision of psychological services. *American Psychologist, 43,* 184–188. http://dx.doi.org/10.1037/0003-066X.43.3.184

George, L. K. (1993). Sociological perspectives on life transitions. *Annual Review of Sociology, 19,* 353–373. http://dx.doi.org/10.1146/annurev.so.19.080193.002033

Gerolimatos, L. A., Gregg, J. J., & Edelstein, B. A. (2014). Interviewing older adults. In N. A. Pachana & K. Laidlaw (Eds.), *The Oxford handbook of clinical geropsychology* (pp. 163–183). Oxford, England: Oxford University Press.

Gerontological Society of America. (2012). *Communicating with older adults: An evidence-based review of what really works.* Available from https://www.geron.org/publications/communicating-with-older-adults

Gerontological Society of America. (2017). *KAER Toolkit: 4-step process to detecting cognitive impairment and earlier diagnosis of dementia—Approaches and tools for primary care providers.* Retrieved from https://www.geron.org/programs-services/alliances-and-multi-stakeholder-collaborations/cognitive-impairment-detection-and-earlier-diagnosis

Ghaed, S. G., Ayers, C. R., & Wetherell, J. L. (2012). Evidence-based psychological treatments for geriatric anxiety. In F. Scogin & A. Shah (Eds.), *Making evidence-based psychological treatments work for older adults* (pp. 9–46). Washington, DC: American Psychological Association. http://dx.doi.org/10.1037/13753-002

Gonçalves, D. C., Pachana, N. A., & Byrne, G. J. (2011). Prevalence and correlates of generalized anxiety disorder among older adults in the Australian National Survey of Mental Health and Well-Being. *Journal of Affective Disorders, 132,* 223–230. http://dx.doi.org/10.1016/j.jad.2011.02.023

Grabovich, A., Lu, N., Tang, W., Tu, X., & Lyness, J. M. (2010). Outcomes of subsyndromal depression in older primary care patients. *American Journal of Geriatric Psychiatry, 18,* 227–235. http://dx.doi.org/10.1097/JGP.0b013e3181cb87d6

Graham, R. D., Rudd, M. D., & Bryan, C. J. (2011). Primary care providers' views regarding assessing and treating suicidal patients. *Suicide and Life-Threatening Behavior, 41,* 614–623. http://dx.doi.org/10.1111/j.1943-278X.2011.00058.x

Griffin, P. W., Mroczek, D. K., & Wesbecher, K. (2015). Personality development across the lifespan: Theory, research, and application. In P. A. Lichtenberg, B. T. Mast, B. D. Carpenter, & J. Loebach Wetherell (Eds.), *APA handbook of clinical geropsychology: Vol. 1. History and status of the field and perspectives on aging* (pp. 217–234). Washington, DC: American Psychological Association.

Gum, A. M., Areán, P. A., Hunkeler, E., Tang, L., Katon, W., Hitchcock, P., . . . Unützer, J. (2006). Depression treatment preferences in older primary care patients. *Gerontologist, 46,* 14–22. http://dx.doi.org/10.1093/geront/46.1.14

Gum, A. M., King-Kallimanis, B., & Kohn, R. (2009). Prevalence of mood, anxiety, and substance-abuse disorders for older Americans in the national comorbidity survey-replication. *American Journal of Geriatric Psychiatry, 17,* 769–781. http://dx.doi.org/10.1097/JGP.0b013e3181ad4f5a

Hacker, J. S. (2008). *The great risk shift: The new economic insecurity and the decline of the American dream.* New York, NY: Oxford University Press.

Haighton, C. (2016). Thinking behind alcohol consumption in old age: Psychological and sociological reasons for drinking in old age. In A. Kuerbis, A. A. Moore, P. Sacco, & F. Zanjani (Eds.), *Alcohol and aging* (pp. 3–16). Cham, Switzerland: Springer. http://dx.doi.org/10.1007/978-3-319-47233-1_1

Hall, G. S. (1922). *Senescence: The last half of life.* New York, NY: Appleton.

Hamilton, M. (1960). A rating scale for depression. *Journal of Neurology, Neurosurgery, & Psychiatry, 23,* 56–62. http://dx.doi.org/10.1136/jnnp.23.1.56

Hartman-Stein, P. E., & Georgoulakis, J. M. (2008). How Medicare shapes behavioral health practice in older adults in the U.S.: Issues and recommendations for practitioners. In D. G. Gallagher-Thompson, A. M. Steffen, & L. W. Thompson (Eds.), *Handbook of behavioral and cognitive therapies with older adults* (pp. 323–334). New York, NY: Springer. http://dx.doi.org/10.1007/978-0-387-72007-4_21

Havinghurst, R. J. (1961). Successful aging. *Gerontologist, 1,* 8–13. http://dx.doi.org/10.1093/geront/1.1.8

Hayslip, B., Maiden, R. J., Page, K. S., & Dolbin-MacNab, M. L. (2015). Grandparenting. In P. A. Lichtenberg, B. T. Mast, B. D. Carpenter, & J. Loebach Wetherell (Eds.), *APA handbook of clinical geropsychology: Vol. 2. Assessment, treatment, and issues of later life* (pp. 497–511). Washington, DC: American Psychological Association.

He, W., Goodkind, D., & Kowal, P. (2016). *An aging world: 2015* (International Population Reports No. P95/16-1). Retrieved from U.S. Census Bureau website: https://www.census.gov/content/dam/Census/library/publications/2016/demo/p95-16-1.pdf

Heinik, J. (2010). V. A. Kral and the origins of benign senescent forgetfulness and mild cognitive impairment. *International Psychogeriatrics, 22,* 395–402. http://dx.doi.org/10.1017/S1041610209991682

Heisel, M. J., & Flett, G. L. (2006). The development and initial validation of the geriatric suicide ideation scale. *American Journal of Geriatric Psychiatry, 14,* 742–751. http://dx.doi.org/10.1097/01.JGP.0000218699.27899.f9

Hess, T. M., & Auman, C. (2001). Aging and social expertise: The impact of trait-diagnostic information on impressions of others. *Psychology and Aging, 16,* 497–510. http://dx.doi.org/10.1037/0882-7974.16.3.497

Hicks, C. L., von Baeyer, C. L., Spafford, P. A., van Korlaar, I., & Goodenough, B. (2001). The Faces Pain Scale—Revised: Toward a common metric in pediatric pain measurement. *Pain, 93,* 173–183. http://dx.doi.org/10.1016/S0304-3959(01)00314-1

Hillman, J. (2012). *Sexuality and aging: Clinical perspectives.* New York, NY: Springer. http://dx.doi.org/10.1007/978-1-4614-3399-6

Hillman, J., & Hinrichsen, G. A. (2014). Promoting an affirming and competent practice with older lesbian and gay adults. *Professional Psychology: Research and Practice, 45,* 269–277. http://dx.doi.org/10.1037/a0037172

Hinrichsen, G. A. (1985). The impact of age-concentrated, publicly assisted housing on older people's social and emotional well-being. *Journal of Gerontology, 40,* 758–760. http://dx.doi.org/10.1093/geronj/40.6.758

Hinrichsen, G. A. (2008). Interpersonal psychotherapy as a treatment for depression in late life. *Professional Psychology: Research and Practice, 39,* 306–312. http://dx.doi.org/10.1037/0735-7028.39.3.306

Hinrichsen, G. A. (2010). Public policy and the provision of psychological services to older adults. *Professional Psychology: Research and Practice, 41,* 97–103. http://dx.doi.org/10.1037/a0018643

Hinrichsen, G. A., & Clougherty, K. F. (2006). *Interpersonal psychotherapy for depressed older adults.* Washington, DC: American Psychological Association.

Hinrichsen, G. A., Emery-Tiburcio, E., Gooblar, J., & Molinari, V. M. (2018). Building foundational knowledge competencies in professional geropsychology: Council of Professional Geropsychology Training Programs (CoPGTP) recommendations. *Clinical Psychology: Science and Practice, 25,* e12236. http://dx.doi.org/10.1111/cpsp.12236

Hinrichsen, G. A., Kietzman, K. G., Alkema, G. E., Bragg, E. J., Hensel, B. K., Miles, T. P., . . . Zerzan, J. (2010). Influencing public policy to improve the lives of older Americans. *Gerontologist, 50,* 735–743. http://dx.doi.org/10.1093/geront/gnq034

Hoge, M. A., Karel, M. J., Zeiss, A. M., Alegria, M., & Moye, J. (2015). Strengthening psychology's workforce for older adults: Implications of the Institute of Medicine's report to Congress. *American Psychologist, 70,* 265–278. http://dx.doi.org/10.1037/a0038927

Holt-Lunstad, J. (2017). The potential public health relevance of social isolation and loneliness: Prevalence, epidemiology, and risk factors. *Public Policy & Aging Report, 27,* 127–130. http://dx.doi.org/10.1093/ppar/prx030

Hummert, M. L., Garstka, T. A., Shaner, J. L., & Strahm, S. (1994). Stereotypes of the elderly held by young, middle-aged, and elderly adults. *Journals of*

Gerontology: Series B. Psychological Sciences and Social Sciences, 49, P240–P249. http://dx.doi.org/10.1093/geronj/49.5.P240

Inouye, S. K., van Dyck, C. H., Alessi, C. A., Balkin, S., Siegal, A. P., & Horwitz, R. I. (1990). Clarifying confusion: The confusion assessment method: A new method for detection of delirium. *Annals of Internal Medicine, 113,* 941–948. http://dx.doi.org/10.7326/0003-4819-113-12-941

Institute of Medicine. (2008). *Retooling for an aging America: Building the health care workforce.* Washington, DC: National Academies Press.

Institute of Medicine. (2012). *The mental health and substance use workforce for older adults: In whose hands?* Washington, DC: National Academies Press.

Interprofessional Education Collaborative. (2016). *Core competencies for interprofessional collaborative practice: 2016 update.* Retrieved from https://www.ipecollaborative.org/resources.html

Iversen, T. N., Larsen, L., & Solem, P. E. (2009). A conceptual analysis of ageism. *Nordic Psychology, 61*(3), 4–22. http://dx.doi.org/10.1027/1901-2276.61.3.4

Jacox, A., Carr, D. B., & Payne, R. (1994). New clinical-practice guidelines for the management of pain in patients with cancer. *The New England Journal of Medicine, 330,* 651–655. http://dx.doi.org/10.1056/NEJM199403033300926

Jaffe, I. (2014, June). *NPR survey reveals despised and acceptable terms for aging.* Retrieved from https://www.npr.org/2014/07/08/329731428/npr-poll-reveals-despised-and-acceptable-terms-for-aging

James, J. W., & Haley, W. E. (1995). Age and health bias in practicing clinical psychologists. *Psychology and Aging, 10,* 610–616. http://dx.doi.org/10.1037/0882-7974.10.4.610

Jin, K. (2010). Modern biological theories of aging. *Aging and Disease, 1,* 72–74.

Johns, M. W. (1991). A new method for measuring daytime sleepiness: The Epworth Sleepiness Scale. *Sleep, 14,* 540–545. http://dx.doi.org/10.1093/sleep/14.6.540

Joiner, T. E., Jr., & Katz, J. (1999). Contagion of depressive symptoms and mood: Meta-analytic review and explanations from cognitive, behavioral, and interpersonal viewpoints. *Clinical Psychology: Science and Practice, 6*(2), 149–164. http://dx.doi.org/10.1093/clipsy.6.2.149

Karel, M. J. (2011). Ethics. In V. Molinari (Ed.), *Specialty competencies in geropsychology* (pp. 115–142). New York, NY: Oxford University Press.

Karel, M. J., Gatz, M., & Smyer, M. A. (2012). Aging and mental health in the decade ahead: What psychologists need to know. *American Psychologist, 67,* 184–198. http://dx.doi.org/10.1037/a0025393

Karel, M. J., Holley, C. K., Whitbourne, S. K., Segal, D. L., Tazeau, Y. N., Emery, E. E., . . . Zweig, R. A. (2012). Preliminary validation of a tool to assess competencies for professional geropsychology practice. *Professional Psychology: Research and Practice, 43,* 110–117. http://dx.doi.org/10.1037/a0025788

Karel, M. J., Teri, L., McConnell, E., Visnic, S., & Karlin, B. E. (2016). Effectiveness of expanded implementation of STAR-VA for managing dementia-related behaviors among veterans. *Gerontologist, 56,* 126–134. http://dx.doi.org/10.1093/geront/gnv068

Karlin, B. E., Ruzek, J. I., Chard, K. M., Eftekhari, A., Monson, C. M., Hembree, E. A., . . . Foa, E. B. (2010). Dissemination of evidence-based psychological treatments for posttraumatic stress disorder in the Veterans Health Administration. *Journal of Traumatic Stress, 23,* 663–673. http://dx.doi.org/10.1002/jts.20588

Kastenbaum, R. (1964). The reluctant therapist. In R. Kastenbaum (Ed.), *New thoughts on old age* (pp. 139–145). New York, NY: Springer. http://dx.doi.org/10.1007/978-3-662-38534-0_9

Katz, S., Downs, T. D., Cash, H. R., & Grotz, R. C. (1970). Progress in development of the index of ADL. *Gerontologist, 10,* 20–30. http://dx.doi.org/10.1093/geront/10.1_Part_1.20

Kaye, L. W. (2017). Older adults, rural living, and the escalating risk of social isolation. *Public Policy and Aging Report, 27,* 139–144. http://dx.doi.org/10.1093/ppar/prx029

Keller, M. B., & Shapiro, R. W. (1982). "Double depression": Superimposition of acute depressive episodes on chronic depressive disorders. *American Journal of Psychiatry, 139,* 438–442. http://dx.doi.org/10.1176/ajp.139.4.438

Kingson, E. R., & Checksfield, M. W. (2015). Advancing a retirement income security agenda for all generations. *Public Policy and Aging Report, 25,* 47–51. http://dx.doi.org/10.1093/ppar/prv005

Kite, M. E., Stockdale, G. D., Whitley, B. E., & Johnson, B. T. (2005). Attitudes toward young and older adults: An updated meta-analytic review. *Journal of Social Issues, 61,* 241–266. http://dx.doi.org/10.1111/j.1540-4560.2005.00404.x

Kite, M. E., & Wagner, L. S. (2002). Attitudes toward older adults. In T. D. Nelson (Ed.), *Ageism: Stereotyping and prejudice against older persons* (pp. 129–161). Cambridge, MA: MIT Press.

Knight, B. G. (2018). Commentary on "Building foundational knowledge competencies in professional geropsychology." *Clinical Psychology: Science and Practice, 25,* e12239. http://dx.doi.org/10.1111/cpsp.12239

Knight, B. G., Karel, M. J., Hinrichsen, G. A., Qualls, S. H., & Duffy, M. (2009). Pikes Peak model for training in professional geropsychology. *American Psychologist, 64,* 205–214. http://dx.doi.org/10.1037/a0015059

Knight, B. G., & Pachana, N. A. (2015). *Psychological assessment and treatment with older adults.* Oxford, England: Oxford University Press. http://dx.doi.org/10.1093/med:psych/9780199652532.001.0001

Kotlikoff, L. J., Moeller, P., & Solman, P. (2016). *Get what's yours: The secrets to maxing out your Social Security* (Rev. ed.). New York, NY: Simon & Schuster.

Krause, N., & Hayward, R. D. (2015). Social perspectives: Support, social relations, and well-being. In P. A. Lichtenberg, B. T. Mast, B. D. Carpenter, & J. Loebach Wetherell (Eds.), *APA handbook of clinical geropsychology: Vol. 1.*

History and status of the field and perspectives on aging (pp. 259–299). Washington, DC: American Psychological Association.

Kroenke, K., Spitzer, R. L., & Williams, J. B. W. (2001). The PHQ-9: Validity of a brief depression severity measure. *Journal of General Internal Medicine, 16,* 606–613. http://dx.doi.org/10.1046/j.1525-1497.2001.016009606.x

Kuerbis, A., Sacco, P., Blazer, D. G., & Moore, A. A. (2014). Substance abuse among older adults. *Clinics in Geriatric Medicine, 30,* 629–654. http://dx.doi.org/10.1016/j.cger.2014.04.008

La Rue, A., & Watson, J. (1998). Psychological assessment of older adults. *Professional Psychology: Research and Practice, 29,* 5–14. http://dx.doi.org/10.1037/0735-7028.29.1.5

Langa, K. M., & Levine, D. A. (2014). The diagnosis and management of mild cognitive impairment: A clinical review. *JAMA, 312,* 2551–2561. http://dx.doi.org/10.1001/jama.2014.13806

Lawton, M. P. (1990). Residential environment and self-directedness among older people. *American Psychologist, 45,* 638–640. http://dx.doi.org/10.1037/0003-066X.45.5.638

Lawton, M. P., & Brody, E. M. (1969). Assessment of older people: Self-maintaining and instrumental activities of daily living. *Gerontologist, 9,* 179–186. http://dx.doi.org/10.1093/geront/9.3_Part_1.179

Lawton, M. P., & Cohen, J. (1974). The generality of housing impact on the well-being of older people. *Journal of Gerontology, 29,* 194–204. http://dx.doi.org/10.1093/geronj/29.2.194

Lee, G. R., & Shehan, C. L. (1989). Retirement and marital satisfaction. *Journal of Gerontology, 44,* S226–S230. http://dx.doi.org/10.1093/geronj/44.6.S226

Levinson, D. J. (1986). A conception of adult development. *American Psychologist, 41,* 3–13. http://dx.doi.org/10.1037/0003-066X.41.1.3

Levy, B. R. (2001). Eradication of ageism requires addressing the enemy within. *Gerontologist, 41,* 578–579. http://dx.doi.org/10.1093/geront/41.5.578

Levy, B. R. (2009). Stereotype embodiment: A psychosocial approach to aging. *Current Directions in Psychological Science, 18,* 332–336. http://dx.doi.org/10.1111/j.1467-8721.2009.01662.x

Levy, B. R., Zonderman, A. B., Slade, M. D., & Ferrucci, L. (2009). Age stereotypes held earlier in life predict cardiovascular events in later life. *Psychological Science, 20,* 296–298. http://dx.doi.org/10.1111/j.1467-9280.2009.02298.x

Lewin, K. (1951). *Field theory in social science.* Chicago, IL: University of Chicago Press.

Lichtenberg, P. A. (2010). Introduction. In P. A. Lichtenberg (Ed.), *Handbook of assessment in clinical gerontology* (2nd ed.; pp. xi–xvii). San Diego, CA: Academic Press.

Luoma, J. B., Martin, C. E., & Pearson, J. L. (2002). Contact with mental health and primary care providers before suicide: A review of the evidence. *American Journal of Psychiatry, 159,* 909–916. http://dx.doi.org/10.1176/appi.ajp.159.6.909

Luong, G., Charles, S. T., & Fingerman, K. L. (2011). Better with age: Social relationships across adulthood. *Journal of Social and Personal Relationships, 28,* 9–23. http://dx.doi.org/10.1177/0265407510391362

Magai, C. M. (2001). Emotions over the lifespan. In J. E. Birren & K. W. Schaie (Eds.), *Handbook of the psychology of aging* (5th ed., pp. 399–426). San Diego, CA: Academic Press.

Markus, H., & Nurius, P. (1986). Possible selves. *American Psychologist, 41,* 954–969. http://dx.doi.org/10.1037/0003-066X.41.9.954

Mast, B. T., & Gerstenecker, A. (2010). Screening instruments and brief batteries for dementia. In P. A. Lichtenberg (Ed.), *Handbook of assessment in clinical gerontology* (pp. 503–530). San Diego, CA: Elsevier. http://dx.doi.org/10.1016/B978-0-12-374961-1.10019-3

Mast, B. T., & Yochim, B. T. (2018). *Alzheimer's disease and dementia.* Boston, MA: Hogrefe.

McCann, R., & Giles, H. (2002). Ageism in the workplace: A communication perspective. In T. D. Nelson (Ed.), *Ageism: Stereotyping and prejudice against older persons* (pp. 163–199). Cambridge, MA: MIT Press.

McCombe, G., Fogarty, F., Swan, D., Hannigan, A., Fealy, G. M., Kyne, L., . . . Cullen, W. (2018). Identified mental disorders in older adults in primary care: A cross-sectional database study. *European Journal of General Practice, 24,* 84–91. http://dx.doi.org/10.1080/13814788.2017.1402884

McCrae, C. S., Roth, A. J., Zamora, R., Dautovich, N. D., & Lichstein, K. L. (2015). Late-life sleep and sleep disorders. In P. A. Lichtenberg, B. T. Mast, B. D. Carpenter, & J. Loebach Wetherell (Eds.), *APA handbook of clinical geropsychology: Vol. 2. Assessment, treatment, and issue of later life* (pp. 369–394). Washington, DC: American Psychological Association. http://dx.doi.org/10.1037/14459-014

McCrae, R. R., & Costa, P. T., Jr. (2008). The five-factor theory of personality. In O. P. John, R. W. Robins, & L. A. Pervin (Eds.), *Handbook of personality: Theory and research* (3rd ed., pp. 159–181). New York, NY: Guilford Press.

McCurry, S. M., Logsdon, R. G., Teri, L., & Vitiello, M. V. (2007). Evidence-based psychological treatments for insomnia in older adults. *Psychology and Aging, 22,* 18–27. http://dx.doi.org/10.1037/0882-7974.22.1.18

McDonald, W. M., & Vahabzadeh, A. (2013). Electroconvulsive therapy and neuromodulation in the treatment of late-life mood disorders. In H. Lavretsky, M. Sajatovic, & C. F. Reynolds, III (Eds.), *Late-life mood disorders* (pp. 406–431). New York, NY: Oxford University Press.

Mental health: Does therapy help? (1995, November). *Consumer Reports,* 734–739.

Miller, M. D. (2009). *Clinician's guide to interpersonal psychotherapy in late life: Helping cognitively impaired or depressed elders and their caregivers.* New York, NY: Oxford University Press. http://dx.doi.org/10.1093/med:psych/9780195382242.001.0001

Miloyan, B., Byrne, G. J., & Pachana, N. A. (2014). Late-life anxiety. In N. A. Pachana & K. Laidlaw (Eds.), *The Oxford handbook of clinical geropsychology* (pp. 470–489). Oxford, England: Oxford University Press.

Moeller, P. (2016). *Get what's yours for Medicare: Maximize your coverage, minimize your costs.* Waterville, ME: Thorndike Press.

Mohlman, J., Sirota, K. G., Papp, L. A., Staples, A. M., King, A., & Gorenstein, E. E. (2012). Clinical interviewing with older adults. *Cognitive and Behavioral Practice, 19,* 89–100. http://dx.doi.org/10.1016/j.cbpra.2010.10.001

Montross, L. P., Depp, C., Daly, J., Reichstadt, J., Golshan, S., Moore, D., . . . Jeste, D. V. (2006). Correlates of self-rated successful aging among community-dwelling older adults. *American Journal of Geriatric Psychiatry, 14,* 43–51. http://dx.doi.org/10.1097/01.JGP.0000192489.43179.31

Moore, A. A., Karno, M. P., Grella, C. E., Lin, J. C., Warda, U., Liao, D. H., & Hu, P. (2009). Alcohol, tobacco, and nonmedical drug use in older U.S. adults: Data from the 2001/02 national epidemiologic survey of alcohol and related conditions. *Journal of the American Geriatrics Society, 57,* 2275–2281. http://dx.doi.org/10.1111/j.1532-5415.2009.02554.x

Moore, A. A., Kuerbis, A., Sacco, P., Chen, G. I., & Garcia, M. B. (2016). Screening and assessment of unhealthy alcohol use in older adults. In A. Kuerbis, A. A. Moore, P. Sacco, & F. Zanjani (Eds.), *Alcohol and aging* (pp. 169–180). Cham, Switzerland: Springer. http://dx.doi.org/10.1007/978-3-319-47233-1_11

Mosqueda, L., & Olsen, B. (2015). Elder abuse and neglect. In P. A. Lichtenberg, B. T. Mast, B. D. Carpenter, & J. Loebach Wetherell (Eds.), *APA handbook of clinical geropsychology: Vol. 2. Assessment, treatment, and issues of later life* (pp. 667–686). Washington, DC: American Psychological Association. http://dx.doi.org/10.1037/14459-026

Mroczek, D. K., Spiro, A., & Griffin, P. W. (2006). Personality and aging. In J. E. Birren, K. W. Schaie, R. R. Abeles, M. Gatz, & T. Salthouse (Eds.), *Handbook of the psychology of aging* (6th ed., pp. 363–377). San Diego, CA: Elsevier. http://dx.doi.org/10.1016/B978-012101264-9/50019-7

Mueller, A. E., Segal, D. L., Gavett, B., Marty, M. A., Yochim, B., June, A., & Coolidge, F. L. (2015). Geriatric Anxiety Scale: Item response theory analysis, differential item functioning, and creation of a ten-item short form (GAS-10). *International Psychogeriatrics, 27,* 1099–1111. http://dx.doi.org/10.1017/S1041610214000210

Munk, K. P. (2014). Transitions in later life. In N. A. Pachana & K. Laidlaw (Eds.), *The Oxford handbook of clinical geropsychology* (pp. 144–160). Oxford, England: Oxford University Press.

Nasreddine, Z. S., Phillips, N. A., Bédirian, V., Charbonneau, S., Whitehead, V., Collin, I., . . . Chertkow, H. (2005). The Montreal Cognitive Assessment, MoCA: A brief screening tool for mild cognitive impairment. *Journal of the American Geriatrics Society, 53,* 695–699. http://dx.doi.org/10.1111/j.1532-5415.2005.53221.x

National Center for Health Statistics. (2011). *Health, United States, 2010: With special feature on death and dying* (DHHS Pub No. 2011-1232). Hyattsville, MD: U.S. Department of Health and Human Services, Centers for Disease Control and Prevention, and National Center for Health Statistics.

National Institute on Aging. (n.d.). *Health topics: A–Z.* Retrieved from https://www.nia.nih.gov/health/topics

National Institute on Aging. (2016). *Aging well in the 21st century: Strategic directions for research on aging.* Retrieved from https://www.nia.nih.gov/sites/default/files/2017-07/nia-strategic-directions-2016.pdf

National Institute on Alcohol Abuse and Alcoholism. (n.d.). Alcohol and your health: Older adults. Retrieved from https://www.niaaa.nih.gov/alcohol-health/special-populations-co-occurring-disorders/older-adults

Neimeyer, R. A., & Holland, J. M. (2015). Bereavement in later life: Theory, assessment, and intervention. In P. A. Lichtenberg, B. T. Mast, B. D. Carpenter, & J. Loebach Wetherell (Eds.), *APA handbook of clinical geropsychology: Vol. 2. Assessment, treatment, and issues of later life* (pp. 645–666). Washington, DC: American Psychological Association.

Nelson, T. D. (2005). Ageism: Prejudice against our feared future self. *Journal of Social Issues, 61,* 207–221. http://dx.doi.org/10.1111/j.1540-4560.2005.00402.x

Nelson, T. D. (2011). Ageism: The strange case of prejudice against the older you. In R. L. Wiener & S. L. Willborn (Eds.), *Disability and aging discrimination: Perspectives in law and psychology* (pp. 37–47). New York, NY: Springer. http://dx.doi.org/10.1007/978-1-4419-6293-5_2

Neugarten, B. L. (Ed.). (1968). *Middle age and aging.* Chicago, IL: University of Chicago Press.

Neugarten, B. L. (1982). *Age or need? Public policies for older people.* Beverley Hills, CA: Sage.

Ng, S. H. (2002). Will families support their elders? Answers from across cultures. In T. D. Nelson (Ed.), *Ageism: Stereotyping and prejudice against older persons* (pp. 295–309). Cambridge, MA: MIT Press.

Norris, M. P. (2015). Evolutions and revolutions in Medicare policy and reimbursement of geropsychology services. In P. A. Lichtenberg, B. T. Mast, B. D. Carpenter, & J. Loebach Wetherell (Eds.), *APA handbook of clinical geropsychology: Vol. 1. History and status of the field and perspectives on aging* (pp. 45–69). Washington, DC: American Psychological Association. http://dx.doi.org/10.1037/14458-004

North, M. S., & Fiske, S. T. (2015). Modern attitudes toward older adults in the aging world: A cross-cultural meta-analysis. *Psychological Bulletin, 141,* 993–1021. http://dx.doi.org/10.1037/a0039469

Nyenhuis, D. (2015). Vascular cognitive impairment. In P. A. Lichtenberg, B. T. Mast, B. D. Carpenter, & J. Loebach Wetherell (Eds.), *APA handbook of clinical geropsychology: Vol. 2. Assessment, treatment, and issues of later life* (pp. 209–226). Washington, DC: American Psychological Association. http://dx.doi.org/10.1037/14459-008

Older Americans Act of 1965, Pub. L. 89-73, 79 Stat. 218, 42 U.S.C. §§ 3001–3058ff.

O'Shaughnessy, C. (2011). *The aging services network: Serving a vulnerable and growing elderly population in tough economic times* (Background Paper No. 83). Washington, DC: National Health Policy Forum. Retrieved from the George Washington University website: https://hsrc.himmelfarb.gwu.edu/sphhs_centers_nhpf/251

Pachana, N. A., Byrne, G. J., Siddle, H., Koloski, N., Harley, E., & Arnold, E. (2007). Development and validation of the geriatric anxiety inventory. *International Psychogeriatrics, 19,* 103–114. http://dx.doi.org/10.1017/S1041610206003504

Palmore, E. B. (1988). *The facts on aging quiz: A handbook of uses and results.* New York, NY: Springer.

Pasupathi, M., & Löckenhoff, C. E. (2002). Ageist behavior. In T. D. Nelson (Ed.), *Ageism: Stereotyping and prejudice against older persons* (pp. 201–246). Cambridge, MA: MIT Press.

Perlis, M. L., Jungquist, C., Smith, M. T., & Posner, D. (2008). *Cognitive behavioral therapy of insomnia: A session-by-session guide.* New York, NY: Springer.

Petkus, A. J., Reynolds, C. A., Wetherell, J. L., Kremen, W. S., Pedersen, N. L., & Gatz, M. (2016). Anxiety is associated with increased risk of dementia in older Swedish twins. *Alzheimer's & Dementia, 12,* 399–406. http://dx.doi.org/10.1016/j.jalz.2015.09.008

Plassman, B. L., Langa, K. M., Fisher, G. G., Heeringa, S. G., Weir, D. R., Ofstedal, M. B., . . . Wallace, R. B. (2008). Prevalence of cognitive impairment without dementia in the United States. *Annals of Internal Medicine, 148,* 427–434. http://dx.doi.org/10.7326/0003-4819-148-6-200803180-00005

Portacolone, E. (2017). Structural factors of elders' isolation in a high-crime neighborhood: An in-depth perspective. *Public Policy & Aging Report, 27,* 152–155. http://dx.doi.org/10.1093/ppar/prx025

Prigerson, H. G., Horowitz, M. J., Jacobs, S. C., Parkes, C. M., Aslan, M., Goodkin, K., . . . Maciejewski, P. K. (2009). Prolonged grief disorder: Psychometric validation criteria proposed for *DSM–V* and *ICD–11. PLoS Medicine, 6,* e1000121. http://dx.doi.org/10.1371/journal.pmed.1000121 (Erratum published 2013, *PLoS Medicine, 10.* http://dx.doi.org/10.1371/annotation/a1d91e0d-981f-4674-926c-0fbd2463b5ea)

Qualls, S. H., Segal, D. L., Norman, S., Niederehe, G., & Gallagher-Thompson, D. (2002). Psychologists in practice with older adults: Current patterns, sources of training, and need for continuing education. *Professional Psychology: Research and Practice, 33,* 435–442. http://dx.doi.org/10.1037/0735-7028.33.5.435

Radloff, L. S. (1977). The CES-D scale: A self-report depression scale for research in the general population. *Applied Psychological Measurement, 1,* 385–401. http://dx.doi.org/10.1177/014662167700100306

Rebok, G. W., Parisi, J. M., Gross, A. L., Spira, A. P., Ko, J., Samus, Q. M., & Holtzman, R. E. (2012). Evidence-based psychological treatments for improving memory function in older adults. In F. R. Scogin and A. Shah (Eds.), *Making evidence-based psychological treatments work for older adults* (pp. 131–165). Washington, DC: American Psychological Association.

Resick, P. A., Monson, C. M., & Chard, K. M. (2016). *Cognitive processing therapy: A comprehensive manual.* New York, NY: Guilford Press.

Rix, S. E. (2006). Work in the new retirement. *Public Policy and Aging Report, 16*(3), 9–15. http://dx.doi.org/10.1093/ppar/16.3.9

Roberto, K. A., & Blieszner, R. (2015). Diverse family structures and the care of older persons. *Canadian Journal on Aging, 34,* 305–320. http://dx.doi.org/10.1017/S0714980815000288

Roberto, K. A., & Weaver, R. H. (2019). Late-life families. In B. H. Fiese, M. Celano, K. Deater-Deckard, E. N. Jouriles, & M. A. Whisman (Eds.), *APA handbook of contemporary family psychology: Foundations, methods, and contemporary issues across the lifespan* (pp. 631–647). Washington, DC: American Psychological Association. http://dx.doi.org/10.1037/0000099-035

Rook, K. S., & Charles, S. T. (2017). Close social ties and health in later life: Strengths and vulnerabilities. *American Psychologist, 72,* 567–577. http://dx.doi.org/10.1037/amp0000104

Rosenzweig, A., Prigerson, H., Miller, M. D., & Reynolds, C. F., III. (1997). Bereavement and late-life depression: Grief and its complications in the elderly. *Annual Review of Medicine, 48,* 421–428. http://dx.doi.org/10.1146/annurev.med.48.1.421

Rosow, I. (1976). Status and role change through the life span. In R. H. Binstock & E. Shanas (Eds.), *Handbook of aging and the social sciences* (pp. 457–482). New York, NY: Van Nostrand Reinhold.

Rowe, J. W., & Kahn, R. L. (1998). *Successful aging.* New York, NY: Pantheon Books.

Ryerson, M. L. (2017). Innovations in social connectedness. *Public Policy and Aging Report, 27,* 124–126. http://dx.doi.org/10.1093/ppar/prx031

Ryff, C. D. (1991). Possible selves in adulthood and old age: A tale of shifting horizons. *Psychology and Aging, 6,* 286–295. http://dx.doi.org/10.1037/0882-7974.6.2.286

Sachdev, P. S., Mohan, A., Taylor, L., & Jeste, D. V. (2015). *DSM–5* and mental disorders in older individuals: An overview. *Harvard Review of Psychiatry, 23,* 320–328. http://dx.doi.org/10.1097/HRP0000000000000090

Satre, D. D., & Wolf, J. P. (2015). Alcohol abuse and substance misuse in later life. In P. A. Lichtenberg, B. T. Mast, B. D. Carpenter, & J. Loebach Wetherell (Eds.), *APA handbook of clinical geropsychology: Vol. 2. Assessment, treatment, and issue of later life* (pp. 121–144). Washington, DC: American Psychological Association. http://dx.doi.org/10.1037/14459-005

Schaie, K. W. (1989). The hazards of cognitive aging. *Gerontologist, 29,* 484–493. http://dx.doi.org/10.1093/geront/29.4.484

Schaie, K. W. (1994). The course of adult intellectual development. *American Psychologist, 49,* 304–313. http://dx.doi.org/10.1037/0003-066X.49.4.304

Schaie, K. W., Willis, S. L., & Pennak, S. (2005). An historical framework for cohort differences in intelligence. *Research in Human Development, 2,* 43–67. http://dx.doi.org/10.1207/s15427617rhd0201&2_3

Schulz, J. H., & Binstock, R. H. (2006). *Aging nation: The economics and politics of growing older in America.* Westport, CT: Praeger.

Scogin, F. (2007). Introduction to the special section on evidence-based psychological treatments for older adults. *Psychology and Aging, 22,* 1–3. http://dx.doi.org/10.1037/0882-7974.22.1.1

Scogin, F., & Shah, A. (Eds.). (2012). *Making evidence-based psychological treatments work for older adults*. Washington, DC: American Psychological Association. http://dx.doi.org/10.1037/13753-000

Segal, D. L., Coolidge, F. L., & Rosowsky, E. (2006). *Personality disorders and older adults: Diagnosis, assessment, and treatment*. Hoboken, NJ: Wiley.

Segal, D. L., June, A., Payne, M., Coolidge, F. L., & Yochim, B. (2010). Development and initial validation of a self-report assessment tool for anxiety among older adults: The Geriatric Anxiety Scale. *Journal of Anxiety Disorders, 24,* 709–714. http://dx.doi.org/10.1016/j.janxdis.2010.05.002

Seitz, D., Purandare, N., & Conn, D. (2010). Prevalence of psychiatric disorders among older adults in long-term care homes: A systematic review. *International Psychogeriatrics, 22,* 1025–1039. http://dx.doi.org/10.1017/S1041610210000608

Shah, A., Scogin, F., & Floyd, M. (2012). Evidence-based psychological treatments for geriatric depression. In F. Scogin & A. Shah (Eds.), *Making evidence-based psychological treatments work for older adults* (pp. 87–130). Washington, DC: American Psychological Association. http://dx.doi.org/10.1037/13753-004

Shanas, E. (1979). Social myth as hypothesis: The case of the family relations of old people. *Gerontologist, 19,* 3–9. http://dx.doi.org/10.1093/geront/19.1.3

Sheppard, H. L. (1976). Work and retirement. In R. H. Binstock & E. Shanas (Eds.), *Handbook of aging and the social sciences* (pp. 286–309). New York, NY: Van Nostrand Reinhold.

Siddiqi, N., House, A. O., & Holmes, J. D. (2006). Occurrence and outcome of delirium in medical in-patients: A systematic literature review. *Age and Ageing, 35,* 350–364. http://dx.doi.org/10.1093/ageing/afl005

Silverman, P. R. (2004). *Widow-to-widow: How the bereaved help one another* (2nd ed.). New York, NY: Brunner-Routledge. http://dx.doi.org/10.4324/9780203020975

Simoni-Wastila, L., & Yang, H. K. (2006). Psychoactive drug abuse in older adults. *American Journal of Geriatric Pharmacotherapy, 4,* 380–394. http://dx.doi.org/10.1016/j.amjopharm.2006.10.002

Snowdon, J., & Almeida, O. P. (2013). The diagnosis and treatment of unipolar depression in late life. In H. Lavretsky, M. Sajatovic, & C. H. Reynolds III (Eds.), *Late-life mood disorders* (pp. 79–103). New York, NY: Oxford University Press.

Sperling, S. A., Geneser, A. C., & Manning, C. A. (2015). Parkinson's disease dementia and dementia with Lewy bodies. In P. A. Lichtenberg, B. T. Mast, B. D. Carpenter, & J. Loebach Wetherell (Eds.), *APA handbook of clinical geropsychology: Vol. 2. Assessment, treatment, and issues of later life* (pp. 227–245).

Washington, DC: American Psychological Association. http://dx.doi.org/10.1037/14459-009

Spitzer, R. L., Kroenke, K., Williams, J. B., & Lowe, B. (2006). A brief measure for assessing generalized anxiety disorder. *Archives of Internal Medicine, 166,* 1092–1097. http://dx.doi.org/10.1001/archinte.166.10.1092

Stanley, B., & Brown, G. K. (2012). Safety planning intervention: A brief intervention to mitigate suicide risk. *Cognitive and Behavioral Practice, 19,* 256–264. http://dx.doi.org/10.1016/j.cbpra.2011.01.001

Steffen, A. M., Zeiss, A. M., & Karel, M. J. (2014). Interprofessional geriatric healthcare: Competencies and resources for teamwork. In N. A. Pachana & K. Laidlaw (Eds.), *The Oxford handbook of clinical geropsychology* (pp. 733–752). Oxford, England: Oxford University Press.

Sterns, H. L., & Dawson, N. T. (2012). Emerging perspectives on resilience in adulthood and later life: Work, retirement, and resilience. *Annual Review of Gerontology and Geriatrics, 32,* 211–230. http://dx.doi.org/10.1891/0198-8794.32.211

Sterns, H. L., & McQuown, C. K. (2015). Retirement redefined. In P. A. Lichtenberg, B. T. Mast, B. D. Carpenter, & J. Loebach Wetherell (Eds.), *APA handbook of clinical geropsychology: Vol. 2. Assessment, treatment, and issues in later life* (pp. 601–616). Washington, DC: American Psychological Association. http://dx.doi.org/10.1037/14459-023

Stewart, S., O'Riley, A., Edelstein, B., & Gould, C. (2012). A preliminary comparison of three cognitive screening instruments in long term care: The MMSE, SLUMS, and MoCA. *Clinical Gerontologist, 35,* 57–75. http://dx.doi.org/10.1080/07317115.2011.626515

Strupp, H. H. (1996). The tripartite model and the *Consumer Reports* study. *American Psychologist, 51,* 1017–1024. http://dx.doi.org/10.1037/0003-066X.51.10.1017

Strupp, H. H., & Hadley, S. W. (1977). A tripartite model of mental health and therapeutic outcomes. With special reference to negative effects in psychotherapy. *American Psychologist, 32,* 187–196. http://dx.doi.org/10.1037/0003-066X.32.3.187

Substance Abuse and Mental Health Services Administration. (2012). *Older Americans behavioral health issues brief 3: Screening and preventive brief interventions for alcohol and psychoactive medication misuse/abuse.* Retrieved from National Council on Aging website: https://www.ncoa.org/wp-content/uploads/Issue-Brief-3-Screening-Brief-Intervention_508_Color.pdf

Teri, L., McCurry, S. M., Logsdon, R., & Gibbons, L. E. (2005). Training community consultants to help family members improve dementia care: A randomized controlled trial. *Gerontologist, 45,* 802–811. http://dx.doi.org/10.1093/geront/45.6.802

Tinetti, M. E. (2003). Preventing falls in elderly persons. *The New England Journal of Medicine, 348,* 42–49. http://dx.doi.org/10.1056/NEJMcp020719

Travis, L. A., & Kimmel, D. C. (2014). Lesbian, gay, bisexual, and transgender aging: Considerations for interventions. In N. A. Pachana & K. Laidlaw (Eds.), *The Oxford handbook of clinical geropsychology* (pp. 776–796). Oxford, England: Oxford University Press.

The U-bend of life: Age and happiness. (2010, December 18). *Economist, 33*–36.

U.S. Census Bureau. (2011). *The older population: 2010* (2010 Census Briefs). Retrieved from https://www.census.gov/prod/cen2010/briefs/c2010br-09.pdf

U.S. Office of Disease Prevention and Health Promotion. (2016). Healthy People 2020. DIA-1: Increase the proportion of adults aged 65 years and older with diagnosed Alzheimer's disease and other dementias, or their caregiver, who are aware of the diagnosis: About the data. Retrieved from https://www.healthypeople.gov/node/4158/data_details

van Hees, M. L., Rotter, T., Ellermann, T., & Evers, S. M. (2013). The effectiveness of individual interpersonal psychotherapy as a treatment for major depressive disorder in adult outpatients: A systematic review. *BMC Psychiatry, 13*, 22. http://dx.doi.org/10.1186/1471-244X-13-22

Van Humbeeck, L., Piers, R. D., Van Camp, S., Dillen, L., Verhaeghe, S. T. L., & Van Den Noortgate, N. J. (2013). Aged parents' experiences during a critical illness trajectory and after the death of an adult child: A review of the literature. *Palliative Medicine, 27*, 583–595. http://dx.doi.org/10.1177/0269216313483662

Ventry, I. M., & Weinstein, B. E. (1983). Identification of elderly people with hearing problems. *ASHA, 25*, 37–42.

Wallace, M. (2003). Sexuality. *Dermatology Nursing, 15*, 570–573.

Weissman, M. M. (1979). The myth of involutional melancholia. *JAMA, 242*, 742–744. http://dx.doi.org/10.1001/jama.1979.03300080040023

Weissman, M. M., Markowitz, J. C., & Klerman, G. L. (2018). *The guide to interpersonal psychotherapy* (Updated and expanded ed.). New York, NY: Oxford University Press.

West, L. A., Cole, S., Goodkind, D., & He, W. (2014). *65+ in the United States: 2010* (Current Population Reports No. P23-212). Retrieved from U.S. Census Bureau website: https://www.census.gov/content/dam/Census/library/publications/2014/demo/p23-212.pdf

Wetherell, J. L., Hershey, T., Hickman, S., Tate, S. R., Dixon, D., Bower, E. S., & Lenze, E. J. (2017). Mindfulness-based stress reduction for older adults with stress disorders and neurocognitive difficulties: A randomized controlled trial. *Journal of Clinical Psychiatry, 78*, e734–e743. http://dx.doi.org/10.4088/JCP.16m10947

Wetherell, J. L., Petkus, A. J., Thorp, S. R., Stein, M. B., Chavira, D. A., Campbell-Sills, L., . . . Roy-Byrne, P. (2013). Age differences in treatment response to a collaborative care intervention for anxiety disorders. *British Journal of Psychiatry, 203*, 65–72. http://dx.doi.org/10.1192/bjp.bp.112.118547

Whitbourne, S. K., & Connolly, L. A. (1999). The developing self in midlife. In S. L. Willis & J. K. Reid (Eds.), *Life in the middle: Psychological and social development in middle age* (pp. 25–45). San Diego, CA: Academic Press. http://dx.doi.org/10.1016/B978-012757230-7/50021-3

Whitbourne, S. K., & Hulicka, I. M. (1990). Ageism in undergraduate psychology texts. *American Psychologist, 45,* 1127–1136. http://dx.doi.org/10.1037/0003-066X.45.10.1127

Williams, B. C., Warshaw, G., Fabiny, A. R., Lundebjerg, N., Medina-Walpole, A., Sauvigne, K., . . . Leipzig, R. M. (2010, September). Medicine in the 21st century: Recommended essential geriatrics competencies for internal medicine and family medicine residents. *Journal of Graduate Medical Education, 2,* 373–383. http://dx.doi.org/10.4300/JGME-D-10-00065.1

Yang, J. A., Garis, J., Jackson, C., & McClure, R. (2009). Providing psychotherapy to older adults in home: Benefits, challenges, and decision-making guidelines. *Clinical Gerontologist, 32,* 333–346. http://dx.doi.org/10.1080/07317110902896356

Yesavage, J. A., Brink, T. L., Rose, T. L., Lum, O., Huang, V., Adey, M., & Leirer, V. O. (1982–1983). Development and validation of a geriatric depression screening scale: A preliminary report. *Journal of Psychiatric Research, 17,* 37–49. http://dx.doi.org/10.1016/0022-3956(82)90033-4

Zarit, S. H., & Heid, A. R. (2015). Assessment and treatment of family caregivers. In P. A. Lichtenberg, B. T. Mast, B. D. Carpenter, & J. Loebach Wetherell (Eds.), *APA handbook of clinical geropsychology: Vol. 2. Assessment, treatment, and issues of later life* (pp. 521–551). Washington, DC: American Psychological Association. http://dx.doi.org/10.1037/14459-020

Zarit, S. H., & Zarit, J. M. (2007). *Mental disorders in older adults: Fundamentals of assessment and treatment* (2nd ed.). New York, NY: Guilford Press.

Zeiss, A., & Karlin, B. (2010). Transforming mental health care for older veterans in the Veterans Health Administration. *Generations, 34*(2), 74–83.

Zijlstra, G. A. R., van Haastregt, J. C. M., Ambergen, T., van Rossum, E., van Eijk, J. T. M., Tennstedt, S. L., & Kempen, G. I. J. M. (2009). Effects of a multicomponent cognitive behavioral group intervention on fear of falling and activity avoidance in community-dwelling older adults: Results of a randomized controlled trial. *Journal of the American Geriatrics Society, 57,* 2020–2028. http://dx.doi.org/10.1111/j.1532-5415.2009.02489.x

Zinbarg, R. E., Craske, J. G., & Barlow, D. H. (2006). *Mastery of your anxiety and worry: Therapist guide* (2nd ed.). New York, NY: Oxford University Press.

Index

About the Author

Gregory A. Hinrichsen, PhD, ABPP, has spent his entire professional life in the field of aging, beginning with a first job out of college as a social services outreach worker to older adults. Over the course of his 40-year career, he has provided mental health services to older adults and their families, conducted research, directed psychology internship and geropsychology fellowship programs, and contributed to public policy. He has held leadership positions in geropsychology professional organizations and received the Award for the Advancement of Psychology and Aging from the American Psychological Association (APA) Committee on Aging. He has expertise in interpersonal psychotherapy and coauthored (with Kathleen Clougherty) *Interpersonal Psychotherapy for Depressed Older Adults.*

Dr. Hinrichsen is an associate clinical professor in the Department of Geriatrics and Palliative Medicine, Icahn School of Medicine at Mount Sinai, New York City, where he provides mental health services to older adults in primary care, teaches, and supervises. He is also an adjunct professor in the Department of Counseling and Clinical Psychology, Teachers College, Columbia University, New York City, where he teaches and collaborates on interpersonal psychotherapy, global mental health, and military service veteran research studies.